Mediation of
PATRIARCHY AND SEXISM
by Women in
South Africa

Boatamo Mosupyoe
University of Washington

The McGraw-Hill Companies, Inc.
Primis Custom Publishing

New York St. Louis San Francisco Auckland Bogotá
Caracas Lisbon London Madrid Mexico Milan Montreal
New Delhi Paris San Juan Singapore Sydney Tokyo Toronto

McGraw-Hill Higher Education

A Division of The McGraw-Hill Companies

Mediation of Patriarchy and Sexism by Women in South Africa

McGraw-Hill's Primis Custom Publishing Series consists of products that are produced from camera-ready copy. Peer review, class testing, and accuracy are primarily the responsibility of the author(s).

1 2 3 4 5 6 7 8 9 0 QSR QSR 9 0 9

ISBN 0-07-239029-8

Editor: Julie Kehrwald
Cover Designer: Kyle A. Zimmerman
Printer/Binder: Quebecor Printing Dubuque, Inc.

CONTENTS

4

5

LIST OF TABLES

To the memories of my late husband Simmy and son Thamsanqa. Your death on the same day and at the same time that I was expecting one of your daughters and sister was very painful. But not in vain. Your spirit will live in all the endeavors that the three of us undertake.

Acknowledgment

My daughters Palesa and Lesego for their patience, support, love and understanding. I highly appreciate their understanding when I left them in different places to pursue my academic career. My mother and late father for their never ending faith in my abilities. My late brother in-law, Nkanyezi, whose untimely death left a vacuum in my life. I will miss his in put in my work, his love and support. My sister Mary Grace who always has had faith and believed in me. My sister Winnie, brothers Thabo and Tshepo who took turns to drive me to places where I conducted field research, and never complained. Instead wondered why their big sister would endure "loud church services" and to be sprinkled by water every time she entered a church or a place of a high priest. My sister Mmule who took it upon herself to locate and tell me of any ZCC women member that she came across. Professors John Ogbu, Mariane Ferme, Tabitha Kanogo for their input this study. I cannot forget Professor Shack, for patiently yet sternly guiding my career at Berkeley. He has been a part of my academic life in ways that I appreciate more than he can ever know. Special thanks to all of my informants. I cannot mention all of you except but a few, including, Mr. Lentsoane, Mrs. Dimpe, Mr. and Mrs. Mathibedi, and Mr. Lentinti.

LIST OF ABBREVIATIONS

ANC	African National Congress
AIC	African Initiated Church
AICs	African Initiated Churches
AID	African Independent Churches
AZAPO	Azanian People's Organization
FEDSAW	Federation of South African Union
RDP	Restructuring and Development Program
SAMWU	South African Municipal Union Workers
ZAC	Zion Apostolic Church
S.A.Z.C.	South African Zionist Apostolic Church
ZAFM	Zion Apostolic Faith MissionZCC
ZCC	Zion Christian Church

Some Abbreviations on Chart 1:2-1:4
I explain in the text how I use the abbreviations that refer to the names of informants.

Prophet.	Prophetess
Adult. Liter.	Adult Literacy
Att/ville	Atteridgeville
Compl. Hs	Completed High School
DO	Drop Out
FW	Factory Worker
Hammans.	Hammanskraal
Hosp.	Hospital
Nurs.Ass.	Nursing Assistant
PR.	Place of Residence
Union Aff.	Union Affiliation

FOREWORD

Three interdependent main factors motivate my interest in the Zion Christian Church (henceforth ZCC). The first is personal and dates back to my childhood years. The second, also to a certain degree personal, pertains to the political events of the 1990 in South Africa, specifically the call to a non sexist society. The two came to heavily bear on my choice of a topic for this study, thus making my third interest academic. The multitude of anthropological literature on leadership on churches of the ZCC type further motivates my academic interest. The literature focuses mainly on male leadership in these churches. This is so in spite of the fact that in most of these types of churches women constitute the majority. I felt the need to examine gender and leadership in the domain of the ZCC in particular.

This study focuses on the ZCC women's conception and mediation of patriarchy and non sexism with their education and social reality. Mediation refers to the way in which individuals negotiate and reconcile the conflict between the concept of non-sexism with their reality. Although the study builds on my graduate work that culminated in two theses, my involvement with the ZCC as an area of interest predates my graduate years. I lived with my parents as a child for years as a neighbor of ZCC members. One of our neighbors occupied a position as a high priest in the church. He conducted services at his house that took place every night during the week. Curiosity always prompted my brothers and I to attend or when chided by parents, who disapproved of the church, sat where we could listen and observe without attendance. The explanation of my parents cautious attitude and lack of respect for the church can partially be placed within the purview of the larger key concerns in modern social theory.

Biko (1986: 54-60)) and later Jean and John Comaroff (1991: vol. 1) observe that the missionaries introduced Christianity in Africa as a 'superior' lifestyle meant to replace the indigenous clothing, customs, beliefs, which were in turn erroneously depicted as "pagan" and " barbaric". They all further note its role in the division of people as the converted and the pagans. The Comaroffs (1991: 311-2) continue to discuss in explicit terms how additionally the infusion of complex European cultural forms fostered modes of consciousness that precipitated new social divisions based on class. Class here, is created by both the relations of work and wealth and relative acquisition of monetary gains, as well as systems of signs and practices.

Thus from the aggregation of that social field emerged distinct imageries of personhood, that is, the ZCC as the other versus the majority of the Black population. The ZCC as a distinct entity, was viewed as marginal, suspicious, dangerous, and fit for ill informed and uneducated people. Important to note, even the sector of the Black population that had very minimal school education but were affiliated with the mission churches[1] still held the view of the ZCC as uneducated. This "class awareness" to use Giddens term (Giddens 1974: 111) later found further articulation by the Comaroff's (1991 and 1997: 216) as an unintended by products of missionaries' activities in South Africa. Although never expressed in these particular words, my parents view of the ZCC were in concert, both in content and form, with those of the larger social environment.

My mother always reminded us that the ZCC's teachings were not for us. She herself has very little school education. She also previously worked as a maid. Compelling reasons that made her focus on making sure that all her six children be educated beyond high school. She also took great pains to try and limit our exposure to the nightly loud preaching by encouraging us to read at the time of the church services. The proximity of the two houses made it impossible for us not to hear. Moreover, our curiosity always prompted our discrete defiance to my parent's orders. My father, on the other hand, was a relatively well educated man. He also enjoyed a lot of respect in the community. He however, constantly entered into heated arguments with our neighbor, the ZCC high priest. The arguments always centered around my father accusing the ZCC priest of having sprinkled his "water" on him and my mother's bedroom window and our yard. The priest would never deny the charge. He would instead tell my father that a real man would not be afraid of the 'ZCC water.'

Such arguments always culminated in my parents deciding to turn to their own religions to counteract this deed. In my parents' house we practiced the Roman Catholic and 'the living dead' or *Badimo* religion.[2] Ironically, then the Catholic Church condemned the believe in *Badimo* as "heathen superstition."[3] Nevertheless, similar to the Comaroff's (1991 vol. 2 p89) account of Sechele, the Batswana king[4] my parents never saw a discrepancy in the co-existence of the two religions. The belief in Jesus Christ would not make them abandon their *Badimo*. Even more interesting my family[5] was never subjected to the same ridicule as the ZCC members for practicing the two religions.

Anyway, my mother would summon the Roman Catholic priest to our house. He would diffuse the strength of the ZCC water by sprinkling the Roman Catholic 'holy water' on the window and part of the yard touched by the 'ZCC water.' An act which made it very clear that the 'ZCC water', in my parents minds, carried some kind of ill-luck that would do harm to us. The fear was so profound that my parents would in addition call upon the family traditional doctor, *ngaka* to reinforce the effects of the 'Roman Catholic water.' *Ngaka* would perform an elaborate ritual in which the whole family would participate. The ritual included calling on *Badimo* and offering snuff to them around the 'family tree.'[6] Furthermore, *ngaka* would make small cuttings on our wrists with a razor blade. He would then put a black ointment on these small cuttings of which I still bear visible scars. The ritual culminated with the *ngaka* appealing to our ancestors to avert or remove the potential harm administered by the 'ZCC water' on us. He also sprinkled his own water on the 'afflicted' parts of the house and the yard.

Thus the water from three religious sources battled with one another on my parents' yard and bedroom window. They would all assume the dual symbolic meaning of dissolving evil and harm while simultaneously "distilling the force of God's moving message" (Comaroff 1991: 206- 214). The interpretation of course, depended on a distinct frame of reference. This responsive behavior to the ZCC explicitly spelt out my parents' view of the church. The concern superseded lack of education by members. They also controlled 'powerful influential water,' that necessitated the combined power of the traditional and the western in order to defeat and diffuse its effect.

The second reason that accounted for my parents' view of the ZCC also falls within the purview of social theory. Numerous scholars like Oosthuizen (1968), Barret (1968), and Pauw (1960) a long time ago, argued that the Zionists types of churches lack an overt political agenda against the structures of racism. Later Ramose (1988) and Nthabu (1989) amongst others, would argue that the ZCC did not oppose the apartheid regime. This view of the ZCC as lacking an agenda against the apartheid regime persisted. This was shared by the majority of the South African Black community. My parents together with other neighbors would complain about the nightly noise made by the ZCC only to be ignored by the authorities. The latter preferred the peaceful ZCC and could not understand why anybody would be against the church unless they were 'terrorists.' Therefore, on one level my parents resented the noise and the favoritism displayed to the ZCC by the police who were organs of the apartheid regime.

All these notions and experiences about the ZCC formed part of my knowing and thinking that I carried with me to College. I received my Bachelors degree from University of the North, in Pietersburg, an area in Lebowa, within the walking distance of the headquarters of the ZCC. The proximity served to satisfy my never-ending curiosity and interest in the church. I would visit the area during weekends and Easter. I hoped to gain an in-depth understanding about what was then called "these strange apolitical people who are delaying the struggle." Later on, as a young married woman before my first husband passed away, my parents moved and gave us the house in Atteridgeville. Thus I continued my association almost on a daily basis with some members of the church.

All that involvement with the church motivated my graduate work, that is my Masters and Ph.D. work at University of California, Berkeley, on the examination of how the church's social, political and religious structures, symbolically parallel or diverge from those of the pre-colonial Bapedi, the group from which the ZCC emerged. The host of anthropological literature on leadership and the symbolic aspects of sex differentiation in churches like the ZCC specifically in Africa, but also in other parts of the world, provided a further interest. In discussing this topic, I will first review the literature and proceed by situating the ZCC within these scholarly debates.

A review of literature on the aspect of leadership dates far back in time and reflects a heavy northern[7] influence. The influence finds expression through the male focus in the discussion of leadership structures in these churches.[8] Leadership as a male axiom gains even more primacy with Sundkler (1948) initially, and subsequently Oosthuizen (1968), Beyerhaus (1967) and Martin (1964). Using gender specific nomenclature they differentiate between chief type and prophet type leaders. Sundkler punctuates the process by ascribing physical characteristics to the two types of leaders. The former he depicts as a solidly built 'man'[9], taciturn, and dignified able executive bold in the struggle against the whites with leadership that parallels the traditional diviner. The latter on the other hand, he describes as the prophet type that either accepts Jesus as savior or usurps his position.[10]

Martin West (1975) later questions the chief and prophet type dichotomy. He maintains that the paradigm lacks utility and fails to explain the different pattern of the churches that he studied in Soweto. Furthermore, West questions Sundklers' analogy between the traditional leadership systems and these churches leadership in urban areas. In the absence of the traditional structures in the urban areas, church leadership should be assessed on its own merit, West asserts.

Daneel (1987) counteracts and contends that West undermines the aftermath of the traditionally determined leadership concepts in the urban areas. He cites as an example, the correlation between the exercise of authority in traditional rural courts and in the church councils of urban churches. Daneel (1987: 12-13) also demonstrates by an examination of Mutendi and Sengwayo churches in Zimbabwe that the chief type and prophet type cannot be applied as neatly as Sundkler and the others suggest.

Daneel's position on the impact of the traditional structures on the churches is later affirmed by Bond, Johnson and Walker (1979), Comaroff (1980). Lukhaimane (1989) and Nthabu (1989). Bond, Walker, and Johnson (1979)[11] expand the argument by drawing our attention to the function of these churches as 'adaptive institutions' (1979: 166) that provide a vehicle for the achievement of status, prominence, and leadership. Traditionalized and routinized charisma as a determinant in the achievement of visible status becomes a perceptible variable in the analytical framework. This focus on the charismatic authority balances the discussion of gender in this domain, albeit with a heavy northern feminist orientation.

Women's roles in the churches and churches founded by women now come full force into the discourse. With Max Weber (1947) as the pioneer, anthropologists and other scholars[12] agree to the pivotal role of charisma in attracting and sustaining membership in the churches. The presence of charisma as the allure for membership prompts scholars to wrestle with identifying its location in the scope of members. Some still with a focus on males posit that the prophet carries the charismatic authority, and the bishop the judicial authority.[13]

Others in the Weberian sense, note that the charismatic potential for women is routinized in the group as a whole but not with respect to their specific cultural contributions. The charismatic promise also sustains the female leadership positions. The latter dynamic finds expression in the Gaudencia Aoko's movement. Aoko's career as a charismatic healer gained her a mass following in Kenya and Tanzania. However, her power decreased with the sudden disappearance of spiritual gifts[14] Yet the leadership of a much less studied church of Mma Nku,[15] in Vereeniging South Africa diverges from the above paradigm. Mma-Nku started and continued to run the church in her own right with no reference to male sponsorship to define the parameters of her power.

Such dynamics provide the bases for scholars to rethink the northern feminist tendency of viewing religious ideology and practice as factors that cause universal oppression of women. Ironically northern scholars like King (1992) Hacket (1984), Brusco (1995), Holden (1983) and Toulin (1997) following in the footsteps of Chodorow and MacCormack[16] to illustrate the limitation of this paradigm. They all note the impossibility of sustaining generalizations in studying gender in the religious domain. The construction of gender in religion, both inside and outside the Judeo-Christian fields it is as complex as it is ambiguous. Consequently, tenets that define the status of women increase to include viewing the participation of women in these churches as positive vehicles of liberation and empowerment.[17] Within this framework Berger (1976), Steady (1976) and Hoelher-Fatton (1996) note that strategic collective action can accord power and status to women. Moreover temporary positions of authority can be achieved by women through manipulation of the existing gender order within the churches. The Roho church of Western Kenya[18] and the Shona churches of Zimbabwe best exemplify this manifestation. Hoelher-Fatton (1996), Walker (1979) and Daneel (1987) both observe that women can assert their authority and power by speaking in tongues or singing in the middle of the male priests' sermon. The fact that the priests get extremely annoyed by this act goes to prove that they feel intrusion into their power base.

In spite of and/or in addition to the above various anthropologists observe a clear demarcation of the symbolic spheres of men and women in liturgy and ideology in these churches. Hacket (1987) most notably asserts that even in churches founded by women the hierarchical structures do not accord them any particular prominence. The very few political positions occupied by women are either determined by their ceremonial separation or depend upon male sponsorship.[19] Foster (1992) and Toulis (1997) similarly observe that women's position in Black Pentecostal churches in Europe is ephemeral. However there is a slight twist. Acknowledging the complexity of what constitutes legitimate authority and power in the churches, Foster posits that the men hold those positions because the women allow them to. Citing the women's numerical dominance Foster echoes the idiomatic sentiment that paradoxically implies 'behind every successful man there is a woman.'

She does this by making reference to the women's influence that originates from the background. She calls it "silent collusion," to apparently illustrate shared authority. In spite of the latter claim that suggests equality between the sexes, Foster continues to argue that the churches empowered women in the struggle against racism in Europe but failed to address sexism. In fact she characterizes the churches as sexist (Foster 1992: 47-55). The contradictions that permeate Foster's analysis are also present in these kinds of churches in Africa as the landscape and scope of discourse demonstrate. The same paradoxes also speak to the complexity of gender power relations in the religious domain.[20] Berger (1976: 180) describes how in the Nyabingi and the Emandwa of Rwanda and Uganda women were in the higher echelons of the hierarchical structures.

In time men seized the leadership as the historical circumstances changed and resistance to European domination defined prestige and status. Juxtaposing different historical periods Berger views the one in which women were leaders as of "relatively low value" precisely because "possession was more spontaneous and less regulated." We cannot however generalize based on Berger's observations. Other churches present a consistent pattern through historical periods. Alice Lenshina's Lumpa church of Zambia, the Church of Christ led by Mrs. Harrison in Nigeria, the Holy Chapels of Miracles founded by Theresa Offiong, used the model of 'female chieftainship.' Central to their political administration was the 'reverend mother's' position that ranked lower in the hierarchical structures. In addition these churches were unable to provide an authority structure exclusively for women, and their leadership was surrounded and supported by men[21]

Additionally, more often in these churches social relationships cross cut the symbolic differences. Kilton's (1991) description of the Ga medium clearly illustrates this point. While the female medium assists male priests in the performance of the Ga calendrical rites, her authority exceeds that of the male priests, only because it is believed to come from the spirits. Walker (1977) and Breidenbach (1977) find a similar male and female dichotomy in the Harrist Church of West Africa. The perception of Harris as a charismatic authority and a miracle worker, defined the position of the women he associated with as protégés whose symbolic power derived from his. Parsons (1967: 192-219) and Fortes (1966) a long time ago, observed a dual paradox of female expressive control in religion. The very freedom that relieves women from decision making to attend to higher concerns, serves as both her power and powerlessness. The nurturing activities of women become the symbolic rubic through which they express themselves in faith-healing and mediumship. At the same time they are at a loss to express prophetic inspiration. Walker (1979) and Hoelher-Fatton (1996) later notice the same pattern in the John Maranke and the Roho churches. Male leaders in both these churches set the parameters of women's ritual practice. As Walker (1979: 30) posits: *"Bapostolo women show them (men) particular respect and express their control through interaction rather than formal leadership."* These scholars also contend that in these churches women perform the traditional female duties, with men at liberty to send them to run errands

Practices in the ZCC parallel the latter dynamic. ZCC women perform the domestic roles. Women prepare the church, fetch water, sweep the floors and run errands. With regard to the leadership, as this study will later demonstrate the ZCC follows the traditional Bapedi structures. This validates Daneel's claim of the strength of the relationship between some churches' structures and the traditional order. The sons of Lekganyane, the founder of the church, have inherited the leadership of the church as bishops through three generations.

This factor renders Sundkler's ascription of physical traits to leaders problematic. All three bishops differ in physical characteristics, thereby defying Sundkler's stereotypical application of the dichotomous prophet type chief type leaders. All of them, as the evidence will later show adopted a policy of lack of opposition to the apartheid racial structures. If we follow Sundkler's logic then the deceased second bishop of the church, Edward should have stood against the apartheid officials, since his physique fits the description of a leader who Sundkler contends does that. This also can be a matter of perspective.

Members of the church[22] make reference to the charismatic authority of Lekganyane the founder of the church. Although during his reign membership escalated during the time of World War Two, membership in the church reached its greatest numbers during the reign of his son Edward.[23] Some members of the church speak of him as having lesser 'seriti' than his father.[24]. Factors other than charisma account for the increase in membership in the ZCC during Edward's tenure.[25] Therefore, the assertion that membership can only be secured and maintained by the charismatic nature of the leader is not applicable in the ZCC's case. Even more interesting the combined charismatic authority of the founder and the prophetesses could not increase membership at the speed and numbers that the less charismatic Edward managed to achieve. Evidence points to the founder having surrounded himself with charismatic prophetesses more than his son Edward. Maria Sefuthuma, the prophetess who later accurately predicted that the ZCC would split into two after the founder's death gained prominence because of the latter's sponsorship. Her power, of course, also disappeared with his death,[26] making the claim that in some churches the women's power derives from the even more powerful male and his sponsorship, applicable to the ZCC.

That there is a clear demarcation of the symbolic spheres of men and woman in the ZCC is irrefutable. Here also much like in the Western Kenyan and Zimbabwean churches above, the prophetesses exploit the existing gender hegemony. They do this by declaring their immediate need to prophesy. As the study will later show, this happens frequently during sermons delivered by priests. This reversal of power base mirrors Kilton's observation to the effect that the woman's spiritual authority in this case exceeds that of the male. However, there is no evidence to support the contention that males and priests would rebuke women when they so behave. I have observed priests deferring to the prophetess' wishes. Similarly the ZCC departs from the historical pattern that Berger describes in Rwanda and Uganda.

The male leadership design of the ZCC has been consistent through historical periods. Nevertheless, the role these churches have historically played as mediums of social change, makes the Zion Christian Church a very relevant area of focus in the context of working together with other forces to transform the society and move it towards non-sexism. My interest in the developments of the 1990's was sparked within this milieu. The developments of the 1990's in South Africa after three hundred and forty two years of colonialism and apartheid, serve as a further strong motivation for my focus on women in the church. Specifically the call to not only a non-racial but non-sexist South Africa, encourages me to see the need to further explore the role of the Zion Christian Church in the context of patriarchy and non -sexism. I hope this endeavor will contribute towards the transition to a new society. The South African apartheid system divided people on the basis of their color treating the indigenous people as aliens in their own land. The system, declared by the United Nation as a "crime against humanity," simply put, deprived Blacks of their basic human rights. This was done by a series of complex often confusing laws that made it illegal for a Black person to be part of the unions or earn more money than a white person.[27] In addition to this inhumane system, was and still is the prevalence of sexism as a component that forms an important part of the fabric of the South African society.[28]

That some of the differential treatment of men and women emanate from patriarchy that the present African National Congress government inherited from the apartheid system, is irrefutable. Indeed the apartheid system had laws in place that stated, for example, that a woman cannot earn more than a man in the same profession with the same qualifications. Many such like practices were legal.[29] However, in addition to these structural and institutional practices, an order of values manifest in everyday practice, explicitly and implicitly supportive of the notion of sexism, forms part of the larger South African reality, maybe with few exceptions.

A society like the Lobedu of the Northern Transvaal will be one such exception.[30] Arguably, one can posit that this society has managed to maintain some of its pre-colonial cultural elements as a matriarchal society. A series of queens all known as Queen Modjadji have consistently maintained the rule of their subjects, even within the humiliating constrain and effects of the colonial and apartheid structures. But such make up an exception rather than the rule and by and large sexism forms a common thread across ethnic and color lines of the South African reality.[31]

Indeed, the proclamation by political parties to move towards both a non-racial and non-sexist society, lends credence to the above assertion of South Africa as a sexist society. If then patriarchy is not only deeply rooted in social practice but also perpetuated through institutions, the success for the attainment of a non-sexist society depends on several courses of action. Identifying the roots and processes that produce the condition of sexism, makes up one such action. Additionally and most importantly, how women as actors involved in the process of active construction of their reality perceive the concept, forms another. An examination of how women's motives, capacities, behavior, and desires operate in the society as a result of options they make also should play a pivotal part. The Zion Christian Church comprises one of the many important influential South African institutions with powerful tools of socialization[32] that could either promote or discourage sexism.

Located in the Northern Transvaal region of Lebowa, South Africa, the Zion Christian Church makes up one of the largest African Initiated Churches in Southern Africa. Ramose (1988) and Comaroff (1980) observe that from its inception the church has faced predicaments typical to those arising from the conjuncture of multiple structures finding themselves within a single shared context.[33] The "single context" reference in itself somewhat a fallacy, as the environment further proliferates and transforms into multiple milieus, within a single context. In the Zion Christian Church's case, the contradictory relationship emanates from the complex historical process of a conjuncture of internal and external forces.

Internally the church had to reconcile its structures within the context of the entire South African culture. More specifically the Bapedi socio-cultural factors, since it originated and still has its headquarters in Moria, the Bapedi region of Lebowa.[34] In addition, like the rest of the South African indigenous people, the church faced colonial and the apartheid influences. Both of the latter forces threatened its identity and self- determination. Relegated to the periphery like the rest of indigenous South Africans the church had to inject some logic into the apartheid structural constraints, the indigenous order, self- definition and daily practice. By engaging in an ideological and explicit discourse with internal forces that resisted apartheid on one hand, and the apartheid regime on the other hand, the church created a multilevel process of self-determination and articulation.

The articulation marked by a series of experiential paradoxes of conformity and non-conformity culminated in historical periods of transient alliances by the ZCC between the apartheid system, resistance movements, and its own self determination. These flitting alliances though ambiguous, had distinct pragmatic implications for the church and the apartheid regime, while to others, they implied a gross disservice to the struggle and epitomized Karl Marx's (1967) metaphorical "religion opiates the masses." In the context of the move towards non-sexism how will the ZCC face the new challenge? Ideologically the concept of sexism suggests a hierarchical social practice where men enjoy unfair privilege at the expense of women, as mentioned above. Conversely, non-sexism seeks to transform the cognitive view and actual treatment of women as inferior and therefore subordinate to men. Hopefully, the ideology will translate into a new socialization through various means that will eliminate attitudes, behaviors, and values that have created and maintained this cognitive dissonance.

In this way non- sexism hopes to create relational equality for women and men in the post apartheid South Africa. The view of women as secondary and subservient beings, permeates the fabric of South African society, as exemplified by various legislated practices. A case in point, whereas some South African indigenous beliefs recognized man and women as joint owners of the land, the colonial and apartheid orders diminished that cultural element by declaring that a woman can never own property. The introduction of gender differential wages also functioned to undermine the African women's status. Precolonial relationships conferred common cultivation rights, sexual and economic freedom to both genders. The legally enforced euro-model of differential gender relations converted common African property rights into male property rights.[35]

The subsequent female subordination, in concert with anti-feminist northern axiology, places the husband as the provider who demands and receives respect. The secondary European women's status, on the other hand, is that of an ideal woman as faithful, domestic wife and mother, with exclusive focus of her interest and energy on the husband and children.[36] Notwithstanding, I will argue that it should also be acknowledged that pre-colonial South Africa contained cultural practices that could be interpreted as a manifestation of differential treatment between men and women. While seniority in pre-colonial social intercourse between men and women, women and women and men and men determined social hierarchy, elements that today with the course of social change, could be interpreted as differential between men and women existed. All these together with other influences compounded daily practices of gender relations and form/ed the pivotal part of yesterday and still today's South Africa. Various institutions have throughout the years furthered the course of sexism and participated in marginalization of women. The enormous impact culminated in a demand by some women and men for a non-sexist society. The determination and urgency bore fruit through the mandate of Act 106 of 1996 that resulted in the founding provision of the new and recently adopted South African Constitution, stating in part:

> "*The Republic of South Africa is one sovereign democratic state founded on the following values:*
> > *(a) Human dignity, the achievement of equality and advancement of human rights freedoms*
> > *(b) Non-racilialism and non-sexism.*"

Thus punctuated and mandated by the Constitution, post apartheid era dictates a philosophy that will translate into practice that conflicts with the teachings that form the institutional foundations of the ZCC structures. Unlike non-racialism which cuts across gender lines and fostered uniformity in terms of members perceptions about the apartheid system within the ZCC, non-sexism arguably disadvantages women more than it does men. In other words, in the ZCC institution members will have to face how they are treated in the church as women or men, as opposed to how they are treated by the apartheid regime, an outside force. As the apartheid laws are transformed by the new African National Congress (ANC) government to enforce women's upliftment the burden then shifts to the Zion Christian Church structures to reconcile its internal practices with the move towards a new society. As part of the larger South African reality the church cannot ignore the call, or can it?

1

Introduction

The Purpose

This study thus is about the Zion Christian Church women and the concept of non-sexist and non patriarchal South Africa. It examines how these women's perception and their specific construct of the non-sexist philosophy affect primarily their education and then their social mobility. Inherent in the non-sexist paradigm is the assumption of unequal men and women's relationship, or in broader terms patriarchy. A logical inference from the idea indicates that South Africa has problems of unequal men and woman's relationships that adversely affect the society, and therefore, need to be eradicated.

Patriarchy as a locale of the source of gender inequality has been addressed in a number of feminist literature.[37] Hartman defines it as:

> *"a set of social relations which has a material base and in which there are hierarchical relations between men and women, and solidarity among them which enable them to control women. Patriarchy is thus the system of male oppression of women."* (1976: 138).

Other measures work together with patriarchy as the causal factors of unequal men and women's relationships. Amongst them, capitalist organization of labor, which proponents argue that by its very nature of valorizing 'exchange' and not 'use' products, relegates women to secondary dependent status.[38]

Women's work in the domestic sphere, unlike men's work of exchanging labor in the marketplace, does not generate capital. As such, some theorists have argued, women's position in the capitalist world constitutes the exploited and the disproportionate dependents of men. In addition to capitalism, the saliency of forms of socialization plays a part. Parson (1958) described a long time ago socialization as unconscious early childhood process of development of gender roles, that culminate in distinct potentials, values, and motivations specific to males and females.

The process intrinsically contains internalization of these capacities and tendencies that guide adult men and women to make choices appropriate to their particular gender.[39] Finally, developmental paths that stress women as individual active conscious actors in the construction of their lives and life option, also contribute to the problem.[40] Departing from the assumption that circumstance that more or less match definition such as the above serve as a motivation for the strong call of the non-sexist South African Movement, I start by identifying the epistemological foundation of men and women relationships as they exist in the ZCC. This initial step examines the confluence of the structures from which the church derive.

The cultural framework of these relationships as Ramose (1988) and Nthabu (now Mosupyoe) (1989) accurately contend come from a nexus of multiple structures of interdependence and unequal influence. The pre-colonial, specifically Bapedi, colonial, Judo-Christianity, and pre and post apartheid structures all form part of the conjuncture. Consequently, an exploration of how gender relations as articulated in the traditional Bapedi structures find expression in the ZCC structures constitutes an important part of the study. How these ZCC women mediate the limits and/or the opportunities of the structural order and everyday practical experience, to create cultural models and coping strategies that help them function in society, forms an additional and the main purpose of this study.

This study recognizes that these strategies and cultural models arise from societal, individual, institutional, and ideological structures. These structures in turn have the capacity to either constrain or advance ZCC women's self determination, education, and the basic ability to function as self articulating members of the society. Thus in an effort to understand how women shape and mediate their concept for a non sexist society with their educational and social development, this study will examine the following: the extent to which the Bapedi traditional structures influenced gender relations in the ZCC; how ZCC women construct the concept of non sexism and patriarchy in the context of their educational and social development; how they explain and mediate the differences in perception of their church's practices and the call to a non-sexist society; how the women interpret the ZCC differential treatment of men and women with regards to education in general and education initiatives within the church; how they mediate the conflict created by the education they obtain from structures outside the church with education they receive within the church; and how they reconcile the dictates and teachings of their church with those of the constitution that demands equality in gender treatment and education

My attempt to answer the above questions commences with the review of the theoretical framework that shapes my inquiry. The next section explores different key concepts, theories, trends in literature, and paradigms whose relevance emerge to inform my study.

Theoretical Framework

The multitude of literature on the churches historically called African Independent Churches, and recently the African Initiated Churches (AIC singular AICs plural) proves invaluable to my theoretical framework.[41] This study is in concert with the accurate reference to the churches as Independent or African Initiated. The ZCC historical emergence falls within the purview of the definition as independent, African Initiated, and different from the mission churches. The word Independent first appeared in print in an address in Johannesburg in 1904 to the first general missionary conference by a Methodist minister.[42] Barret defines African Independent Church as:

> *"A church that claims Christianity in that it* acknowledges *Jesus Christ as Lord and which has either separated bysecession of an existing AfricanIndependent Church, or has been founded outside the mission churches, as a new kind of religious entity under African initiative and leadership."*
> (Barret 1968, p50) [43]

The churches of this kind were first studied and evaluated by Sundkler (1948). At least his work is the first known study. He differentiated these churches from the "orthodox" or "mission" churches. Mission churches also referred to as western or historical, are ecclesiastical organizations that have developed from the work of foreign missions or missionary societies originating primarily from Europe and the United States. Notwithstanding their autonomy and self government, the continuity of these churches with their Christian past distinguishes them from the many indigenous varieties of African initiated churches.[44]

Other theorists like Barret and (1968, p47), Linnigton (1924), and Pauw (1963), while in agreement with Sundkler, employed the term separatist and schismatic to expose the ignored historical element in these churches, secession. Secession manifest in two forms; secession either from a mission church or from an existing indigenous initiated church. These descriptions also prove relevant to the theoretical framework of this study since the ZCC is not a mission church. It came into being through a secession from an African initiated church.[45] In addition, the church claims Christianity and acknowledges Jesus Christ as Lord.

Further qualifications that elucidate on the origin, nature, and functions of these churches prove invaluable to this study. Theorists have added further classifications with some implicit common threads. These are, expressions of: (i) the desire to create a new social order; ii) a charismatic prophetic figure who mediates between the divine and the human; iii) anchorage among deprived groups," oppressed , the poorest of the poor in cities and towns, populations of colonial countries; iv) amalgamation of the Christian religion with traditional beliefs and concepts., i.e. syncretic.[46]

All of the above definitions specifically apply to the ZCC whose founder desired to create a new social order different from the mission churches. Furthermore, Engenase, the founder, has been described by various scholars as charismatic and has been perceived as mediators between the living and the dead. An additional area of agreement pertains to the reference of the church as poor. There is no question that the church was until recently located in an area that has been described as poor. Most notably, members themselves have articulated the position of other members as such in their writings. Lukhaimane and Mukhondo are two such examples. This study also concurs with the assertion that these churches, including the ZCC, are syncretic in nature. It is however, important to note that Anderson (1992) another member, denies the blend of the traditional elements with the Christian's. Based on this denial Anderson argues:

> "the AIC's are manifestation of true and authentic Christianity they are not syncretic movements in which traditional practices of ancestor worship still continue." (Anderson as cited in Stein, C. 1992, p.4)

Contrary to Anderson's assertion, my research and discussion prove that the blend of the traditional and foreign exists.
My claim is reinforced by Johnson (1994), Williams (1982), and HammondTooke's (1989) findings. Indeed, Mofokeng (1990:47), whose views reaffirm my contention refers to AIC as custodians of African culture and traditional religion. Consequently the churches now define themselves as African Initiated Churches, which are Christian. Without denying their syncretism the churches postulate their rightful place in the arena of Christianity. This study however, parts company with other

disparaging qualifications of these churches. For example, Sundkler continued his assessment by describing and referring to these churches as pagan whose leaders seek to usurp the power of Christ. The phenomenon, Sundkler ethnocentrically concluded, renders the churches a derision to Christianity. Oosthuizen (1968), West (1975) and Camaroff (1985) concurred with Sundkler's evaluation

Along similar lines, literature usage employed a wide range of terminology in describing these kinds of churches, as cults, revivalist, messianic, etc. Oosthuizen (1968) and Martin (1964) punctuated the definition by further depicting these churches as sects, nativistic, and claims of "totally usurping Christ, creating a Black Christ, a deification of the Black messiah and a Black savior." I will argue that these authors use rather strong unacceptable terminology that portrays these churches as deficient and therefore inferior to the mission churches. The theoretical framework of this study departs from the above ethnocentric depiction. The above nomenclature when analyzed against the Christian tradition of seeking to have a visible head of the church on earth suggests double standards. The Christian church tradition accepts a representative of Christ who disappeared from earth on the day of ascension. Such a representative as reflected through the papacy, patriarchy or the archbishopric of Canterbury does not detract from the divine powers of Christ.

Moreover, the representative is neither perceived as having identical powers as nor seizing the power of Jesus. I found this to be true in my research. Certainly, without doubt the AIC leaders and members of the church reject the assertion that they actually claim that their leader is Jesus Christ personified.

> *"His position is that of a representative of the church guided by the holy spirit from god, from Jesus Christ, through the mediation of his ancestors-Engenase and Edward-he is not Jesus, he can never be Jesus."*

One of the members posited.[47]

Furthermore, the identification with biblical figures, and the reenactment of biblical events, I will argue, are in the first place a consequence of the need for Christian authenticity, since the AICs are not accepted in the World Council of Churches. In the second place they reflect African traditional beliefs of relative fluid limit between the living and the dead as further discussions will show, with the basic intention of asserting the ongoing relationship between deceased leaders and the followers.

Inspiration can be drawn from the exemplary life of the leader, which points to the way to heaven. Such statements are an analogy connoting likeness rather than total identification in the sense of a deification of the founder leader. In addition they correlate to African traditional beliefs, including the Bapedi. Later studies by Barret (1968, p50) and Daneel (1974) reinforce the above position which forms part of my theoretical framework.

They object to the appraisals of these churches as "pagan," and "derision to Christianity." They view such an appraisal as derogative and reflective of ethnocentrism. They argue for the acceptance of these churches as authentic Christian churches since they do accept Jesus as Lord. Sundkler (1968) subsequently reviewed his ideas after acknowledging the latter fact. Unlike the above position where he had to revise his views, Sundkler's distinction of these churches as of two types, Zionist and Ethiopian endured. His exploration of the "Zionist" and "Ethiopian" churches in South Africa informs my theoretical framework. His accurate description of the way in which the emergence of these churches against the background of the structures of racial inequality, compels Blacks to search for a meaningful and authentic religious experience outside the Mission Churches, applies to this discussion.

The Ethiopian term according to Sundkler (1961, p38), Turner (1967, p23), and Molland (1955, p6), refers to churches which are fairly western in doctrine, worship, and polity that mirrors northern church organizational forms. Further traits are the maintenance of spiritual independence revealed through the assertion of African traditional patterns in their ethos. Race antipathy towards the whites or pan Africanist ideas and secession from mission churches on racial grounds constitute additional features of Ethiopian churches. The word Ethiopian Sundkler points out, is adopted by Africans of these type of churches because in their understanding it seeks to find the promise and the actual beginnings of an African church in the scriptures.

The ZCC doctrine, organizational form, and worship differ from the Western's. Therefore, Sundkler's distinction of Zionist from Ethiopian churches becomes even more helpful to this study. His differentiation makes the former a more appropriate category for the ZCC. He contrasts Ethiopian churches from Zionist churches by describing Zionist churches as syncretic movements, where healing, speaking with tongues, purification rites, and taboos are the main expression of their faith (p436).

This study also benefits from Eberhardt (1964, p4) more detailed characterization of Zionist churches that complements Sundkler's. Eberhardt (1964) adds the following features to the description: the believer's baptism by immersion; healing through prayer; revelatory messages through prophets and" tongues; African traditional elements in worship, concern to find" land and establish a holy city. These additional descriptive features of the Zionist churches give an even clearer picture of the structure of the ZCC. Anthony Wallace's enduring (1956) theory elucidate on this study in as far as they reflect on uniform phenomenon of major cultural system innovation in the Zionist type churches. The latter paradigm motivated Wallace (1956) to employ the term revitalization as an additional feature of these churches. He maintains that they involve an organized concerted effort by a society to create a more satisfying culture.

Ensuing sociological and anthropological work on African Religious churches, support Wallace's position. Focusing on the mediating role of these churches under conditions of rapid and uneven transformation, they were variously viewed as "a buffer in the wake of social dislocation", "a small reference group in relation to wider society"; "places to feel at home"; as examples of "encapsulating" or "totalitarian syndrome"; and as "the syncretic foci for modification and adaptation."[48] These accurate descriptions derive from the context of racial inequality, that compelled Blacks to search for a meaningful and authentic religious experience outside the Mission Churches. Indeed the ZCC various missions provided a home for members who felt misplaced by dominating northern culture. The church's messages injected meaning and logic into members' existence by reaffirming their traditional practices. It furnished a context from which members could draw when faced with dilemmas bestowed by a confluence of two opposing worlds. This study, however, without denying the racial variable, significantly departs from the racial inequality pattern. The context is a move towards equality between genders as opposed to inequality of ethnic/racial groups.

By focusing on this different context this study initiates a new anthropological debate and offers new perspectives towards the changing role of one of the African Initiated Churches. Further, within the context of the general historical development of these churches, and the ZCC of South Africa in particular, the focus on the potential influence of this church on transformation of gender relations, posits a new paradigm. In discussing these gender relations, the theoretical framework of this study follows Firth's (1949) view that withstood the test of time, on understanding African faith. Firth a long time ago (1949) succinctly argued that a full understanding of the major dimension of African faith depends upon viewing religion as a social system, and within the context of larger social, political and economic order.

Subsequent anthropologists and scholars from other disciplines expand on Firth's analytical framework without abandoning his basic analytical context. That is, they view the AICs as social systems within the broader social-cultural context, and continue to add other elements that provide further tools of analysis. Bond (1979), Johnson (1979), Walker (1979) Stein (1992), and Wilmore (1992), for example, see the AIC's within that milieu as instruments that facilitates adaptation to a changing social scene. Bond Johnson and Walker further argue that the AICs serve as new ways of viewing reality in order to deal with current concerns.

Within that framework, as we have seen, a clear demarcation of the symbolic spheres of men and women's activities has been noted.[49] A similar manifestation exists in the ZCC. Leadership in the church is concentrated in the hands of the men. This study goes beyond that discussion. It examines the way in which the Zion Christian Church views and treats women's education, as well as their social mobility. Against the background and theoretical framework of the age old discourse the study introduces new paradigms that foster redefinition and roles of the AIC in the contemporary world. By focusing on an objective towards equality between gender relations the discourse draws attention to otherwise ignored or neglected issues in these types of churches. More especially it draws attention to their potential in transforming attitudes towards women's education and social development.

Confronting the South African institutional patriarchal culture and its intention of championing a non-sexist society, I will argue, poses a challenge to the non-sexist movement. The ZCC like many other institutions represents institutions that are viewed as patriarchal, albeit by non-members. Thus its development within the transformation to a new society cannot be ignored. Indeed, in my view the ZCC forms a crucial influential institution in various ways. Firstly, one could argue, towards the achievement of a non-sexist future South Africa. It has to be an important component of the process. Or secondly the church could contribute towards the interpretation of what non -sexism means in the African context.

The importance of the ZCC as a crucial socialization body has been demonstrated throughout the years. Although ambivalent and controversial as further discussions will reflect, both the old and new governments acknowledge its potential effective role. In the apartheid era various government officials visited the church during its Easter services, to try and eliminate the possibility of opposition against apartheid, as the study will later demonstrate. Mandela, the current first Black president of South Africa after he was released from prison visited the church and used the occasion to urge the members to support the future non racist and non-sexist ANC ruled South Africa. One would like to believe that the call for a non-racist society favors all members of the ZCC. However, the non-sexist call does not. How seriously the ZCC take this call in as far as transforming its patriarchal structures, is pivotal to this study.

Sources of Information and Methodology

This study draws primarily from data collected through ethnographic fieldwork among the ZCC. My research was supported in part by the Department of Anthropology at UC Berkeley, International Institute of Education and by my own funds. The research focused on ZCC members from different districts of Pretoria, that is Mabopane, Soshanguve, Garankuwa, Atteridgeville, Ratjiepane, Makapanstad. In other instances I interviewed members from Pietersburg. The study also draws heavily from the personal exposure that I have had with the members of the church from childhood. Between the years 1983-1984, I travelled extensively with my late husband to Phalaborwa. On these occassions we would also frequently stop at Moria, the headquarters of the church to converse with the ZCC members.

The Pretoria areas have a substantial number of ZCC members, ranging from high priests to ordinary church goers. In addition, Garankuwa has a church that serves members from Soshanguve, Mabopane and Hammanskraal. Since my home is situated in Pretoria, Garankuwa district, access to the church members and the church was not difficult and ensured interaction with members on a daily basis. I attended the 3.00 p.m. Sunday church services with ease. The distance required quite a bit of walking.

Further one of the most respected high priests and a leader of one of the largest branches in the area resides in Soshanguve. Soshanguve is located about 35 miles from my home. This served as an added advantage, since the proximity allowed me to attend several of their all night services and be there most of the days. This particular priest is a well educated man, some of his education he obtained from the USA. He was a school mate of one of my aunt's and knew my parents very well. I personally did not have any contact with him prior to my research. He displayed a lot of generosity which included me having access to a lot of written material, interviews with women and men elders, arranged meetings for me with elders, and never failed to indulge my curiosity about the history of church, its transformation and himself in particular. He also gave me a book written in Sepedi, the language spoken mostly by people in Lebowa. This book contains invaluable information about the history of the ZCC.

This man is one of the few very highly educated members and a practicing priest of the ZCC. His wife is also well educated and a 'matron' of nurses at Garankuwa hospital. The term 'matron' in the South African context is used to refer to an executive manager of nurses. The individual usually possesses qualifications far beyond just general nursing education. This is the case with this minister's wife. It should be mentioned that the ZCC has not only publicly proclaimed its desire to educate its member, but it has, as this study will show taken significant steps towards that objective. This high priest also facilitated my exposure to even broader ZCC community. I have had opportunities to participate in church sesssions and listen to singing that forms an integral part of everything the ZCC does. Sometimes I self righteously and naively thought that I would have the opportunity to interview women and the singing will cease. It did not always turn out that way. The sessions marked by chanting, singing and dancing so uniquely incredible and creative, made me completely forgot about my intention to interview, sometimes.

The unique syncretic songs reflected improvisation from biblical words, African idioms and indigenous cultural saying that I have never heard before in my life. This exhilarating experience left me with a profound indelible appreciation of participant observation technique. I appreciated the fact that I am an anthropologist and had an opportunity to be among these highly talented women with beautiful voices and strong presence. The presence that gave them integrity and dignity as it affirmed their being. Members greeted one another with *"Khotso"* meaning peace. Indeed, in the history of the church, never was it ever reported that anarchy reigned. The Easter gathering in the ZCC has throughout the years served as the epitome of order and extreme discipline, where no one will have anything stolen from them.

Participant observations in churches, meetings, arbitration sessions, and healing services formed an important part of my methodology. In addition, individual and group interviews both structured and unstructured were conducted with a spectrum of women in the church. The diversity spanned age, level of education, rural, urban, leaders, regular members, healers, married, and unmarried. Men were also interviewed, but not to the same as extent as women.

For the purpose of this study I refer to women between the ages of ten and thirty five (10-35) as younger women. Those between the thirty six and forty nine (36-49) as middle aged, and from fifty and above (50+) as older. My field work employed ethnographic qualitative method of research. In the interest of protecting my informants, I employ code names to acknowledge their contributions. I assigned each of the individuals who I regarded as "primary informants"[50] an alphabet that took into consideration the initial alphabet of either the first or the last name.[51]

Those who share an alphabet I further divide by numerals to distinguish them from one another. To further qualify I use small case letters u, r, to point out whether they are from the rural area or the urban area. I also use small case y or m to qualify them as young or middle aged. The letters with no y or m qualification indicate older women.[52] Therefore the code names for people who are represented by the letter M will look like this: Mu: older urban woman, Mu2: older urban woman number 2, Mmu: Middle aged urban woman Mmu2: Middle aged urban woman number 2; Myu: Younger urban woman etc. Mmr: Middle aged rural woman, Mmr2: Middle aged rural woman number 2; Myr: Younger rural woman etc.; and Mr. older rural woman. The same method is also applied in the identification of priests and male informants, only their code names will be preceded by the prefix Mr. That is Mr. Mr will mean older rural minister, etc.

In instances where the names also appear in public records and published sources real names are used. The study footnotes women and men's code names where the need arises. Most of my informants responded in indigenous languages. This requires that I translate their responses to English in writing this study. Consequently the translations that are indented and written in italics are all mine.

The Structure of the Study

In order to analyze and answer the larger question of how the ZCC women mediate their construct of non-sexism with their education and social reality in South Africa, I proceed from this point by discussing the cultural and historical context of the study. This is achieved by a discussion of the ZCC and Bapedi histories. The Bapedi are the group from which the ZCC has emerged. The founder of the church was a Mopedi. Although the church has spread throughout South Africa, the branches receive their mandate from the Bapedi region of Lebowa. The headquarters of the ZCC is also located in Lebowa. Thus the relationship of the Bapedi and the ZCC structures with the colonial and missionary structures is also discussed. To contextualize and provide a background understanding of why ZCC women's perceptions show continuity with the past, chapter three starts by discussing the symbolic power of the ZCC gender relations. It then continues to discuss the mutual relationship between the Bapedi traditional structures and the Zion Christian Structures. The main argument of the chapter posits that a paradoxical continuity of precolonial practices manifest as they converge and conflict with new practices from other influences. This lays the ground for the discourse to follow, since elderly women evoked the traditional culture together with their religious orientation to authenticate their view of non sexism and patriarchy.

Thus chapter four evaluates how the ZCC women conceptualize and mediate patriarchy and sexism with structures within their church and the broader South African reality. The discussion also explores how women's construction of these concepts affects their educational and social development. Chapter five explores the causal factors in women's decisions to create models and strategies that help them function as minorities outside ZCC school structures. I employ the basic underlying principles of Ogbu and Simons percussive study to investigate the problem, as it affects and has affected mainly ZCC women's decisions in education. Specifically four tools of analysis from Ogbu and Simon's quantitative study on three minorities in the US, prove not only relevant but also invaluable.[53]

How minority are perceived by others and how they perceive themselves, cultural frames of reference, degree of trusting relations with schools, group identity and membership, became factors also in the ZCC women's case, albeit in a qualitative ethnographic manner. Women's construction of, to borrow Ogbu's words, 'cultural models, educational orientation and strategies'[54] were shaped by all of the above conditions in addition to the others.

Logically chapter six examines the influence of the education that ZCC women acquire in their work places on their conceptualization of sexism. The discussion continues to explore how women reconcile the contradictions of the ZCC teachings with the new reality. It also examines the influence of the media on the ZCC women's construction of sexism and patriarchy. Finally chapter seven, provides the summary of the main contributions of the study. The study proves that a discrepancy exists between the ZCC teachings and the call to a non sexist South Africa. This contradiction affects how women perceive their education and social development with relation to men. The study emphasizes that in some other areas especially the rural areas, women's perception can undermine their educational and social development, because of their loyalty to the bishop and the church's teachings. To further elucidate on the bishop's influence and power the discussion on the history of the church becomes necessary. Thus the following chapter focuses on this aspect by tracing the history of the ZCC, Bapedi, and their relationship with the missionaries.

2

Events in History

Early Bapedi History and Christianity

The Bapedi constitute one of the indigenous people of South Africa. Although Bapedi are scattered throughout and beyond the country, Lebowa in the Northern Transvaal has been consistently considered the area where the majority resides. The language of Bapedi makes them distinct. Sepedi, the Bapedi language varies from Setswana and Sesotho languages spoken by the Batswana and the Basotho respectively, the other two constituencies of the South African nations. Despite the mutual intelligibility of the three languages fundamental variations abound, for example, where all Bapedi, for example, say "*aowa*" to signify "no", the South Sotho use *"che"* and the Batswana *"nyaa*," to mention just but one difference [55] Attempts to trace the origin of the Bapedi culminated in three conflicting theories.[56]

Of the three Mönnig's (1969) lends most resonance for my purposes. Mönnig employs nomenclature and notes that the three nations conceives of Mopedi as the common originator of their nations. Since "Bapedi" is the plural form of "Mopedi," Mönnig's theory leads me to think that all the nations collectively referred to as Sotho might well have been originally collectively known as Bapedi, by virtue of their common allegiance to Mopedi.[57] Subsequent nominal differences I will argue, resulted from secessions from the main group. In any case, within the nation that is now known as Bapedi there are amongst others these ethnic groups: the Bakgalaka, Balobedu, Bakhukhuni and the Eastern Sotho [58] The Bapedi's first encounter with a missionary came through Merensky of the Berlin Lutheran Mission during the rule of king Sekwati in the 1800's.

As in other parts of Africa Christianity among the Bapedi was met with resistance. Its introduction as a yard stick against which the cultural norms of the indigenous beliefs and lifestyles had to be devalued, accounts for the resistance. The equation of Christianity with "civilization" and its resultant extreme contempt and marginalization of indigenous thought divided the Bapedi into the converted, *majakane*, and pagans, *bahetene*. This leads me to concur with Ramose (1988) in qualifying Christianity as a quantitative superfluity to Africa, since its seemingly intended purpose of fostering love, neighborlyhood and human camaraderie sharply contrasted with its practical divisive actions. The description of Africans by the missionaries as corrupt, lazy, and lascivious people in need of the civilizing influence of white rule, implicitly validated the colonial advances by the Voortrekkers (Dutch) into Bopedi (Lebowa). The apparent deliberate refusal of the missionaries to link social problems of the Bapedi to the cruelty and injustices they were subjected to by the whites, made Christianity the ideal religion for the colonialization of people. Consequently, among the most Africans, Christianity translated into the ideal religion for the maintenance of the subjugation of the same people. Missionaries were thus considered the essential medium of, and forerunner to, colonial articulation; they were the significant agent of ideological innovation.[59]

It was precisely because of such demeaning attitudes that King Sekhukhuni in 1864, drove Merensky out of Bopedi (Lebowa), and burned down his mission station.[60] Bopedi, then remained without a missionary for 32 years, until in 1892 when Winter, also of the Berlin Mission Society, seceded and formed the Bapedi Lutheran Church. By referring to the church as Bapedi, proved to be a wise successful move on the part of Winter. Unlike his predecessor Merensky, provided a point of reference that the Bapedi could identify with. The "Bapedi" reference spelled out an act of inclusion powerful enough to attract membership despite the still ever present racist colonial trappings of the Bapedi Lutheran Church. Winter's move caused an influx of missionaries in Bopedi, and an acceptance of colonialist versions of Christianity.[61]

Resistance over shadowed the acceptance of Christianity. This was evidenced by the simultaneous mushrooming of various versions of African initiated churches, including Zionist churches, of which the ZCC is an offshoot. My next discussion will thus focus on the historical review of the emergence of the Zionist churches, this will in turn provide an introduction and a context, for the next discussion on the history of the ZCC.

Zionist Churches in South Africa

A review of literature indicates that John Dowie founded the Zionist churches from an apocalyptic church in the United States, the Christian Catholic Apostolic Church. Identified by divine healing, three-fold immersion for baptism, and the second coming of Jesus Christ the church broke into six different American groups. Like missionaries churches one of its overseers, Daniel Bryant, went to Johannesburg and baptized 27 Black South Africans and one Boer, P.L. le Roux in the church he called the Zion Apostolic Church, an act which established the first Zionist church in South Africa.[62]

An important point to be made here is that even though Daniel Bryant's church has characteristics of the African Initiated Churches, it also simultaneously possesses features of the Western Missionaries. The intention of Bryant to come to Africa echoes that of the western Missionaries, that is, 'to evangelize the African heathens.' Likewise following in the tradition of the discriminatory practices of the mission churches in concert with colonialism and the apartheid regime, Le Roux went to work among the white community. He appointed Elias Mahlangu and Joseph Mahlangu to officiate over the Black congregants.

The differential treatment and the marginilization of the Africans and their life style in the church produced the expected consequences, which at this point formed a pattern in South Africa. The Mahlangu brothers broke from the Zion Apostolic Church in the period between 1917 and 1920, because like many other Blacks they did not take kindly to a religion that both rejected their culture, and inverted their active participation in traditional religious ceremonies, turning them into passive listeners. Their secession generated the South African Zionist Apostolic Church (SAZC). This group, in which Blacks and whites were both members, could not agree on management styles, partly because Blacks could not be ministers except in Black townships.

Thus the SAZC a Zionist church came into being through secession and the need among Africans to liberate themselves from religious colonialism. Through indigenization the church empowered Blacks and made the religion relevant to their context. It becomes clear that the ZCC the church of my focus traces its origin to the SAZC, a Zionist church. The discussion that follows on the life history of the founder of the ZCC will further elucidates on the latter fact and offers a context for the emergence of the ZCC from its Bapedi origins.

A Life History of the Founder of the ZCC

The Zion Christian Church was founded by Ignatius Lekganyane. Born in Thabakgone, in 1885 in the area of King Mamabolo, Ignatius was popularly known as Engenase, a Bapedi corruption of Ignatius. This year coincides with the dates given by the surviving contemporaries of Engenase who were interviewed in 1969 by his descendant J.E. Lekganyane.[63] The date was also confirmed by Mr. Du[64] the priest informant that I interviewed. Engenase's father, Barnabas

Matseleng Lekganyane, was married to Sefora, a daughter of a famous medicine man, a fact which would later influence the ZCC.[65]

Engenase, a polygamist, had three wives. With his first wife, whom he married in 1918, Engenase had six children: Barnabas, Talane Reuben (the late Bishop Edward of the ZCC), Maria Masebole and Manku (these were twins, but Manku died at birth), Joseph (the late Bishop of the St. Engenase ZCC) and Makhudu Piet, the only living son.[66] There are several conflicting reports as to the number of Engenase's children. One sensational report by Katesa Schlosser (1958) suggests that Engenase had a son named Jesus, whom he killed and put in a box for several days while praying in vain for his resurrection. Martin (1978), however, says that Schlosser's report is falsified by Engenase's enemies, who were jealous of the rapid growth of the church. Members and priests that I interviewed dismissed this claim as false and reflective of jealousies on the part of Engenase's enemies.[67]

Engenase's school education totaled not more than four years. He however, excelled in religious lessons, hymnal and good behavior. Dropping out of school Engenase worked for a time shooting wild birds in the forest for his father. It was during this period that he began to suffer from what appeared to be an incurable eye disease. It was apparently during this period of his life that while sleeping under a tree he saw a vision. The voice from this vision instructed him to leave Mamabolo for Johannesburg in search of a church in which baptism consisted of triple immersion in water. Joining this church would, according to the vision, cure his eye.[68]

Engenase left for Johannesburg. On his arrival he looked for a job to satisfy the Urban Areas Act forbidding unemployed Blacks to stay in Urban Areas. Once he secured a position, he set about finding the church of his vision. Observing that the baptism of Joseph and Elias Mahlangu, leaders of the Z.A.C., fits the requirements of the dream, he asked the two brothers to baptize him. This happened before the two brothers split from the ZAC. After baptism, Engenase became a powerful member of the congregation and eventually received authorization from Le Roux to preach.

When Engenase had fulfilled his purpose in Johannesburg by the terms of his vision, he left the city to pioneer the work of the S.A.Z.A.C. in Pietersburg (Lebowa) in the Mamabolo area. His ability to preach attracted many members to the church, but because he was not an ordained minister he could not perform baptism. Elias then sent a certain Reverend Mamabolo to help Engenase with baptism.[69] With the growth of the church and the simultaneous old age and ill-health of Reverend Mamabolo, the latter was compelled to request the Mahlangus to ordain

Engenase, so that he could help them in the management of the church. Ordained in 1916, Engenase became the only leader in the Northern Transvaal after the death of Mamabolo in 1918. Engenase's relationship with the Mahlangu brothers deteriorated when he questioned the validity of, and eventually abolished, some of the church practices, like wearing long white robes, growing beards, and taking off shoes when entering the church.[70]

When the Mahlangu brothers felt threatened by the Northern Transvaal congregation's support for Engenase's dissent they decided to demote him. Kruger (1971) states that a primary reason for the break was Engenase's desire to control the church, and insists that the break should be seen in context of a mushrooming of "Black messiahs.". Engenase's charismatic powers drove him to lead rather than follow, like Shembe for Zulus, Motaung for the Southern Sothos, among others, although he hesitated to express complete independence. Engenase temporarily joined, along with a substantial number of his Z.A.C. congregation, the Zion Apostolic Faith Mission (ZAFM), under the direction of Edward Motaung. Engenase's location in the Northern Transvaal was an important advantage for Motaung's church, which was headquarters in Lesotho. Engenase's relationship with Motaung, however, deteriorated when Motaung felt Engenase's diminishing allegiance, and realized the superior financial security of the church in the Northern Transvaal. Motaung summoned Engenase to Lesotho to reprimand him. The ensuing discussion revealed many of the same differences as Engenase's conflict with the Z.A.C., although in the Z.A.F.M. administrative problems seemed to be dominant.

Some members familiar with the history emphasize the fact that Engenase had broken the Z.A.F.M. constitution by marrying a second wife, as well as the probability that, as a sub-leader, he wanted to be in charge of what he sensed was rapidly becoming a mass movement. Others refer to the "God given supremacy" of Engenase's power, a divine gift that necessitated that he becomes a leader and not a follower. One member priest put it like this "Engenase o ne ana le seriti sa masisi." Meaning he was endowed with a tremendous amount of dignity.

Engenase finally broke ties with the Z.A.F.M. and decided to form a new church. The fact that he had a strong following consisting of the men who had been with him both in the Z.A.C. and Z.A.F.M., made it easier. The available evidence shows that scholars do not agree on the exact year of the establishment of the church. Oosthuizen (1968) is almost certain that the church was founded in 1924, while Lukhaimane(1980) suggests that Engenase formalized what was already in existence in 1924. Most of my informants Mr. Lu, Mr. P2r, and Mr. Pr[71] all of them prominent ministers, emphasized that the church was founded in 1910. Newspaper reports, consistently quote 1910 [72] as the year the church was founded.

Indeed, in 1985 the church celebrated its 75th birthday, an occasion that continued to mark the controversial nature of the church, with the invitation of the apartheid leader, Botha. To legitimize the church, I will argue, Engenase told his followers that God revealed himself to him on Mount Thabakgone in the form of a whirlwind, by twice blowing off his hat. On the second occasion the hat was filled with leaves, symbolizing the multitude that would follow him. God then encouraged him to have faith and continue independently. Engenase then named his new church the Zion Christian Church, a name to which he refused to add "Bantu" or "South Africa," because he felt the church would grow beyond the borders of South Africa.[73]

The Growth and Split of the Church

The ZCC membership escalated from an estimate 27,500 in 1942 to between 40,000 and 45,000 in 1943. It was during this period of the second World War when Engenase's power reached its peak. Many converts sought a religion which might help them understand the War. The growth of the church can also be ascribed to the faith healing function which the church provided in abundance. Engenase's health deteriorated after 1945, rendering him incapable of performing his usual functions, which were then executed by his councilors, especially his younger brothers, Adolph and Paulus. [74] On the few occasions that he appeared in public his favorite fifth son, Joseph, would drive him to the conferences, a gesture which to most members indicated Joseph as the successor. This was so despite the stipulation of the constitution. The constitution invested the conference, constituted by ordained ministers and lay preachers, with the right to choose the successor. The latter was to be appointed for life.

Engenase added to the confusion about the successor by prophesying about the church. Prompted by an argument he had with his brothers about the predicted split of his church by Z.A.C. and Z.A.F.M leaders, Engenase summoned while on a visit to Johannesburg, a female prophet to foretell the future of the church. The prophet, Maria Sefuthuma, if you remember, predicted a temporary split, which would be followed by a reunion. This collaborated with Engenase's 1933 prophecy evolving from the two feathers plucked from a dove which first rested on his head and then flew to the roof of his house. The feathers, according to Engenase, symbolized the two churches that would emerge from his church. His indecisiveness about who would be responsible for the split leads one to believe that he wanted to provide for all his sons in a manner mirroring succession in the Bapedi traditional kingship.

Engenase's interpretation of the two stars from the west seems to support the dove's theory. In 1941 he showed his family members, a big and a small star, symbolizing the old and young son, respectively. The smaller star moved towards and eventually swallowed the big star. This symbolized the split. In addition it indicated that though at first the younger son would have a smaller following, he would ultimately possess a greater membership than the older son. Engenase's failure to indicate which of his three elder sons; Barnabas, Edward, and Johannes, was represented by the bigger star caused confusion among members. Shortly before his death, however, Engenase summoned his brothers and the elders of the church, and told them that his brother Paulus would present Joseph as their future leader.

Engenase died in 1948. Satisfying the traditional one year period of bereavement, Paulus delayed the appointment of the successor, an act directly instrumental in the split that followed. Around Pietersburg, most members understood that the mourning period had to be observed. Outside Pietersburg, in the areas around Johannesburg and Pretoria, referred to as the "reef", members grew impatient and interpreted the delay as a tactic on the part of Paulus and some prophets to usurp leadership. The "reef" people wanted Edward as their leader. They were close to and familiar with him. Edward had fallen into disfavor with his father and contrary to his father's wishes had sought employment in Johannesburg, "the reef." They understood the procedure of appointing the new leader from the traditional perspective of the eldest son. Edward used Elija Mamabolo as a link of representation to the people, who in 1949, the year of the ZCC split, hired buses to commute to Pietersburg for the purpose of witnessing the official installation of Edward as the new Bishop.

On arrival, through a dancing pattern known as *mokhukhu*, Edward's followers stamped out opposition, and forced Paulus' group, supporters of the fifth son, to evacuate his home and erect temporary shelters elsewhere.[75] Edward's group also confiscated the band instruments. Today, however, both groups have their own bands. The eldest son Edward had more followers than Joseph, who was installed under a tree with only a handful of disciples, which included all the family members except his uncle Reuben Lekganyane, whose quarrels with Engenase predated the latter's last sick days.

Delivering his first speech, Joseph assured members of his authentic leadership, transmitted to him through the powers vested in the walking stick that he (Joseph) inherited from Engenase. People believed that the walking stick transmitted healing powers from one leader to the other. Joseph's church came to be known as St. Engenase's Zion Christian Church. Contrary to Engenase's prediction to the effect that the small star would eventually consume the bigger star, Edward's church, constitutes a larger membership than Joseph's. Edward's church is now led by his son Barnabas and Joseph's church by his son Engenase. Within five years of Edward's leadership the church's membership had grown into 80,000, and he had built it into a financial giant. By the time of his death in 1967, the membership figure was about 600,000.

In 1980 the members numbered 2.3 million. Despite differences in leadership and symbols of identification, Joseph's/Engenase's church remains virtually identical to the giant ZCC in terms of philosophy and practices. Membership at Barnabase's church is estimated as over five million.[76] This church is the largest church with Black membership, in the whole of the Southern African region. In light of the preceding discussion, I will argue that both the error in omitting exposure to, and the ignorance of most members of the existence of a constitution, resulted in the belief that the appointment of the successor would assume the traditional form, where birth order would determine the leader rather than merit or skill.

Nevertheless, considering the huge success the church enjoys in terms of membership, I will argue that Barnabas, like his father Edward, does have the skills and merit to administer the church. Thus, the split in the ZCC goes beyond a simple power struggle between the two brothers, a factor which significantly departs from the generalized ascription of secessions in Zionist churches to power struggles, as posited by others, throughout the years.[77] The growth of the church can also be ascribed to several additional factors. One is, since its inception the ZCC has consistently embraced the dictates of the South African discriminatory laws, and consciously avoided conflicting with the regime. Consequently, the apartheid regime showed leniency towards the church. The other factor relates to the faith healing mission of the church, which still today attracts even non ZCC members.

The next important factor and most pertinent to the theme of my analysis, relates to the retention and perpetuation of African traditional practices in the ZCC. This too worked to promote the growth of the church. The preservation of African traditional elements in the face of colonialism and apartheid served to give members a sense of authenticity and belonging. The two western structures sought to undermine African culture, the ZCC on the other hand legitimized it through religious practice.

Indeed most ZCC women used the traditional African culture as a frame of reference in framing their understanding of non sexism and patriarchy. In addition the general operation of the church resonates the Bapedi tradition. This continuity with the past as a strong foundation on which views are constructed, calls for an examination of the representation of gender relations of the Bapedi structure in the ZCC structures. The discourse will not only inject some logic in comprehending these women's responses, but will also elucidate on this relationship of complementary opposites, and the degree of mutual influence.

3

Symbolic Gender Relations in the ZCC and Bapedi Structures

Symbolic Aspects of Sex Differentiation

Membership

One of the least studied aspect of the AICs is the question of membership which has a bearing on the most studied leadership question. In order to analyze the symbolic aspects of women in the ZCC looking at membership becomes an important first step. An examination of this factor offers a background that elucidates on sex differentiation in execution of women and men's roles. Barrett (1968); Lewis (1971); Moufuga-Nicolas (1972); Murphree (1971), and Jules-Rosette (1979) noted the predominance of women in the AICs. Their findings are either at a direct variance with or caution the subsequent studies by Lagerwerf (1975) and Hacket (1987) who concur that contrary to popular academic opinion, women do not always outnumber men in the AICs. Kalu subscribes to the latter view, and further asserts that churches with complex bureaucratic and hierarchical structures reflect higher male attendance, at least in West Africa.

In the context of the above varying theories the ZCC presents a unique entity. It has a complex bureaucratic and hierarchical structure partially in concert with Kalu's position. The ZCC however, also diverges from her findings as in part it fits the other scholars' assertion, namely, women in the church do outnumber men. Membership in the ZCC is open to everybody, women, men and children. Children, however, should be 18 or older in order to join on their own, without their parents. Most children become members by virtue of their parent's membership.[78] From its inception women in the ZCC have outnumbered men. Comaroff (1980) in her study about the Tshidi reports that ZCC membership in this particular congregation composes of more men than women. However, on the whole evidence shows that in the ZCC women outnumber men.[79] In spite of the latter, the final determination of who becomes a member rests with the priests.

Both Daneel (1987) and Jules Rosette (1978) note males' pivotal role in sponsoring membership into the church of the Zionist kind. The process of becoming a member as explained to me by a number of ZCC congregants,[80] mirrors Daneel and Jules-Rosette's accounts. To become a member both males and females have to inform a priest, who will then assign a sponsor to the prospective member. The assignment of sponsors is dichotomized along gender lines, with females sponsoring women and males sponsoring men. The sponsorship entails a period of probation and orientation about the church's teachings, rules and regulations. In addition religious attendance to church services and meetings forms a mandatory part of this period for the prospective member.

The church expects compliance with the requirements from everybody regardless of gender.[81] Violation of the prerequisites results in extended period of orientation and probation. A person could be refused membership because of failure to regularly attend meetings and services. Upon completion of the orientation or probation the sponsor informs the minister about the prospective member's readiness and recommends baptism.[82] The prospective member answers questions from elders other than the sponsor. Here too females quiz women and males quiz men to test their knowledge of the church's expectations.[83] The high priest determines the final acceptance of members into the church, by giving his approval in matters of baptism. Baptism by immersion carried out exclusively by male priests confers full membership. The act of baptism initiates an individual into a member of the congregation. It is also viewed as a method of cleansing all of the pollutants that an individual had acquired from the unclean world that he or she associated with before becoming a member.[84]

Comaroff (1980) and Sundlker (1969) both refer to the symbolic meaning of baptism in the AICs. The most important symbolic aspect of baptism centers around the power the male priest possesses. The latter enables him to dissolve the new member of his or her former identity. Through the process the new member symbolically experience the dual transformation of death and rebirth. This could only happen through the power endowed in the priest and transferred onto the new member. Women in the ZCC lack such symbolic abilities of transforming death to rebirth, a factor which gives an additional reason why women cannot even be priests.

After baptism, sponsors then give new members their uniforms. The importance of wearing uniform in the Zionist churches has been noted by Sundkler (1961: 213 ff.), Comaroff (1980: 205), West (1975:

18), and Berglund (1967) among others. Much like in the other Zionist type churches, uniform in the ZCC is believed to be "infused with power that encases the body of the wearer like a shield." (Comaroff 1980: 206). The women reiterated the sentiment and truly believed in the symbolic protective nature of the uniform.[85]

For men the uniform comprises of a kakhi suit, a brown hat, and white boots. Women wear a green and yellow suit, black shoes, and a green scarf.[86] Several women explained the symbolic meaning of the color of their uniform.[87] West (1978:18) explains the importance of the role of color in the Zionist churches' symbolic order. Much like Comaroff (1980), and Sundkler (1948) they attribute the choices of colors to the racial conflict that existed between whites and blacks in the particular areas that they studied. For example West (1978) asserts that black signifies churches of the spirit while white stands for churches of the law. Implying that the black churches represent authentic holiness while white does not.

The explanations that I received from the women in the church depart from that binary racial explanation. The color yellow these women said symbolically represents the sun and a flower like the 'sun-flower.'[88] The sun as a sign of happiness will always shine on the church, Mu3 asserted. Green symbolizes wealth and plenty, implying that the church will continue to grow in membership and members will gain spiritual wealth. Women who sing in the choir wear blue, which signifies the clear sky and clarity of the mind. The symbolic meaning translates into spiritual intelligence of ZCC members.[89]

Although women wear black shoes, black as the color, one member further claimed represents ill luck. The women wear scarves on the head all times especially when attending church services and meetings. In addition they are required to cover the upper part of their bodies, that is, they should not expose their shoulders. The woman's body in the church symbolizes God's temple and should be treated as such, men do not have an equivalent analogy.[90] Both men and women receive the badge after baptism and as further discussions will show, they all have to wear it at all times.

The men wear hats that they take off when entering the house. Women are not allowed to touch the man's hat.[91] Such gender- based practices also find expression in other procedures of the church. Most notably the hierarchical leadership structures show a clear demarcation of symbolic spheres of men and women, like Hacket (1987) posited.

Priesthood, Prophets, and Prophetesses

As earlier discussions have illustrated there is a clear demarcation of the symbolic spheres of men and women's activities in the AICs.[92] Evidence point to monopoly of political and administrative positions by men. Similarly, priesthood in the ZCC is a male domain. Never in the history of the church has a woman ever qualified to be a priest.[93] Neither has the church ever had a male bishop. However, both a man and a woman qualify to be either a prophet or prophetess, respectively. The high priests reported that any man over the age of 21 who exhibits skills and abilities can become a prophet. In addition to the skills, they further posited, the man must have "a call." The latter is a spiritual calling that causes an individual to experience change. The transformation entails a new social and spiritual identity, a symbolic rejuvenation that connects the player to the direct powers of the "living dead,"[94] the bishop and God.

Jules-Rosette (1977) observes that in the AICs a woman's power increases after her childbearing period has ended. Daneel (1970) concurs with Jules-Rosette. In his observation of the AIC among the Shona in Zimbabwe he equates the phenomenon to the traditional Shona custom. He contends that Shona custom already contained precedents of an older 'neuter' medium figure through whom God spoke, thereby removing all of her sexual characteristics. I found a similar paradigm in the ZCC.

Only post- menopausal women can be prophetesses. Menstruation period symbolically translates into placing a woman in the state of impurity and therefore disqualifies them from becoming prophetesses, and even priests. This paradigm could present dual purposes, I will argue. It could on one level, represent the symbolic order that seems to reform rather than reinforce the natural qualities of a woman. On another level, however, it could have the power to reverse the hegemonies by moving women from the periphery to the center. In addition, despite the fact that a woman past menopause has to go through the same spiritual experience as a man in order to be accepted as a prophetess, charismatic attributes could give her an advantage over a prophet.[95] Charisma has also accorded a woman eminence, admiration, and respect in the ZCC. The charismatic promise of several prophetesses sustained their female leadership positions.

That notwithstanding, both men and women who wish to be in those prophets or prophetesses have report their experiences to either one of the elders or priests. A male prophet would then be assigned to apprentice the woman into the profession, since males primarily take ritual precedence over women.[96] Although the church has more prophetesses than prophets, only prophets serve as apprentices. The orientation involves an elaborate process of observation and practice. One could also become a prophet or prophetess through a vision seen by either the bishop or one of the priests or prophets. This ensures an accelerated way of being ordained by the church.

When women appear in such visions or dreams they are immediately assigned a sponsor for apprenticeship.[97] Such orientation could take fewer than three months[98] since the endorsement came through the power of the vision affirmed by a male. This differs from instances where a woman proclaims herself that she has to be ordained. In such cases a number of prophets and prophetesses need to verify her claim. The process could take several months as others would sometimes say they need more time in order to see clearly whether she qualifies. A man on the other hand is immediately assigned an apprentice. The standards for ordination also seem to be higher for women.[99]

I observed a process where prospective prophetesses were trained and accepted. They had to prove their visionary, divining skills as well as their ability to prescribe *ditaelo*[100] in an effective way. To prove their visionary and divining power women engaged in the process of relating to the higher priests facts about members of the congregation picked at will and randomly. Mu explained how the acceptance into ordination depended on the number of affirmative responses the prospective prophetesses' received for her re-counts. Their ability to prescribe *ditaelo* also had to be proven by members who will attest to having experienced healing or change after taking either water or coffee that was prescribed by the prophetess.

While people most of the time responded positively, the disparity lay in the fact that prophets are exonerated from the process. They receive ordination on the basis of what their sponsor says. Instances of prophetesses attaining prominence through a male sponsorship in the ZCC abound. Lukhaimane (1980) gives an account of the famous Maria Sefuthuma. Maria became a prophetess and was frequently sought after. She became Engenase's favorite and achieved prominence in the church. If you remember she accurately predicted the splitting of the church into two.

Through Engenase's endorsement and sponsorship she achieved prominence and enjoyed a great amount of respect, one priest from Atteridgeville explained. However, after the death of Engenase her prominence diminished. She was replaced by others during Edward's tenure. The pattern continues even to the present. I also observed in various locations that those women who were favored by priests commanded a lot of respect. The privilege and power these women enjoy as mediums of revelation act as leveling mechanism within the hierarchical framework of the church.

Some women prophetesses acquire prominence by virtue of their marriages to high priests. Here we find the familial symbolism that Jules-Rosette observes (Jules-Rosette 1976b). Indeed in the ZCC too the familial connection legitimized Du2.[101] authority, while at the same time it reaffirmed the division between female spiritual authority and historical male supremacy and political control. Such dual paradox of the prophetesses' power and powerlessness occurs in other instances as well. For example, the prophetesses cannot administer *diatelo*, unless in the absence of a minister and in cases of emergency,[102] only prophets can. Yet only the prophetesses can prescribe what a 'patient' should take to heal his/her ailment, the prophet cannot. In addition the prophetesses are not allowed to hear and mediate disputes while prophets can. Further, while prophets can marry additional spouses after they appear to them in their dreams, the same is not expected from the prophetesses.[103]

Despite the above limitations the prophetess's position also commands power and respect. The prophetesses enjoy respect and deference by virtue of their age. Both men and woman display obeisance to them. Priests of a younger age as well as any younger male member also defer to their authority. In this particular case, the focal role of their divining, visionary prescriptive abilities in this symbolic process make them 'masters' of ritual power. The latter is possible because in the Zionist symbolism such skills construct the human form into the prophetesses' image of the world according to a revealed vision of agency, power, and collective well being.

Church services can also become the domain of power for the prophetesses. During mixed gender church services women enter through the back door, sit on the left side of the church and are excluded from preaching. Only males can preach. However, I have observed a prophetess interrupting priests' sermons by just raising a hand to declare her intention to divine and testify about an important member of the congregation. Even the highest ranking priest defers to this action when it happens. Such testimony, which Sundkler (1961: 192) noted a while ago and still true today, "replaces formal preaching or clerical exegesis."

By this action the prophetess transfers her position from the periphery to the center. In this event her authority exceeds that of the male priest because it is believed to come from the spirits. This phenomenon departs from the above idiom of familial symbolism where the influential position of the prophetess either come from the male sponsorship or marriage to a priest. While prominence does depend on male sponsorship in most instances their symbolic power in other spheres we cannot ignore.

Thus within the ZCC we find positions of the prophetesses assuming an ephemeral form which they can alter through mediation to achieve the central focus. In the context of the theme of mediation towards non sexism, evidence supports the claim that such negotiation cannot be divorced from the broader traditional, social and political mix. The possibility of the role of the prophetesses in the ZCC to be used as a strategic and symbolic vehicle to achieve non sexist goals, should be assessed within that background.

Theorists like Daneel (1987) insists on equating such dichotomous binary positions of power in the AICs to African traditional practices. Other scholars in much more detail than Daneel continue the debate about the equation of the tradition and the symbolic power of women in the AICs. Jules-Rosette (1977) argues that parallels between social change and the freedom of women in the AIC exist, but require careful approach. Fabian(1974) on the other hand denies such correlation. Robins (1975) underscores Fabian's assertion.

My findings in the ZCC follow Robins' and Jules-Rosette's contention that complexities of the complementary gender situation in the AICs sometimes lead to traditionalistic revitalistic responses. In such cases some women tend to want to reassume the trappings of the conventional roles,[104] as this study will later show, with more force than before. One could argue that such is a symbolic effort to hangon to the familiarity of tradition or reconstitutes a lost sense of community. However, the study will also reflect that other women opted to become prophetesses as an alternative to pursuing school education. This manifestation in slight contrast to the above traditional revivalistic responses, implicitly reflects the women's ability to discern the potential of traditional practices to transform into the symbolic rubic through which change could occur.[105] The women saw possibilities of advancement of their social status in becoming prophetesses.

Such a possibility in these women's minds was analogous to that achieved through formal education.[106] It is important to note that their choice was conscious and derived from their familiarity with the traditional functions of the position. Becoming a prophetess requires skills and a "spiritual call," as we have learnt in the discussion about membership. However, possessing such attributes as a prerequisite did not seem paramount to these women. Becoming a prophetess presented such a viable promising future that obstacles would be tackled as they occur. The latter suggests that these women saw the possibility of engaging in a process of simultaneous social reproduction and transformation, reaffirming Jules-Rosette (1977) and Daneel's (1987) argument of the strong links between the traditional structures and activities in the AICs. The following discussions that juxtapose the ZCC and Bapedi structures offer further information on the correlation and the symbolic position of women.

Gender Relations in Social Structures

A comparison of both social structures reflects that while archetypes of fundamental Bapedi structures are reproduced in the ZCC, sometimes the less complex and complete end product as manifest in the ZCC becomes a facsimile rather than a prototype of the Bapedi social structure. This is so because of the dynamic nature of cultures, and the fact that the ZCC constitutes part of and not all of the social dimension of the lives of the Bapedi members. Systems of prohibitions and preferences as revealed in the ZCC social systems illustrate cultural elements that are based upon and similar to, but less comprehensive than, those of the Bapedi.

Like in most societies the choice of a marriage partner among the Bapedi was and still is socially organized and controlled. The system of prohibition and preferences which governed marriage depended primarily upon patrilineal and secondarily on matrilineal line of descent. This did not imply that marriage requirements necessarily derived from biological and classificatory considerations, but rather from social conceptions which valorize direct lines of patrilineal descent. For example, historically, while a man used the same term *kgaitsedi* to refer to his father's brother's daughter and sister, the marriage with the former was preferred and a union with his sister was prohibited. In the common case where two brothers married two sisters, a son from the union was allowed to marry a daughter from the other marriage. In this case the Bapedi argued that the emphasis was on the father's brother's daughter's relation and not on the mother's sister's daughter.[107]

Historically, the difference between biological and social determination was reflected in the contradictory prohibitions associated with, on the one hand, marriage, and on the other, sexual intercourse. The levirate custom.[108] permitted, for example, marriage, while the intercourse law prohibited sexual intimacy, between a man and his late brother's widows.[109] Meant to perpetuate the family name, the marriage redefined biological relationships, so that what northerners[110] would call a step or half relation translated into an original and direct relation. What was, for example, a fraternal relation became filial when a man married one of his brother's widows with a child. The new husband was considered, without semantic qualification, "father", as if he had completely replaced the true biological father. The lack of qualifiers implied a biological relation. The valorization of the patrilineal over the matrilineal in a need to maintain a protectively coherent familial structure, points to the primacy of the men's line of descent over the women's.

An extended family benefited from maintaining its wealth through marriages between patrilineally-related family members, while avoiding matrilineal-related alliances. In addition to the primary marriage, the Bapedi contracted secondary unions which fell out of the nature of the dual function of marriage as both the establishment of alliances between two groups of relatives and enabling procreation. Consistent with these functions, the Bapedi practiced the sororal[111] and the levirate customs, but without making a clear distinction between the two.[112] Based on the evidence, it would seem that the two customs were inextricably interwoven. They translated into the right or privilege of a man to marry his wife's sister, the right or privilege of a man to claim his wife's sister as a substitute, and the right or privilege of a man to claim his deceased wife's sister as an ancillary.

Although the principle underlying these unions intended to perpetuate marriage, protect orphaned children, as well as produce children with the objective of preserving the name that would have otherwise died in case of barrenness or death, [113] I will argue that it has other implications. The woman or a widow did not have the same right or privilege accorded a man or a widower. To the extent that the practice is confined to men only and excludes women it falls within the purview of the current definition of sexism within the context of South Africa. The same principle extends to "ghost marriage", in which the brother of the deceased king married, in the name of the deceased, what should have been the deceased's principal wife, defined as the daughter of a neighboring nation's king.

This kind of marriage was contracted for a king who died without issue, especially one who died without having married his principal wife.[114] Pertinent to the focus of this chapter, the custom still excluded women from receiving the same right, again rendering it sexist. Although the discussion thus far may have suggested monogamy as a uniform practice among Bapedi, polygamy as a form of marriage co-existed with the latter, with a few still practicing polygamy today. Polygamy gave rise to a complex family, in which each wife from a primary marriage had her own homestead, and in which each unit functioned as a separate family with the husband as a common and uniting factor.

The polygamous marriage was disparate, since each wife had her own independent status, and the wives were not equal in rank.[115] The basis of the ranking of wives depended on the date of marriage, and the assignment of status to the individual depended on this ranking. In less comprehensive ways marriages in the ZCC are socially organized and controlled by the church to a certain extent. Polygamy is allowed, Engenase, the founder was himself a polygamist. The genealogy of Jesus' birth vindicates polygamy as a sanction from God, the church believes. Each of the prospective wives of a male member will most likely be revealed to him in visions from, originally, Engenase, or Edward, and more recently from Barnabas, Ignatius or God. Polygamy formed an attraction to members who sought to perpetuate this valued Bapedi custom in danger of displacement by northern cultural imposition. The ZCC accommodates polygamy much more explicitly than one found both in terms of the South African Apartheid Civil Law, and in other African Initiated Churches. I will even further argue that, the apartheid laws rendered this African custom a necessity.

While polygamy formed a cultural practice, the division of Black families by various Section 10 Apartheid laws[116] which prohibited husbands and wives to live with each other, culminated in men having multiple wives. Arguably it also provided the second wife as a care taker for all the children, since the principal wife and the father worked as living employees, who on the meager salary offered could not afford to travel home and see their children, except once a week. Similarly because of the apartheid it would be illegal for the children to visit their parents at their places of employment.

Most ministers are polygamists; this facilitates their work. Since the church required minister to abstain for three months from eating food prepared by an impure woman who had given birth, and not to come into contact with or eat food prepared by a menstruating woman, polygamy allowed them to stay with other wives while serving the church as well. Members of the church see this as a fulfillment of God's requirement contained in the bible chapter of Leviticus 12:1-5. As one woman, Du2 a wife to one of the minister's said:

> "My marriage to my husband was sanctioned by God. He was not the only one who saw a vision--directing him to marry me--I did too. The same vision directed me to be a prophetess. My husband is a priest, God requires that apriest should have several wives to perform his duties efficiently--contact with "hot" women preventssuch efficacy."

While this particular woman completely accepts the practice, and the church expects chosen wives and first wives to comply with the wishes of such dreams, others defy it. I witnessed a case where a priest's wife[117] from the Pretoria area vehemently objected to her husband taking a second wife. The woman said she's been married to the man for twenty years, in which period she bore children for the marriage. During that period the man efficiently executed his priestly duties and never did once complain about the woman obstructing his priestly duties because of the fact that she menstruates and bears children.

She pointed out that they always knew how to comply with the church's requirements without violating the "ban." She viewed her husband's declaration of a vision as a fabrication prompted by his mother, who unsuccessfully tried to control their finances for the past five years. She continued to say that her mother-in law perceived her as an obstacle that prevents her (mother-in-law) from gaining control of their finances and now she her only recourse was to push her out. When the man reiterated the sincerity of his vision a host of instruction ensued directing the woman to obey and facilitate the legitimization of the second marriage.

She was to form part of the family that was going to complete the marriage process. Her unmistakable defiance prompted the council to allow the man to go ahead and marry without her participation. The man later revealed to me that he contracted a church exogamous marriage, a factor which he viewed as a disadvantage. Marrying endogamously, he said, secures sustainable marriages. Exposure from an early age to the church's expectations of gender roles minimizes the differences in perceptions and expectations. Consequently, such a marriage will be less controversial and troublesome.

The woman's attitude, I will argue, reflects the dynamic nature of church's and traditional structures. In addition, it points to the diverse held views and paradoxes with regard to polygamy in the church and in the South African society in general. While other women and men condemned the woman's action, some agreed with her. Of those who supported her was an elderly woman form the rural area Wr. who said:

> *My child things change--I personally do not wish to say anything bad about her. What she said was not even considered--It is a man's world*

Those who disagreed with the woman from Pretoria said that her actions violate God's, the church's, and the cultural practices of *batho* (people) at large.[118] Indeed, the discussion on the Bapedi reflects that polygamy constituted a cultural practice of the Bapedi and other indigenous South African cultures. One woman reminded me that in accordance with both the traditional Bapedi culture, the *batho* that is human culture and the ZCC, women in such conditions attract polluting heat which threatens the health of others and affects the fall of rain.[119] This again is contained in the teachings of the bible, and can be found in Leviticus as well.

The bishop, Barnabas, who also performs priestly duties, I was told also has to observe the ban. On that basis I logically inferred that Barnabas too must be a polygamist. Nobody would discuss with me the marital status of the bishop. The Pretoria woman later told me that she felt a sense of loss but no regret for having to end her marriage. She did not see anyway that she could tolerate her husband having a second wife. The fact that she disbelieved the authenticity of the dream made her even more determined in her actions. She alluded to the fact that on many occasions she has dreamed of being married to different men, and wondered if her wishes will be granted. She looked forward to the non-sexist South Africa, where there will be gender equality.

An examination of how marriage is contracted, how boys and girls are perceived, and how familial relations function in both social structures reveals in some instances a more fundamental reproduction than the above discussion. The discussion of these issues reveals a pentimento where the lines which trace the portrait of a Christian family also mirror, even as they alter and suppress, the hidden, shapes of an older, original portrait.

The Bapedi traditional marriage custom emerges from and revolves around *magadi*. *Magadi*, forms Bapedi traditional marriage custom by which a man and his family exchange with the bride's family originally cattle but recently money to establish a marriage relationship. Departing from earlier misinformed and ethnocentric description of similar customs throughout Africa that viewed this practice as wife purchasing, Ogbu laid the argument to rest when he accurately and convincingly describes this African cultural practice as African way of legitimizing marriage, in the same way as northerners sign a piece of paper.[120]

The Bapedi social structure emerges from and revolves around this contract, which in addition establishes paternity, confers the husband and wife with conjugal rights, and defines the powers, duties, and obligations of two groups of relatives involved. As it defines a series of relationships between individuals, and by extension, their families, *magadi* produces the framework, finally, of the whole social structure.[121] With some modifications because of changes, the family among the Bapedi, as elsewhere, remains a cohesive, corporate group, practicing its own subsistence economy and performing its internal religious and jural functions. Consistent with the patrilineal organization of the Bapedi, inheritance and succession are still largely patrilineal, residence mainly patrilocal, the system of naming predominantly after the father's relatives, and authority over the family continues to be vested mainly in the father. The interest of the family as a group extends to the interest of the larger kin group, predominantly the father's since the husband remains primarily the member of his own group and the wife joins his group.

The children, although related to the mother's relatives, become mainly members of the father's group. Lately, women take hyphenated names, but the offspring still use the father's and not the mother's name. If a case exists where the children assume a hyphenated name, my research did not uncover such an instance. Clearly this further demonstrates the ascendancy of men over women in familial relationships. The family's internal functions, obligations, and duties are intertwined with the communal functions, obligations, and duties which it performs within the larger social groups to which it belongs. Rather than considered or discussed as primarily a separate social unit, the family formed an extension of the existing kin group, and the main vehicle for the continued existence of the group as such. Even with cultural changes, the survival of the old tradition can still be found in the current Bapedi culture.

Similarly, kinship system extended to all people among whom some genealogical connection could be established. In practice, the whole wide network of an individual's relatives had little impact on his or her daily life. The ties of kinship, as expressed in terms of mutual interdependence, were effective mostly in the close categories of relationships associated with the family.[122] For the Bapedi closer relatives fell into three major categories: agnatic maternal, and affinal. Within each of these categories the Bapedi distinguish degrees of relationship.

Within the primarily important group of agnatic kin, in which patrilineality determined a person's relationship a closer unity existed between those descended from one mother categorized as children of one breast, *bana ba letswele*. Despite the hierarchical arrangement of relationship within this group, with the older brother considered superior to the younger brother, an obvious strong bond and reciprocity of service manifested among them. A strong and socially determining bond also existed between a person and his/her cognates. This group, *ba ga malome*, those of my mother's brother, also included persons directly descended from the maternal grandmother referred to as *bana ba mpa e tee*, the children of one womb, and the children of co-wives who were sisters. Characterized by great mutual affection, gift exchange and mutual sympathy, the maternal relationship took precedence over the affinal, the least significant kin group.[123]

Generally, the assignment of status to the individual was based on the basic kin group, the patrilineally related children of one mother, from where it radiated out to the position of this group within the compound family, and the position of the compound family within the agnatic group. Among full parallel siblings, two individuals could never be of equal status, and this fact was recognized through the system of age-grading, where full parallel siblings belonged to different age-grades to underline the difference in their status.   Like the traditional Bapedi structures, the Zionists require the birth of a son to carry on the father's surname and family. Succession in the church depends in practice, if not in theory, on, to a great extent, Bapedi succession rules. The birth of sons in ZCC has guaranteed and continues to sustain longevity as well as continuity of the top structures of the church. Since its inception women never succeeded to head the church.[124]

On the other hand, the function of the badge, one of the primary symbols of the ZCC symbolizes much the same that *magadi* does. Introduced in 1928 by Engenase as a form of recognition, identification, solidarity and unification, as well as loyalty to the church, it symbolizes the social contract among members of the religious community, like magadi in the Bapedi community. Coming across somebody wearing a badge immediately establishes a brother and sister relationship in Lekganyane, *metswalle*, which translates into relatives, in much the same way as *magadi* establishes a network of relations in the Bapedi social structure.

The badge has multiple functions. It serves as disciplinary measure, functions as an interdict of bad behavior, and shields against peril. Members wearing it will supposedly not dare to smoke or drink intoxicating liquor. They also help each other find employment. Members hold the conviction that wearing the badge all the time precludes mishaps such as being robbed. The idea follows from, I believe, the inherent unreasonableness of robbing someone in one's own family. Traveling through South Africa, at taxi ranks, train stations, and bus stations the affinity among people wearing the badge becomes as apparent as the filial relationship established by *magadi*. The following remarks by some members affirm the extent of the badges' function:

"A fellow ZCC member is my family member"

"Seeing someone wearing a badge like me, is like seeing my mother, brother, father or sister--no mistake ther"[125]

Throughout the years different emblems were used. The current one replicates the original that was substituted, without any given reason, by a light pink badge with a red round top. Fear of familiarity and difficulties in obtaining the material prompted church authorities to revert to the original light green badge with a round Black top. The 1949 schism resulted in two churches using two different emblems; Edward chose the five point star, struck from metal and superimposed on the Black and green material as an emblem while Joseph's followers sport a metal dove on a similar material.[126]

The badges, given to every member after baptism, also served to work against the preferred South African Apartheid Government policy of divide and rule, because of their panethnic nature. The badge, worn by a baptized church member of any ethnic group effectively achieves such unity, even if not so intended by the ZCC hierarchy. The uniforms associated with the ZCC, like the badges, both create and reproduce the social contract among its members. In addition the badge constitutes one of the few symbols that attempt to bridge the gap between genders. All members use a single identical badge with no differentiation based on gender. The same cannot be said about other things like the uniform, for example, khakhi suits distinguish male members from women who in turn wear green and yellow uniform.

Nomenclature also plays a role, the ZCC greeting, achieves the same as the badge in terms of gender relations. The greeting *khotso*, peace, followed by a response *A e ate*. "let it spread" used by every member, fosters solidarity. The significance of the greeting finds concrete testimony in the peaceful behavior of the mass gatherings at Moria, especially during Easter Weekend and September. Despite the potential danger of unruliness of such a gathering of millions of people, the total lack of thuggery and theft, further indicates the familial bond reflected in the ZCC's material and metaphorical expressions of solidarity. Thus the contact of the two organizations transformed the nature of the social structures through a complex process of complementary and contradictory reproduction of cultural elements.

A similar image appears in the leadership structures and functions of the traditional Bapedi and the ZCC. As the two establishments articulate their divergence and convergence with external, internal and mutual forces, paradoxical ideological and experiential realities become revealed. An examination of the political hierarchy, the quintessential contradictory parallel, leads the discussion on the broader topic of leadership structures.

Gender Relations in Leadership Structures

The power of the Bapedi king was complex, and in his various roles he depended on the assistance of office holders whose co-operation he needed for the effective exercise of that central power. He ruled through a severely restricted central authority by means of various institutions that included councils and the hereditary or appointed offices held by other members of the nation group. Thus the composite centralized authority became counter balanced by the large measure of autonomy exercised by the constituent groups in the nation group.

The whole network of the political structure worked not only for the operation of the nations' affairs, but also for the protection of law and the control of all abuse of power. The various councils and office holders allowed for the representation, directly or indirectly, of both sectional and majority interests in the conduct of government. On all levels there were men who were entitled to be consulted by the king or other office holders, and without whose active support no measures would have any force.[127] In the execution of his central authority the king was assisted in his various roles by a number of special functionaries who were not only appointed to these offices, but who were entitled to them by virtue of their birth, rank, and status.[128]

In these offices lay most of the executive functions. Foremost of these officials was *mokgomana*, literally, the highest noble male member of the group. *Mokgomana*, who by virtue of his rank and status was inferior only to the exclusive class of the kingdom, led the nation in the capacity of this lifelong position. *Mokgomana* could be substituted during his absence and illness by the next man in rank, *molatedi wa mokgomana*, the follower of mokgomana, and often when the principal office holder became very old such a follower frequently deputizes for him. A host of other executive positions existed. To name but a few, e.g. *morongwa* also a male member, occupying a minor non-hereditary position assisted *mokgoma*, by procuring services of the rainmaker during a period of drought. *Mofa-masemo*, the giver of land a noble male member of considerable seniority controlled the agricultural activities of the nation.[129]

An assistant or follower to mofa-masemo called *molatedi wa mofa masemo* usually the younger brother or relative substituted for him in his illness or absence. High ranking male servants formed part of the ruling body. Some of these were, *mohlanka wa lapa*, servant of the household, *moletsa phalafala* caller or crier, *mohlanka wa kgoro*. These blood relatives usually half brothers of the king or his father's did not themselves do menial work but enjoyed considerable amount of status. Their positions were hereditary through the male line of descent. The latter servant officials were respectively responsible for control of the households of the king, the entertainment of the king's guests and blowing of the king's war horn, which assembled the men, and not women. Moreover, a more formalized council of men, called *lekgotla la teng la kgosi* or *kgosi le bo tatagwe*, the inner council of the king, or the king and his fathers, respectively, assisted the king.

This private and secret inner council consisted of *mokgoma*, the *kgoro* and *lapa* servants, and the *mofa -masemo*, helped the king to formulate policy and discuss before hand, any measure which was later referred to wider councils. In instances of great importance and confidential nature, the king and the inner council consulted a wider body of male councilors known as lekgotla la thopa, private council.

This council confirmed policy decisions taken by the inner council, but also added its advice, and thus could accept, modify or reject such decisions.[130] The private council, therefore, sanctioned policy or laws, and could be described as the ruling nucleus of the nation. In theory the king could override the decisions of this council, but rarely attempted to do so, as such action would have led to a fission in the nation group. The co-operation of this council was essential for the successful government of the nation group, and the council provided possibly the greatest check on the behavior of the king. All matters of public concern were finally dealt with before a general assembly of men. A slight distinction existed between two types of nation gatherings. The first, informal gathering called *lekgotla la banna*, council of men constituted a court of law, attendance at which was not compulsory. The men present at the king's gathering place could also discuss nation affairs in an informal manner and may thus initiate political activities.

The second formal type of general assembly, called *pitso*, was assembled by the king and attendance was compulsory. Any man who did not attend or who had not previously arranged to be excused on sufficient grounds was liable to be fined by the court. Such formal nation gatherings met to discuss and finally accept new laws or nation policy. The king, who normally did not participate in the discussions, opened the proceedings by putting the matter which he had previously discussed with his inner council before the meeting.[131] Any man could take part in the ensuing debate; generally the nation would find itself in agreement with the king and his councilors, and very little debate would follow after the king had outlined the matter. Where differences of opinion became apparent, the official councilors of the king attempted to bring the men around to their opinion. Often the weight added to arguments and their positions normally prevailed.

Should there be great differences of opinion and very strongly expressed feelings on an issues, the king would judge the majority opinion, and allow discussions to proceed until he had a fair indication. He would then close the discussions and give his decision accordingly. Many instances can be quoted of kings acting contrary to their own desires but in keeping with the wishes of their nation groupsmen. The opposite was rarely the case. The above discussion demonstrates the extent to which the official running of the Bapedi nation was men's domain. Arguably the ZCC leadership structures appear to follow along similar lines of authority.

In comparison with the Bapedi king, the ZCC Bishop's authority, said to be derived from the inspiration of the holy spirit, seems absolute. Although assisted in his duties by only the male prophets, ministers and inner council (constituted mainly by members of his family), the Bishop alone interprets the church's laws of procedure, proclaims and implements new rituals, and punishes violators. He does not normally adhere to the drawn constitution, for a number of reasons, including the fact that until the most recent Bishop none were fully schooled in the western sense, and the fact that the constitution was created, primarily, to comply with governmental regulations, and not to satisfy an internal need of the church. The obvious similarity of the constitution of both leadership structures by councils of male relatives with no women, does not preclude the more fundamental deviation expressed through the autocracy of the Bishop.

In addition to appointing and ordaining ministers and prophets, the Bishop has the power to veto the council's discussions and to suspend or expel any member who disagrees with or disobeys him. Any opposition warrants expulsion, synonymous with excommunication. The latter action impacts members so severely that one woman described it as "comparable to expulsion from heaven". Thus the Bishop's power reflects a significant transformation of the more consensual and democratic methods employed by Bapedi kings. Furthermore, the power of the bishop reveals the level of internalization by the ZCC church leaders of the authoritarian tendencies of the previous South African apartheid system of rule. It becomes very obvious that the ZCC axiologies were created through a process that oscillated between the traditional structures, the church's initiatives, as well as the apartheid regimes influence.

There are, in addition to these differences, equally or more powerful parallels to the traditional Bapedi political structures. One of the most striking finds expression in the ties of kinship responsible for the unification of various nation units. The distinction of the political role of the division of sexes, and force deriving from the age differentiation system, form additional similarities. The cleavage of wealth, privilege, and status synonymous with the distribution of power and authority was founded on the ties of kinship originating in the king. This network of kinship formed the basis of all power and authority throughout the nation structure categories of the church's authority. The traditional concept of king-ship among the Bapedi revolves around kinship. *Kgoro*, composed around a core of such kin, formed the most significant political unit. Political authority within *kgoro* tallied with the kinship ties within the unit. The political hierarchy in the whole nation group ascended in similar fashion towards the senior unit of the homogeneous core around which the nation group was constituted, where it attained its summit in the position of the king. The proximity of each unit to the king defined the extent of its political authority.

As the whole political structure emanated from ties of kinship, the web of kinship supported the kingdom, and the private advisers, who were the close relatives of the king, upheld his power if he was incompetent or a waster. They would protect him lest one should supplant him. Any change or alteration would have inevitably altered the entire structural order. Similar to the traditional Bapedi structure, the leadership structures in the ZCC are based on ties of kinship. The ZCC bishop rules the church with the assistance of a family council made up of brothers and uncles. Second to the family council, there is the church council, made up of the local elders of the church, (who are mostly blood relatives of the Bishop) appointed by and responsible to the bishop. The elders, who live near the bishop's headquarters, attend to matters brought about by different congregations to the council for arbitration.[132]

The council applies severe judgment as a repellent to disobedience, and fixes fines in the same way as nation court fines. The manner of address between the ZCC Bishop and his congregation evokes that of the traditional king and his nation. The king was always treated with great respect. He was ceremonially addressed by different honorific personification titles such as, *sebatakgomo*, or *tau*, which means wild beast and lion respectively., and his deeds were exalted in special laudatory poems recited at important assemblies. The king's functions were wide and varied and united as a single whole in the kingdom. A strong fusion of his priestly, political duties, executive office, and his ritual duties existed. His description as the father of the nation effectively reflected the reciprocal relationship between the nation and king. He was not only the executive head of his group, but also the legislator, the supreme judge, and the religious and ceremonial leader.

Like the king, who was addressed by various honorific titles in which he personified various noble animals, the ZCC bishop is often publicly addressed as, for example, *Sebatakgomo*, (Wild Beast), and other emotionally emulative terms which elevate him to, simultaneously, the status of representative of God and king. Thus, the congregation's prayers are often characterized by, "*Baranabase Morena*," (Barnabas King). This points to the ZCC's philosophy of religion.

Another area in which the ZCC follows the pre-colonial kingly authority was that of succession based upon kinship rather than, as occurs in other African Initiated Churches, on religious charisma. With very few recent exceptions, traditionally the order of succession to all political office among the Bapedi kingdom , was hereditary in the male line of descent, in accordance with the normal principles of the kinship system. The manifestation of sex differentiation was highly visible in the Bapedi political system. The principal sanction of the king was manifest in his command of the regimental system evolving from the system of age grading. In this manner the king was in command of all organized forces in the nation group. However, this was often interpreted as beneficial to the majority of the community. To avert disputes commonly related to succession, the Bapedi distinctly prescribed succession to kingdom unilineally within a royal descent group, with membership of the dynasty transmitted only through the male line. The limitation of eligibility through the designation of one son and heir served as a buffer from confusions that might arise from the complexities evolving from polygamy, I will argue.

The only eligible heir was the eldest son of the principal wife *mohumagadi*. *Mohumadi* is/was not necessarily the first married wife because marriage happened through accession on the advice of the king counselors. In addition, the whole nation figuratively married *mohumahadi* by virtue of their contribution towards her *magadi*. It was required that she be a daughter of a king, a factor which makes the marriage exogamous. To emphasize her royal status that distinguished her marriage from ordinary marriages, a symbolic renewal and rebirth of the whole nation became a necessity. Hence the extinguishing and re-lighting of all fires during her marriage ceremony in the group achieved the purpose.

Accordingly, succession in the ZCC church depends in practice if not in theory on, to a great extent, Bapedi succession rules. The children from Engenase's two subsequent marriages, were not recognized as rightful heirs to the church leadership, although they were permitted to participate in the brass band, an important position in the church. As Comaroff (1980) rightly points out, the long line of ZCC leadership follows directly in the Lekganyane line a fact which reaffirms Sundkler's assertion that the king-type leadership, in as far as African Initiated churches are concerned, lasts longer than the prophet-type, thereby resolving the problem of establishing the hereditary legitimacy of charisma.

By treating succession to leadership in the ZCC as hereditary, Lekganyane was extrapolating from the traditional Bapedi kinship system, primarily because, he was, at the very minimum, remotely connected with the Bapedi kingdom line. However, he regards himself as the king of his church and, as a Mopedi himself he found it relatively easy to apply the traditional Bapedi principles of succession to his church. In light of this, Bapedi tradition took precedence over the constitution as far as succession was concerned. In both leadership structures the visibility of women leaves a lot to be desired. The principal wife of the Bapedi king held political office and authority only over female activities. She arranged free labor of the women who have to weed and harvest the king's land. In the performances of her tasks the *mohumagadi* was assisted by one or more women known as the servants of the principal wife.

These servants were usually also wives of the king who come from the same nation as the principal wife and accompanied her during the time of her marriage. The youngest of the servants attended to the homestead of the principal wife and cooked the food for her and her children or arranged for the cooking and maintenance of the homestead. Similarly, it is inconceivable for women in the ZCC to be part of the inner and church councils. The post menopause prophetess' power is largely confined over other women. In cases where women do exercise their power over all, it is superseded by that of men. The following statements from interviews demonstrate how men justify the exclusion of women in the councils:

> " if led by a woman, it falls into a pit,
> "There are never two bulls in the kraal"
> "Women have their own role to play, which in this church they know, and are satisfied about. It is not us men who wanted it that way, but God--and women in this church know that" "Look at it   this way-women are impure-they go to the moon (meaning theymenstruate)--how can you expect a persowith such

a handicap to perform such an important duty as to serve in the council-[133]

Gender Relations in Religious Structures

The Bapedi and ZCC gender relations in the religious structures also mirror as they conflict with one another. The conception of God as male in both structures forms the appropriate commencement point. Mönnig states that before Christianity the Bapedi accepted without doubt the existence of a Supreme Being, a creator, *Kgobe*. After the introduction of Christianity the word *Modimo* substituted the word kgobe. The Bapedi conceived of *Modimo* as male, who fathered only one son, *Kgobeane*, which is the diminutive of *Kgobe.* Bapedi God, in its original conception, had very little direct practical personal relationship to humanity, a perspective clearly different from Christianity's. In proximity Badimo, the living dead (the departed) were nearer to God than the living, and thus acted as mediators. Even in God's capacity as creator of life and death, he is not attributed with the termination of life in its particular manifestation on earth.

This distance of Bapedi God from humanity, I will argue, extended into Bapedi conceptions of death. Bapedi did not believe that God can create people only to punish them eternally after a short period on earth. Before the Christian influence, the concept of hell was not an aspect of death to Bapedi, and indeed to the entire South African indigenous cultures. Their model of the hereafter, like the rest of the indigenous people of South Africa, reflects a comfortable place where the dead, looked over the well-being of the people on earth.

The ZCC structures reveal the impact of the above African heritage. The ZCC conception of God and Jesus Christ replay the traditional religious structures of Bapedi, as does the style of interaction between God, *Badimo* and the living. In this case male Jesus Christ claimant to the second personhood of a triune male God head, forms the object of Christian religious faith. Jesus Christ occupies the center of this faith. In earlier times of the ZCC Jesus Christ was conceptualized in the same way as Bapedi Supreme Being, the creator, *Kgobe* or *Modimo*, with the personal contact and relationship mediated by *Badimo*. Though the ZCC, in its early constitution, acknowledged the presence of Jesus Christ and Engenase often preached about Him, some few confused followers placed Jesus Christ and Engenase at par. Others believed that God empowers the Bishop, who mediates between Christ and the congregation like the *morongwa*, the traditional Bapedi messenger who mediated between the Chief and the nation. Or like *Badimo* mediated between the living and God.

In both structures, God is remote and his impact on human life comes through mediation. The distance here does not preclude, however, an opposite but equally important characterization of the relationship between God and people, on another level, as profoundly intimate, or even almost equivalent. I'm referring to a ZCC dynamic, which equates God and humanity in the person of the Bishop as God's representative. This dynamic recalls, as it emerges from, the way in which Bapedi traditionally maintained a relatively fluid limit between the living and the dead, and I will argue that most indigenous South African cultures still do. The Pope recently announced that the Roman Catholic Church should make the religion relevant to the context of the people. Although I believe the Pope is way too late, the South African Catholic churches, indeed, now also call upon *Modimo le Badimo*--God and Badimo. Whereas people used to belittle the ZCC for refusing to see a conflict between Badimo (the living dead) and Modimo (God), the majority is now arguing for the same position that the ZCC has long stood for. There is a lot to learn from this church.

Bapedi held that the living and the dead reciprocally influence one another, so that souls of the dead people become living spirits, *Badimo*, which ultimately find their way to an undefined world, similar to, but superior than the living world. The influence of the living on the dead, though limited, formed a fundamental element of all rites linked with the living dead spirits. The unlimited nature of the living dead on the living's behavior became evident through good health and prosperity to the respectful and obedient. To those who neglected the prevailing social code, of which they were the guardians, their influence manifested in the form of sickness, economic loss or some other misfortune. Hence, in order to retain their favor they had to be particularly propitiated.

Regarded as intermediaries of God, the powerful *Badimo* communicated with the living through dreams, by means of *moya* and *seriti,* which were: two real life giving attributes which each person receives from God. Detached from the body through death, *moya* could speak, while seriti, was a configuration of the deceased manifest in the dreams of the living only.[134] When Badimo repeatedly occurred in a person's dream that indicated discontent and a need to be appeased. *Badimo* sometimes could also pronounce their desire through whirlwind and hail, which signified displeasure and omen respectively. Sacrifice constituted the only means of appeasing God and *Badimo*.

Only the senior male head conducted ceremonies because he was logically "nearest" in terms of proximity to death in the world of the living to *Badimo*. The head of the family, almost exclusively a male, sacrificed and called upon *Badimo* at their graves whenever they reveal themselves through dreams or calamity, or in some other form that the diviner interpreted as a signal of offense. The manner of address to *Badimo* mirrored the way peers addressed each other among the living, a familiarity which reflected a fluidity of the limits between the living and the dead. Although all other *Badimo* were called upon for help, those of the rulers related to living kings were particularly honored. To the extent that the king and his relatives guided their fortunes on earth, so spirits of the rulers from whom he descended were held by Bapedi to afford supernatural protection and assistance to the people they had once ruled.[135]

We find a similar fluidity in the ZCC mode of prayer, which characteristically invokes God and the bishop's name simultaneously, e.g. "O God of Engenase, I stand here in front of you" or, "I will end here in the name of Barnabas". This tendency to metaphorically aggrandize the Bishop's powers derives from, I would argue, a perception among ZCC members that the Bishop wields exceptional, even divine, healing powers. Accounts of his miraculous healing skills, kept reverently present in common memory, constitute the core of the ZCC philosophy of religion and, more pertinent to my theme of comparison, parallel the traditional Bapedi valorization of male divine healing and healers.[136]

That the parallel is profound and virtually complete seems to me clearly evidenced in an equality of what may be the most fundamental characteristic of both Bapedi and the ZCC faiths; in both, the accounts of miracles performed by divinely gifted men and women healer simultaneously constitutes and "prove" (by reasserting the miracle stories as true) the presence of a higher power. We can thus begin to shape an understanding of the ZCC's deeply rooted perception of the Bishop's supernatural healing capacities, enabling the same faith for which members not only visit Moria, the church's headquarters, in Lebowa, (which can be compared to Muslims Mecca) to receive all these benefits from their "Messiah's representative", but also to roll down where the bishop has passed to be healed or blessed.

Even though the ZCC members also use the name of Jesus Christ, as the son of God when they baptize, there is no clear distinction between Father and Son. Baptism is mainly understood, by the followers, to mean admission into the church, and not a reconciliation between God and humans. However, after Engenase's death the position of Jesus Christ was slightly altered. Members try to revive the name of Jesus, by constantly calling his name. In pragmatic terms, the holy spirit in the ZCC is a replication of the *Badimo* spirit or the living dead. The concept of the holy spirit *moya o mokgethwa* in the ZCC translates into God's guidance, and differs in meaning from *moya*, which could mean air.

Although in some instances confused with, and often subordinated to *Badimo*, the holy spirit plays a dominant role in the development of the ZCC Engenase, and, currently, his successors are construed to have complete control over the holy spirit which endows prophets with preaching skills. It should be noted that women prophets are perceived as having less spiritual powers than male prophets. The Bishops possesses the power to extract the spirits from prophets, thereby terminating their profession. The holy spirit is often manifested in its power to heal, ability to exorcise evil spirits from possessed persons, and in the "ability" to prophecy.[137]

Both Bapedi and ZCC religious structures are explicitly, inextricably tied to concepts like impurity, taboo, witchcraft, magic, divination and medicine, which are in other religions often only implicit. I mean to explore the associative chain which links the conventional to the less conventional aspects of both religious organizations, beginning with Bapedi's. The concept of the supernatural among the traditional Bapedi extended into the condition of impurity, signified by the word *ditshila*. *Ditshila*, referred to a state of impurity exclusive of moral consideration of proper or sinful conduct. This infectious condition posed a threat to the social order. Impure conditions included, for example, a woman giving birth, an unborn child, the placenta, and the house where birth has taken place, a woman who has had a miscarriage, a woman who has intentionally had an abortion, children who are born with teeth, breech (children who are born with feet first), pregnancy through prostitution, and sickness and death.

According to this logic the condition of *ditshila* primarily occurred in women and children, and men could be contaminated through contact, or loss of a spouse. To the extent that the latter logic follows the dichotomous association of women with nature and men with culture, I will argue, it constitutes sexism. Death rendered both men and women *ditshila*, however, for women an additional standard different from men's functioned to isolate them. In case of women their biological makeup and bodily functions over which they have no control operate to isolate and stigmatize them in society, like pregnancy, abortion etc. since contact with a person in such a condition culminated in contamination, which necessitated purification.[138]

The condition of impurity was closely linked to the dual concepts of heat and coolness, drought and rain. To Bapedi rain symbolized goodness while drought denoted all hardships, suffering and evil. *Ditshila* implied, then, heat and drought, and needed to be made pure by means of ritualistic application of coolness emanating from rain. Cutting across the concepts of impurity, heat, and coolness was the concept of taboo. Its embodiment of both the condition and the act of impurity made it distinct from *ditshila*. In fact, taboo, I will argue, served the purpose of preventing or avoiding contact with impurity.

It was prohibited, for example, for a "pure" man to have intercourse with menstruating woman, a woman who has had an abortion, miscarriage, a pregnant prostitute, or a widow, all considered "hot". It was also taboo for any person in a condition of impurity to enter the cattle kraal, to work on the lands, or to be present at any religious rite. It was as if *Badimo* sanctioned actions which were willfully taken, in a way that they did not for conditions of impurity, in which the individual had no particular will. Rectification of a broken taboo, therefore, included both sacrifice to *Badimo* and magical action, where purification of impurity depended only on magical ritual involving coolness.

Emerging from the combination of taboo and impurity was the concept of *boloi*. *Boloi*, witchcraft, like taboo, related to both the action and condition of impurities. The witches were willful conductors of heat, an innate trait with which they were born. Similar to impurity, witchcraft derived its charge from socially threatening transitional states between, for example, walking and sleeping, or inside and outside. The two kinds associated with witches both embodied combinations of distinct categories. *Dithuru*, for example, were objects made from dead people's bodies, and had no will of their own, but depended on the will of the witches. They were, as it were the dead brought to life. *Dithongwa*, combined savagery and civilization, in that they were animals like wild cat, dogs, snakes, owls, and bats which could be made docile by the witches, and served as their sentries and steeds.

The Bapedi distinguished between day witchcraft and night witchcraft. Day witchcraft, which was practiced mainly by men, involved the learned ability of the application of magical and medicinal practices solely to the detriment of others. Night witchcraft, on the other hand, practiced mainly by women, evolved from the incomprehensible or complex inborn trait of heat and a unique ability of performance; for example, a night witch's infant had the ability of cats to cling to the wall. Thus the difference between the two lay in the methods employed and not in the time of operation. Protection against witchcraft was provided by a medicine man *ngaka*. Since most events were interpreted in terms of supernatural sources, ngaka had to possess a keen foresight and proper avertive methods to have genuine control over forces of witchcraft.[139]

Ngaka, or diviner and healer, who was usually male, enjoyed a prominence endowed by the plurality of causes attributable to various supernatural forces. His various functions included inter alia, the divination of causes of events, the recommendation of remedies or aversion measures, the naming of witches, the prescription of protection measures against the witches, the cure of damage done by the witches, and the divination of the wishes and prescription of sacrifices to Badimo. The diviner was the dispenser of leachcraft, and possessed the knowledge of good magic to the advantage of those who employ his services.[140]

Of the various methods of divination the most common by far was the use of bones, called *dikgagara* or *ditaola*, which could be broken down into a number of groups. Pertinent to my theme of comparison and exposure of mutual reproduction of gender relations, the selection of *ditaola*, reflected equality in terms of gender representation, i.e. in most cases every male part was matched by a female part. Consequently, the fundamental, indispensable group was a set of four pieces representing a man, his wife, their son and daughter. The pieces for a man and a woman were pyramidically shaped, and were cut from the tip of a hoof of a bull and a cow respectively.[141]

The two pieces for the son and daughter were flat oblong pieces, formerly made from ivory, and currently from the tibia of a bull or cow, or the fang of a pig.[142] Less essential units of the set derived from the astragali of various animals. One important pair taken from a male and female baboon, represented witches and provided information on witchcraft. Unfortunately, the sole male ant-bear piece presented a deviation. The piece upset the whole almost perfect picture of gender equality in ditaola. By associating the ant-bear piece with only the male diviner perpetuates gender hegemony. In addition, the perception of and reference to this piece as modimo, God and a symbolic representation of the diviner himself, further punctuates the ascendancy of men over women, I will maintain..

Very few women become *dingaka*. In fact *dingaka* normally came from a family of diviners, although anyone who wished to pay a price of a beast to a ngaka of his acquaintance may also learn by apprenticeship. A significant exception to the rule of apprenticeship is the king, who was automatically considered to be the principal ngaka, inheritor of a ceremonial divination set. Because he lacked the skills of interpretation, his position was also ceremonial and he relied on the expertise of his subordinates for his readings. The position of the diviners was both honored and respected in Bapedi society, and second only to the king's in power and influence.

In addition to the diviners, *Bapedi* had *Mapale* or *Malopo*, who divined through direct spiritual contact with Badimo. In contrast with diviners, *Mapale* were frequently women, and their task involved exorcising spirits sent by Badimo and witches, from possessed people. The possessed person was simultaneously cured, and initiated to become *Mapale*, by means of intensive dancing which culminates in the consultant falling into a trance and a chant, both interpreted as a communication with Badimo. Perhaps because her duties were more restricted than that of the diviner, or because of attitudes towards women, *Mapale* did not share the special status attached to *ngaka.*[143]

ZCC immersed in healing that assumes primarily two forms, i.e. divine and faith healing, I will suggest, depends upon and recreates, as it emerges from Bapedi traditional concepts of the supernatural, expressed through; taboo, impurity, witchcraft, magic, divination, and medicine. Divine healing, initially practiced solely by the founder of the church, who as you remember was a male, evolved into and eventually duplicated faith healing. Both methods of healing involve the use of symbols, as will become clear in the discussion that follows.

Divine healing in the ZCC followed a similar pattern as in all the Zionist and Ethiopian churches, as described by Hanekom (1975) and Sundkler (1976): through laying bare hands on consultants. The basis of this practice is found in both St. Mark 16:17,8, and St. Matthew 10: 7,8. where it is expressed that people will be cured through the laying of hands on them. In the ZCC, however, the idea pragmatically assumed a different dimension. The concept interwoven with traditional traits, involves certain taboos that govern the laying of hands on consultants. Ministers who had attended a funeral cannot lay hands on people and have to observe a period of seven day abstinence before they can continue with the execution of their duties. Similarly, living with and eating food prepared by a woman with less than a three months old baby constitutes a threat to the social order, and prohibits ministers to lay their hands on people.

If you remember, the latter accounted for a large number of polygamists among ministers and prophets, since it provided for an alternative wife, and avoided forestalling of duties. The ban on menstruating women based on the book of Lev.12:1-5, not only prohibits such women to shake hands with ministers and to mix with the congregation, but also forbids ministers who have had such contact from the execution of their duties. At businesses owned by the ZCC such women used to be allowed to work only after seven days.

The laying of bear hands was discontinued in 1930, because it threatened Engenase's power. Ministers who were successful in healing consultants through laying hands, took credit for the deed, and healed consultants were more inclined to believe in their power. To counter this Engenase banned the use of bare hands, and to ensure that all power of healing in the church will be attributed to him, he introduced pieces of khakhi cloths that were blessed by him. The cloths regarded as the only legitimate healing tools, could be confiscated by Engenase in case of a disqualification. With the increase of membership, these pieces proved expensive, and were substituted by ordinary green papers or newspapers.[144]

Faith healing is inextricably interwoven with the utilization of tools believed to possess healing powers. One faith healing method involves pricking by a needle which is especially designed and blessed by the Bishop, used in conjunction with a six centimeter long and one-and-a-half centimeter thick wood, kotana. The use of the needle, also the confine of male prophets, serves to extract impure blood by piercing primarily the elderly patients' legs and hands.

Kotana serves to apply healing through hitting all painful parts of the body. This method of healing is comparable to the traditional method of extracting blood perceived as a source of general bodily pain, headache, and eye disease, from a person's body, by sucking through a cut artery or joint, called *lomega*. As an alternative to pricking, coffee and tea, with or without milk, also serve as blood purifiers. The effect of water as a healing implement in the ZCC primarily depends on its source, type, and availability. Water drawn directly from distant seas and rivers, is said to produce more satisfying results than water from taps, for example. Members go to great lengths to fulfill instructions of obtaining such water, not only because of their belief in its effect, but also because water from taps falls short of curing specific sicknesses. Blessed water from whatever source heals through various forms. One important form is through drinking, called *mogabolo*.[145]

Most members drink such water every morning and evening as both a form of averting misfortunes and diseases, and in helping barren women to become pregnant. Sprinkling water on people and objects is believed to have a purifying effect. Blessed water or *meetse a thapelo* can also be used in cooking and washing one's body. Salted water is used to get rid of excessive bile through vomiting. In addition water mixed with sand is used to sprinkle homes, businesses and even crops to ward off witchcraft and misfortunes. Ashes sometimes substitute water in use.

Blessed walking sticks and strings or strips of waist cloths, served as a form of protection against mishaps and witchcraft, respectively. Engenase, the founder of the church, is said to have healed a cripple in Johannesburg through the powers of his walking stick and the music from his band. Members gave accounts of similar miracles performed by Barnabas, the current bishop. The strips of waist cloths, on the other hand maintained their protective powers, for as long as they were not washed with soap. In addition to this, a blue square cloth called *khouseane*, meaning hidden, is attached in a hidden place inside the clothes served to protect individuals from assaults and lightning.

Mr. Lr2[146], one of the high priests suggests that this is associated with Act 19:12 in the Bible, where Paul's clothes are used to cure the diseases. The church members cling to the believe that power is transferred first from the objects, and then go to the person.[147] Barrenness which, to a certain extent still holds a detrimental effect in terms of the perpetuation of a marriage, comprises one of the most important reasons of faith healing in the ZCC. Apart from healing this through water, Bishops utilize a small blessed twig, thupana, which barren women look at and make a knot, representing the child, in their small blankets.

Members who have been through this profess the authenticity of the whole process. Some of the ZCC bishops, especially the founder, Engenase, are said to possess the power of making rain. An example is cited where he made rain for a certain chief Matlala, who testified about this in front of the congregation. This act attracted and still attracts more members to the church. Various other methods are used: Newspapers cut into strips and blessed, are burned in the faces of the consultants to purify objects, stop fights between husbands and wives, and to heal. Most houses of the church members could be identified by blessed copper wires above entrances of homes to safeguard against lightning. Sanctified papers are used to bless the food. All these methods have to be prescribed by prophets, priests and bishops, in an interaction that evokes that of traditional diviners.[148]

Summary

The above discussion on the symbolic reproduction and contradiction of African cultural elements in the ZCC reflects a continuity of patriarchy, albeit in altered forms in some instances. It can be argued that the similarities in both structures presents a continuity in cultural practices. Logically the ZCC members will be influenced by both since it can also be argued that most members joined the church precisely because of the retention of African traditional practices. The badge and *magadi*, two different entities achieve the same purpose of unifying the groups within these two institutions. *Magadi* establishes in-law relationships where such relatives refer to one another as *metswalle*, as does the ZCC badge. ZCC members identified by the badge refer to one another as *metswalle*. In this case symbols produce what can be perceived as equality in gender relations. However, other symbols perpetuate patriarchy.

African systems of prohibitions and preferences, for example as they occur in both structures reflect persistent gender inequalities. While Bapedi structures involved an extensive and more complex construct that included the sororate, levirate, ghost, and preferred marriages that also transformed the fraternal relationships into filial relationships, the ZCC reflects a similar but less complex structure. Visions through dreams controlled a choice of marriage partners in the ZCC.

Common to both is the valorization of patriarchy over matriarchy. Polygamy and not polyandry constitutes the cultural norm, the birth of a son translates into a completion of marriage, patrilineality as manifest in whose surname the children assume, and who inherits and ascends to power has primacy over matrilineality. Patrilocality still constitutes a preferred residence after marriage. In addition, even in the face of cultural change, authority of the family centers around the father, the continuity of the male relatives through the retention of the name remains paramount. Women always take the men's name, albeit in a hyphenated fashion, my research has never uncovered a case where a man chose to take over the woman's name.

Contradictory parallels also abound in leadership structures. Although the Bapedi leadership structure proves to be more democratic and consensual than the autocratic ZCC's, males dominate in both structures. Inner councils and decision making bodies constitute male confines. In both structures the network of kinship central to the running of both institutions also reflect patrilineal preferences over matrilineality. Both structures place high value on succession through patrilineal kinship structures, with no history of a woman ever succeeding to the highest leadership position. Correspondingly, in both structures men's prominence overshadow women's authority. Mutual sayings in both institutions such as "If led by a woman it falls into a pit," "there are never two bulls in a kraal" curtail women's visibility in areas where they have authority.

Moreover, the conception of God as male in both religious structures points to the mutual perception of women. Indeed, only women possess heat and are receptacle of impurity necessitating their isolation until purified. Men make up important diviners and prophets while women occupy peripheral positions such as *Mapale*. Perhaps the most telling sexism manifest in the ZCC's requirement of women to reach menopause before they can hold pivotal positions as prophets. The logical implication then becomes, I will maintain, that the absence of menstruation in menopause equals purity. Since men can hold office at all times with proper qualifications, I can only assume that their biological constitution, obviously devoid of menstruation, translates into a symbol of purity that gives them an unfair advantage over women.

The discussion contains all the reasons why patriarchy has persisted over the years. For example, the division of labor, the association of men with culture and women with nature, and modernization as in the hyphenated surname. Modernization still fails to resolve the actual primacy of men over women, like I have alluded before, still the continuity of the men's family becomes paramount. The importance of the influence of the two structures on women's perceptions of non-sexism cannot be relegated to the margins. The variety of their responses derive from both social structural forces as well as socialization, or from a combination of both.[149] Also the influence of the developmental approach to non-sexism molded some answers, I am referring to conscious efforts women make to reach decisions that construct and reconstruct their perception of social and educational reality.

The same trends are evident in how women perceive and construct patriarchy and sexism. Thus to maintain continuity and consistency, focusing on the ZCC women's perception of these concepts becomes the relevant and logical next step.

4

ZCC WOMEN'S PERCEPTION OF PATRIARCHY AND NON-SEXISM

The overall objective of the study centers around an evaluation of ZCC women's conceptualization and mediation of patriarchy and sexism with their education and social development. The abundance of literature on gender socialization and women's subordination developed through time, reflects an in-depth discourse of convergent and divergent views. These ideas in turn reveal a variety of substantive paradigms that attempt to understand how men and women relate and have related throughout history. Some anthropologists like Chodorow (1978) stress the psychodynamic process of development of the unconscious as a determinant in how different genders arrive at decisions. Mead (1949) on the other hand refers to the importance of the psychological conditioning, with little emphasis on the unconscious. Subsequently other anthropologists like Ortner (1974) follow de Beauvior (1952) in subscribing to the universal association of men with culture and women with nature as the influential force that drives men and women to the kind of decisions they make.

These authors posit that because universally women' s opportunities to advance become curtailed precisely because of their biological make up, i.e. getting pregnant and lactating babies afterwards, cultural biases develop into social values that guide decision making.[150] Reskin and Padavic (1994) see the existence of the paradigm in employers' practices for instance. Most employers adopt an informal segregation code that keeps women from supervising men.[151] These authors believe in the universality of the practice.[152] Troubled by the assumption of universal oppression of women, anthropologists like MacCormarck (1977), employed Levi-Straus' structural approach to prove the fallacy of the concept of universal oppression of women based on the hierarchical binary association of men with culture and woman with nature.

Discussing the Sande of Siera Leone she shows how women predominantly regulate nature and sexual behavior by restricting sexual intercourse to sanctioned places, times and partners.[153] Thus cultural specificity focus, defined as autonomy theory came into being. As the discourse continued inquiry into individual life histories became an additional tool of analysis of understanding gender decisions. This theory that owes its origin to Wright Mills (1959: 143), examines how biographies and histories intersect with social structures to persuade decisions among genders. The analyses of the women's varied responses defy and de-naturalize any one theory as sufficient in the comprehension of how ZCC women construct and mediate factors that make up their world.

Their conception and process of articulation of the concepts cannot be represented as a neat unitary formation (Foster-Carter 1978), but rather it is a set of complex conceptual order motivated by a variety of factors. The women's responses reflect the validity of McCormarck's (1977) claim of the need for cultural specificity, I will also add of individual particularity, as well.

Foundations that Shapes Women's Perceptions

Religious Instruction

The construct and conceptualization of the concept of non-sexism by women in the ZCC produced answers that varied according to age, level of education, degree of exposure and commitment to the ZCC religious instruction, as well as rural/urban dichotomy. Conducted through participant observation and interviews. Women's varied and diverse responses displayed an evident epistemological foundation occasioned by the interpretation of religious instruction. Religious instruction and the theme of peace *khotso* as both the sources of knowledge production and the construct of cultural logic, play a pivotal role as mechanisms of socialization that shape how members construct the concept of non-sexism.

On frequent occasions women will refer me to the bible and biblical teachings as expressed in the church to affirm their answers. In addition to the bible they will also refer to the traditional practices of the Bapedi as to further authenticate their beliefs and practices. [154] The common response from elderly and middle aged women would be:

> *The Bible is my guide, and what I do not understand the bishop and ministers will clarify.*"[155]

These women believed that the ministers when involved with the word of God cannot go wrong, since they are inspired by the holy spirit. When I asked about the elements that might affect them adversely as a result of the religious practices of the church, they ascribed the differences to the division of labor saying:

> *"it is just like in the work place. You have a manager, a supervisor, and a subordinate. This does not translate into oppression, but a natural division of labor"*

In attending church services, it became apparent that though seniority defined by relative age assumes primacy with regard to the role that church members play, the role of gender as an organizing principle still manifests. For example, while there are male ministers across the age range who show deference to and respect of the elderly ministers, there are no women ministers. Priesthood in the ZCC is a male preserve, as we have learnt.

Consequently, only males can preach during church services, women cannot even by virtue of their age preach to a mixed audience that included males. Responses like the following were commonplace among both middle aged and older women:

> *"we do not envisage a stage where a woman will be a priest or a bishop in the church"* and *"it really does not matter whether a woman becomes a priest or a bishop"* [156]

When I inquired as to whether the call of non-sexism by the government will at some stage compel the church to change its position and ordain women as priests a lot of skepticism punctuated the varied answers.

Thus a general passive resignation among some women to the monopoly of priesthood by men persists. Women seem to have internalized their role as distinctly different from men with total disregard to the differential treatment.[157] The prospect of a non-sexist society loudly and clearly also advocates priesthood for women. To a few women in the church the possibility exists, to others especially the elderly it is an impossibility that will only attract God's wrath and poverty for women.

The latter follows the social value that finds expression in the New Testament and reads: "Let a woman learn in silence with all subjection. But I suffer a woman not to teach, nor to usurp the authority over the men, but to be in silence."[158] Violating such a command to some ZCC women will invite poverty. Yet to most, its reality and success will depend on the directive from the bishop, who will have a vision that will define the context within which the transformation to a non-sexist society should be addressed.

If the bishop sees a holy vision that sanctions that women can be priests that will be accepted without question. The latter view proves the instability of the socialization process as Gerth and Mills (1953) succinctly posit. During period of accelerated social change people do not usually draw from childhood experiences of socialization, but act to fit their present circumstances. These women hope that the bishop will act accordingly to the demand of the moments' requirement.

Similarly, conditions in the church sometimes dictate responses that breach church practice, and induce behavior and responses appropriate to the demands of the immediate needs. Functions of male and female elders demonstrate this. ZCC women elders regardless of their status still relationally enjoy respect and deference from younger males, including younger ministers. The deference however, does not extend to the realm of responsibilities like *ditaelo*.

Ditaelo refer to directives inspired and conferred by the holy spirit on male ministers to prepare and administer medicine prescribed by the prophetesses to cure and rectify afflictions. However, in case of emergencies, like in a death threatening situation, where a member needs urgent medical attention and a male minister cannot be found, a woman elder can administer "*ditaelo*." As a 62 year old woman elder, who has been in the church for thirty four years, Mrs. Lr,[159] and supports herself and family by selling food to school children asserted:

> *"I have personally witnessed older women handling coffee, tea and other healing devices where a male priest could not be found. The women have to be past menopause"*

Women prophetesses and elders can only prophesy and preach at women only services, that are held on Wednesdays. Even then, these meetings are opened by a male elder priest, who regardless of his relative age to the woman elder, possesses the privilege of opening the women's meetings. Women elders assume that role only in the absence of a male. Further, I have alluded to the practice where on Sundays and Wednesdays are not allowed to use the front door to enter the church, and only male ministers, male church elders, and dignitaries can use the door. All the other ordinary male members have to observe the same practice as women, meaning, they do not use the front door to enter the church. Older and middle age rural women members gave no credence to this practice. They perceive it as a commonplace practice where dignitaries everywhere enjoy special privileges like walking on the red carpet. The absence of women in the midst of those dignitaries constitutes no offense, neither does it in their eyes diminish their status as women. Some women contended:

> *"when you travel with the president*
> *you do not expect to get the same treatment.*
> *He is the president you are a common person.*
> *It is done everywhere. It is not unique to the*
> *ZCC."*[160]

These women members perceive this interplay of gender and seniority as relational and not necessarily hierarchical. At variance with Chodorow's (1978) theory of the unconscious as determining choices, these women see their perception as deriving from the level of consciousness. One woman elder a fifty four year rural woman Mrs. Mu who married into the church and has been a member for more than fifteen years, remarks that what other people perceive as male privilege, like male ministers opening services points to the division of labor with no reference to male power. That God's reception of and answer to prayers is non discriminatory since it gives equal hearing to prayers of anybody who prays to him, legitimizes her claim, she posited.

Another much older rural woman, Rr,[161] gave a more specific response that may suggest men's superiority to women:

> *"men are the head of the household. It is not only cultural but*
> *the Bible also states so. It has been like that all my life. There*
> *are things that I do that men cannot do. And things that I can do*
> *that they cannot"*

A general agreement with the above view prevailed, while views diverged as to whether a transformation should be effected to conform with the concept of a no-sexist South Africa. This woman and most women in her age group do not feel the need to oppose the practice. Opposing the practice violates the basic principle of peace that constitutes the fabric of the ZCC structure. She conceived the move towards non-sexism as a danger to peace or *khotso* and as a potential precipitator of fights that are not tolerated in the church. The majority of the middle aged women on the other hand, would welcome change achieved within the parameters of the church's dictate or/and through a vision seen by the bishop from God.

Further, while all males can potentially become prophets, only women past menopause as indicated before qualify as prophetesses.[162] In this case power as conferred by women's seniority manifest in a situational and relational fashion. As the discussion has demonstrated the prophetess enjoys enormous authority and respect from any younger members and congregants, regardless of gender. In addition to civility, seniority endows in women prophetess a measure of control that guarantees obedience from all subordinates and reinforces their position of leadership.

Here again the ZCC religious organizational structure reflects both seniority and gender as organizing principles that determine power situationally and relationally. For males both seniority and gender constitute criteria that confer leadership status, while for women only seniority plays a pivotal role in determining leadership. Charisma, while it works for men too to a lesser extent, it can also play a pivotal role in enhancing a woman as a leader, as stated earlier

Like in other African Initiated Churches in West and East Africa, the Harrists movement and Legio Maria respectively, the ZCC shows occasions of the ephemeral rise of women to leadership with the support of a male kin.[163] In the Weberian (1947) sense the charismatic potential for women is routinized in the group as a whole, but not with respect to their specific positions or cultural contributions. Usually the charismatic promise sustains the female leadership positions.

For most men and women the amount of years of school education is minimal. Most of the male ministers have less than four years of school. Ngubane (1977) argues that the ZCC like many other AIC vindicated the superiority of their religious and cultural value by referring to practices and symbols in the bible. The initial lack of interest in school can be traced from such roots. Mr. A.M. Kgathi a staunch member of the ZCC who not only holds two college degrees, but is also an advocate of providing school education to church members writes:

"The Bible is central to all teachings of the ZCC. Unfortunately not all members of the clergy have been trained in the ministerial work. In fact the majority of the priests are not literate." (ZCC Messenger, September 1985)

In concert with the above assertion traditionally in the ZCC the acquisition of education was not considered a prerequisite for ministry. As one member of the congregation Mr. M of Garankuwa put it:

> *"Jesus never attended school, preaching*
> *comes through the inspiration of the holy spirit--you do not need*
> *school for that."*

This pervasive conceptualization of knowledge production resonates with the Bapedi cultural logic that rationalizes that the production of knowledge, wisdom and efficacy derives primarily from seniority. In addition it affirms that both gender and seniority function together in determining positions of authority, albeit differentially. Obeisance to superiors is highly visible and seems to facilitate acquiescence with the church's religious prescriptions. Similarly peace as a preeminent religious mandate and the foundation of the cultural logic in ZCC social, political and religious intercourse facilitates conformity with the teachings of the church, as becomes clear in the next discussion.

Peace-Khotso

That the base of the ZCC's axiological logic on all levels derives from the peace or *khotso* theme, becomes evident in the writings, amongst others, of one of the staunch members of the ZCC, Jan Mukhondo who asserts:

> *"Some joined us and boarded the ZCC peace train*
> *whereas others did not because they despised our*
> *Church. Some went amok thinking that they had better*
> *mechanisms for bringing peace in their territory, homes*
> *and at their work, but up to now they have not yet*
> *brought peace in their environments. Why? Because*
> *they are not turning their hearts and souls to Jesus who*
> *is the only Prince of Peace"* (II Thessalonians 2: 14-17)
> (ZCC Messenger 1992, Issue No 22, p8)

Mukhondo goes on to posit in the same issue that the church believes in Jesus Christ as the only prince of peace and it invites anybody who seeks peace to join them and they will achieve everlasting peace.[164] All teachings, in church, schools and meetings are preceded by the greetings of peace. Consequently peace as the fundamental epistemological basis for the ZCC sociocultural logic necessarily entails varied construction of meaning by the members. By some members, mostly older members, the thematic translation includes acceptance of the church's teachings without any opposition, while others, like younger members, contrary to the latter, apply its usage to advocate transformation.[165] The latter factor became very clear when I asked members if they agreed or disagreed with any teachings of the church.

The most common response emphasizes the centrality of the bishop, thus if the church mandates an order through the holy guidance of the bishop, nobody has any business to even suggest an opposing stance. At one instance a younger male university student, as the discussion will later reflect, questioned the management of the bursary fund by the committee members appointed by the bishop. The response from one of the male elders of the church echoed the notion that what has been mandated by the bishop equals infallibility.

Such manner of settling thorny and controversial issues, frequently manifested in most elderly women's responses to their perception of the fate of a non-sexist South Africa. These women in their late fifties and sixties cannot bring themselves to accept the call. Their acceptance and non-acceptance will be mandated by the bishop. In this way uniformity that ensures peaceful interaction will be maintained, they argued.

One woman, Lu.[166] went to great lengths to explain to me the advantages bestowed by the consistent observance of the peace theme, as well as its relevant application to men and women relationships within the church. Congruent with the notion of *khotso* she asserted, the bishop and the church highly condemn physical abuse of women and children by men. She reminded me of the many times I have been to church services with her and heard ministers preaching about the fact that a man who engages in physical abuse of his family, loses the power of peace, and will never ever be eligible to be a priest. She further remarked that the new South Africa is aspiring for an element of gender equality which the church has long achieved, because of peace. Women are also encouraged to resolve problems with their children through communication, and to resort to spanking only in extreme cases. Spanking does not comprise abuse but depicts a form of acceptable discipline.

Women with regard to this practice referred me to the traditional practice where they *bata* disobedient children.[167] Indeed, the word does not connote cruelty but is a method of calling a child to order with very mild spanking. Again they drew my attention to the age old tradition which could not mean that they were wrong. It was at this stage that one of these women drew my attention to the fact that the whole country debates the issue of polygamy, an element of the ZCC cultural practice sanctioned by the bishop and God, according to these women. Bishop Tutu, the Nobel Laureate and Archbishop of the Anglican Church recently argued for the practice to be accepted by the World Council of Churches as an authentic African cultural practice, one woman reminded me.[168] I then solicited their response to the practice within the church. A sixty two year old rural woman, Br who also supports herself and family by selling food to school children offered her response:

> "I know of men who practice polygamy in the church for a reason. The reasons could be a barren wife or a lazy one."

Others agreed with her. They saw polygamy as an authentic African cultural practice that agrees with the teachings of the ZCC. Polygamy in AIC as a form of an expression of spiritual independence, and an assertion of freedom for African traditional practices as against monogamy of the west, has been noted by many scholars.[169] Indeed, in concert with these findings, to these elderly women in the ZCC, monogamy posits a lot of disadvantages that engender conflict in marriages. To them monogamy as the only marriage option of cultural practice translates into an imposition from the north. Even then northerners themselves cannot practice what they preach. They parctice polygamy in a form of cheagamy, i.e. having extra marital affairs.

Northerners redefined polygamy into bigamy, thereby transforming an agreeable cultural practice into a criminal act. The women continued to direct my attention to the prevalent infidelity in monogamous relationships. In addition they related at great lengths the stress that accompanies confronting a cheating spouse. In such situations they all agreed, women have to fight to preserve the resources, like when a cheating spouse spends money on a mistress. Furthermore, they contend, the injured woman has to go for therapy. Whereas in polygamous marriages the first wife will be informed of the husband's intention and where she gives her consent she plays a pivotal role in officializing the marriage. As one of the two co-wives of one minister Du2 succinctly put it:

> "We do not have to worry about a husband who sneaks out and wastes money on entertaining another woman. We have each other for support. We do not need to pay money to speak to psychologists or psychiatrists.

*Thesupport that we need is right here. I would not sit
here and listen to people putting down ourculture.".*

These women's responses partially typify some of the responses
stated previously. As these more matured and mostly rural women, some
in monogamous and others in polygamous marriages accept the practice,
as younger women opposed it with the same amount of vigor.[170] They
discern the custom as not only insensitive to women, but also as
according men even more undeserved privileges. These young women
referred me to the healing practice in the ZCC that uses water as a
healing device. One, Jyu2,[171] reminded me that one of the reasons for a
man to take a second wife has to do with the claim of a woman's
incapability to conceive, in other words her barrenness.
In cases where a couple cannot conceive the woman bears the blame.
Men's sterility on the other hand never comes up as a factor to be
acknowledged and addressed.[172] Motivated by the above information, I
engaged in participant observation where healing was conducted. I
observed several ministers about this issue. Among those I observed
were two high priests.[173] They attended to many patients some of whom
had problems with conception. Indeed, in concert with what the younger
women had said, women and not men were said to have the problem of
conceiving, in cases where couples did not have children. In all these
cases water was prescribed as a form of cure. The water had to be taken
through a drinking process called *mogabolo.* The drinking of such water
every morning and evening averts misfortunes and diseases, and helps
barren women to become pregnant. I was curious to know if the water
ever helped a sterile man. To this effect I asked one of the minister's.
His answer was preceded by a detailed account of his involvement with
the church.

He told me he is not an actively practicing economist. Instead he
currently operates as one of the few highly educated priests of the ZCC.
He was born in the church which he abandoned in his youth. Later
because of the constant misfortunes that he encountered and the vision
through a dream of his deceased parents, he decided to go back to be an
active member of the church of his "father and mother". Then he finally
gave an answer which deserves to be reported in its entirety. He
responded as follows to my question as to whether men can be sterile:

   *"God intended everybody to have children--there is technically
no sterile man as much as there is nobarren woman--something
happens that blocks a woman's tubes and prevents her from
getting pregnant--our water serves the purpose of unblocking the*

dirt that blocks the woman's tube and enables her to   *have*
children."

I then asked if a man can be blocked, and consequently require the blessed water to unblock him. He then impatiently answered in the negative and emphasized the efficacy of the ZCC water in this regard. The efficiency that even, as far as he is concerned, supercedes Prof Mokgokong's ability. Professor Mokgokong is a celebrated South African gynecologist, who was based at Medical University of South Africa, and has helped women with the problems that prevented them from conceiving.

The other minister's answer though slightly different also implied the same sentiments. He emphasized that the church never had a case where it was a man's fault. If such a case should come to their attention, he assured me the ZCC will do for the man what it does for the women. In addition the church has never failed to help women to conceive. He told me that the blessed water in the ZCC does something that the hospital can never do for anyone. The water works in conjunction with belief and the friendly attention of the priests who attend to these women consultants. They relax and they also believe that they are going to be helped by the God of Engenase, Edward and Barnabase, and that produces results.

It is to such interpretation that the younger women object and also view as differential to women. They contend men can be sterile like women can be barren. In their opinion such views violate peaceful gender existence and interaction, and the basic principle of peace as espoused by the church. To the contention that a man can take a second wife if the first one exhibits laziness, they unanimously agreed that they would like to be accorded the same privilege. After all one maintained, Queen Modjaji of the Lobedu nation, in one of the South African Province has had several husbands. She practices polyandry[174]

Therefore they concluded, polyandry forms an authentic African cultural practice that should not be viewed as foreign and should also be applied to women. These women perceived both polygamy and polyandry as legitimate African practices. Practicing both forms of marriage in the South African culture would engender equality for both men and women. The differential right of men to have more than one wife as happens in polygamy will be balanced by the right of women to have more than one husband as manifest in polyandry.

This will be in line with the concept of non-sexism that the government advocates, as well as the peace principle of the ZCC. The discourse on the dress code expectations followed the same pattern of response.

Body as God's Temple

Responses on the expectations by the church of dress codes continued to vary according to age. The girls and women are taught to respect their bodies by wearing long skirts and dresses, cover their heads with scarves especially during church services, avoid wearing pants since they expose part of their bodies. Treating their own bodies as temples is emphasized. One elderly woman in her late fifties, Hu[175] explained that a woman's body symbolizes God's temple. Therefore the onus falls on a woman to respect herself so as to be respected by men and the public. The conduct and practice will also ensure that women present less temptation to men.

When I asked about the responsibility of men in terms of controlling their own temptation, several women between the ages of fifty four responded that women should not expose themselves to danger banking on the fact that men will control themselves.[176] While men are indeed expected to take that responsibility, women should also do their part. The fact that women respect their bodies and guarantee their own safety does not, for these women translate into putting an extra burden of expectation on women to the advantage of the men.

To them the practice amounts to taking care of oneself and should not be genderized. They compare this to protecting one's house against thieves by locking your doors. The following remark represent the sentiments of both elderly and middle aged women from both the urban and rural areas:

> "You do not depend on the good will of the
> thieves to take the moral responsibility
> not to steal your belongings"

On the other hand younger urban ZCC members views diverge from the above.[177] They strongly feel that they will wear whatever they want, and their choices of attire should not be sanctioned by fear of being attacked by men. These young urban women perceived this cultural axiology as constructed on social relational hierarchy that endows men with unfair privilege. The absence of an equal expectation from men seems to be a point of reaffirmation for these women's views. One even maintains: Clearly younger women would like to see an equivalent expectation of dress code for men, while older women see a relational and not a differential practice of dress code.

Education

Women's General Views on Education

Some priests had preached that a woman should not be more educated than a prospective husband or a husband. Quotes from the bible predominated to reaffirm the assertion that God intended a woman to be subordinate to a man. The saliency of the message from 1 Timothy 2: 11-2 that directs a woman to be subservient to the man also found articulation through quotations from John Knox's expression. Thus expressions such as "The same God that had denied power to the hand to speak, to the belly to hear, and to the feet to see, had denied to woman power to command man," [178] were invoked. Most women from age fifty plus rural and urban with little school education agreed with the idea. To them being more educated than a man precipitates insecurities in a man that results in constant in the household.

This particular view by women supports recent studies done by Blumstein and Schwartz, (1983) and Huber and Spitze (1983), focusing on northern societies, all demonstrate that on average women will enjoy an amount of support for their success from their husbands. However, husbands tend to experience discomfort when wives income equals or exceeds theirs. Important to note, men alone cannot be held responsible for the persistence of patriarchal tendencies, since some women uphold the marriages to protect and accrue their own interest. The above pattern became apparent in the ZCC women's answers.

They considered an environment where a man feels he is the main provider as more conducive to a peaceful and economically prosperous existence than if the opposite holds true. Elevated to an imaginary higher position a man tends to be agreeable and very generous, to a woman's advantage, some women posited. However, this study will later reflect a shift from this way of thinking in younger generations and women who have spent more years in school.

The teachings discourage women from competing with men, both in the domestic and work place. Any woman who strives to be more educated than her husband and possesses overly ambitiousness runs a risk of being called competitive. Such a competition, they contended brings tensions in and instability to marriages because they argued a more educated wife tends to undermine a husband. Women should acquire just enough education to complement and not to compete with men or current husbands.[179] Recently however, the ZCC stresses the importance of education, the stress however proves disparate in favor of men/boys. Boys are told to work hard and get the education that will enable them to provide for their families.

Commonly in the rural areas I encountered women of varied ages who had to leave school after third or fourth grade because of lack of sufficient funds in the family. Their families considered it prudent to continue financing the education of their brothers rather than theirs.[180] The assumption is that church endogamous marriages will guarantee them educated husbands who will care for them. Most of the young women in the rural areas who are in the ninth and twelve grade consider this a good idea. Getting married they said forms an essential inevitable step that every respectable young woman should aspire for. This view was shared by some middle age women with fewer than four years of school.[181] High education in a woman tends to repel and intimidate prospective husbands, they maintained. Furthermore, spinsterhood carries a stigma that engenders isolation and contempt, a risk too high to take. Most of the women feared to be referred to as *lefetwa*, a term which literally translated means, "an individual who has been passed for marriage". *Lefetwa* a nongendered or gender neutral nomenclature, that nevertheless exclusively in usage refers to women who have never been married.

On the other hand men who have never been married are just single, as indicated by the word *lekgwathla*. When subjected to a thorough analysis, the word *lefetwa* is a socially constructed word that evaluatively demeans a woman's status. It carries the implication "she has been passed by men for marriage." Culturally that state of having being passed is looked down upon. Therefore, the word reaffirms the status. Conversely, the word *lekgwathla* is devoid of such implications.

More specifically the word lacks any explicit reference to the contribution of the woman to the man's status. I will argue that such differential and reproachful language if differentially applied constitutes sexism, since it suggests single women lack dignity and respect, but single men on the contrary, are just that single men with no deaming implications.

Most of the young women in the rural areas generally agree with older women. They displayed loyalty to the church's values with which they completely aligned themselves. When asked how they will reconcile the contradictions in their church with a vision of a non-sexist South Africa, which advocates equal amount of education for all, they gave some of the following responses:

"the ministers will tell us if that is okay" (10 yr. old*) "that is not right, because a man is a man*
and a woman is a woman--she is made out
of a man, and she must obey him" (11 yr. old*)*
"even if a woman is clever than a man, but
she is not allowed to rule him--the church and
God say so--you can be clever, but a man has
to rule you--I don't know its the law-" (12 yr. old). [182]

On the other hand the responses of young women of school going age in areas around Garankuwa, Atteridgeville and Mamelodi, were very different. Some responded:

"The Church has an obligation to teach what it has to. I do not have to agree with everything. I am to get as educated as I want. A husband is not going to limit my educational ambition" (17 year old woman)
"Some of the teachings of the church are old fashioned. I love my church and I am going to marry within the church and be more educated than the man" (15 year old young woman). [183]

These young women were less concerned with being spinsters, but more troubled by the terminology employed to refer to women who have never married or those who are at an age considered inappropriate to be single. Inter alia the names include *lefetwa, letekatse, sefebe.* [184] They assert that they could be single, educated and very respectable women. The latter view obviously deviates from those of young women in the rural areas of the same educational standard. In addition to these general perception informed by the church's teachings, the ZCC had to, like other institutions contend with the apartheid laws.

The trichotomous confluence of the indigenous, colonial and apartheid historical periods precipitated a dynamic within the ZCC with its own unique epistemological milieu. The Influx Control Laws as well as the Migratory Labor System affected the ZCC schools like all the others. [185] To contextualize the women's responses to these laws, an overview of the composition of the ZCC schools is in order. All the ZCC schools are in Lebowa within the area of the headquarters of the church. The first school started its first operation in 1964. These schools are mostly served and are staffed by church members. At one time the schools were staffed and served exclusively ZCC members. Other members reported that they joined the church because they wanted their children to have access to the schools. These members highly praised the church and made it a point to let me know that they have not regretted their decisions since.

The ZCC schools are mostly staffed by male teachers at higher levels. Some of the teachers, mostly males are well qualified for their positions. However, others are not well qualified, they just have a junior high school education. The female teachers are mostly confined to primary schools. Male teachers in high schools tend to outnumber females.

Clignet and de Miranda (1977) conclude that the degree and form of labor and education for women stems from social, cultural and historical factors. They employ structural and Marxist analysis to examine women's educational status in the Cameroun, the Ivory Coast and Brazil respectively. Based on that they observe that more often economic development or development in general fails to accord women participation at the same level of equality with men in education and labor force.[186]

Akin to their analysis, the ZCC makes effort to "develop" its members in a way that still reinforces patterns of sexual differentiation. When I specifically pointed out the above disparity in terms of teachers along gender lines to the ZCC women, the responses implicitly resonated the impact of the apartheid migratory labor and influx control laws. Women gave their answers with much care not to indict the apartheid system. They avoided acknowledging the fact that the church cooperated with the apartheid regime, and forbade its members to fight against apartheid. They however admitted that men have no option but to move away from home and work in the mines. The long distance between home and the work place, as well as the low salaries (which were a far cry from their white co-workers), made frequent visit home impossible for the migrant laborers.

It was clear in their carefully worded answers that the influx control system, which made it illegal for a husband's family to move in with or even visit him at his place of employment ensured both the destruction and separation of families. More often men ended up creating new families nearer their place of employment. The responsibility to manage households and send children to schools with meager salaries still falls on women. Encouraging women to marry early as a strategy to lessen the financial burden, develops into a cultural pattern, while young men viewed as a source of security are encouraged to continue with their education. The latter factor played a part in the disproportionate representation of genders with both the teachers and students.

Furthermore, women alluded to the fact that young women and girls are sufficiently qualified after they have acquired women skills like sewing and cooking. The fact that these compose an important part of the school preliminary curriculum to them redeemed their position of withdrawing girls from school earlier than boys. Analyzed within the context of the apartheid laws and Bantu education system, this attitude is also informed and shaped by apartheid laws. With the exception of religious instruction, the school curriculum in the ZCC schools followed the South African Bantu education system syllabus. The Bantu education system, specifically designed for South African Blacks, prepared the latter not to compete with, but to be servants to their white counterparts. From this system of education the regime gained both a huge pool of unskilled and semi skilled Black labor, as well as a small Black professional and managerial class.[187]

Unterhalter (1989) describes Bantu education as a gutter tutelage to the masses specifically produced and fashioned to make it extremely difficult or impossible for Blacks to get out of the gutter of illiteracy and low paid employment. The range of subjects offered clearly reflects Bantu education's ultimate goal. The subjects offered illustrate the intent of the education very clearly. Lower primary schools, i.e. first grade to fourth, for example, offered algebra, needlework, mothercraft, domestic science, Afrikaans, English, Vernacular and Religious Instruction. Designed to generate competent current maids for the white population. I will also argue that the system also produced competent "housewives." Unfortunately such a background provides these women with a frame of reference that advances their justification to perpetuate discontinuance of women's education.

The framework not only justifies their actions but they also feel compelled to make decisions that accounted for this gender incongruity. In addition the women cited the high cost of education, again with great caution not to assign blame to the apartheid laws, however applicable. When I suggested that a great disparity existed in government funding among different racial groups, none of them was prepared to engage me on that level, except to say that that may be, but their main point focuses on the expensive education, and not causal matters.

The fact of the matter is the apartheid government spent $1000.00 annually for every white child's education as opposed to $50.00 for every Black child's.[188] Further Blacks unlike whites had to pay for their education from elementary up to university, while whites had free elementary and high school education. Text books were free for whites and not for the Blacks. In addition, Blacks had to travel for very long distances to reach their schools while whites did not have to.[189]

The gender wage differential that paid men more than women in all labor occupations,[190] professional and non professional functioned as an additional reason why the education of boys was encouraged to that of a girl. An inquiry into how women perceive these differences in the context of the education for women in current non-sexist South Africa again prompted varied answers, divided along age, and rural/urban dichotomous variables. Rural older women's answers proved to be in concert with their urban counterparts as they revealed loyalty and trust in the bishop's ability to guide and lead in matters of policy. These women believed that a vision will be disclosed to the bishop. The answer from one urban middle aged woman, Umu2[191] reads as follows:

> *"Like with everything else the bishop will see*
> *the light that will give us guidance. As of now*
> *things are working just fine. Educating boys*
> *more and not girls is not such a great loss*
> *since both will work together to take care of each other. In fact*
> *it is not a loss at all if you look at it as a matter of*
> *peaceful cooperation and not conflict. What*
> *we have to do is wait, like I said the bishop will tell us what is*
> *right."*

The others nodded in agreement,[192] and Kr further maintained:

> *"Even in your new non-sexist South Africa we*
> *still have Mandela at the top. We have to make decisions in life*
> *that involve choosing one over the other for the benefit of all.*
> *Can you tell me of an instant in life where people are completely*
> *the same?"*

The women further said that they regard the education of women as important as those of men, and that it will be of great pleasure to them if both can be equally educated. However, with the problems that they have presented to me above, like expensive education, they will still make the same decisions. Meaning they will continue to privilege the education of boys instead of girls even in the context of a non-sexist South Africa.

They further reveal their confusion and skepticism about the concept of non-sexism. One remarked that conflict that deviates from *khotso* seems to be deeply embedded in the latter notion. At this stage as I prompted them further by referring to the comparison with the non-racial concept, their dispositions displayed passive resignation as they echoed their faith in the guidance from the bishop. To these women the two calls of non-racialism and non-sexism depict distinct concepts that should not be confused.

They conceptualize gender harmony and equality as dependent upon division of labor, which by and large also dictates decisions about education of boys and girls. Inherent in the sentiment is the belief that in case of a marriage the couple will use their different skills as acquired through education to complement and not compete with each other. Conversely in as far as racialism goes the whites from the beginning had no intention at all to either share or complement Blacks in any way.

Their plan centered around subjugation. Some of them continued to explain that when they met their husbands the intention of staying and working together to raise children was clearly stated. One middle-aged urban woman, Mmu[193] further remarked:

> "*My husband did not say to me: " I want to marry you to subjugate you.' He said I love you and want to marry you, live with you, have children with you that we could raise together, and take care of each other*"

Thus the decision to educate boys over girls, they maintained, in that context does not translate into sexism. I also posed the question about equal remuneration, or differential remuneration based on skills, merit and experience, which could in some cases mean that women earn more than men. Either way for these women is fine as long as one does not humiliate the other. However, they all agreed that if a woman earns more the potential for conflict could increase more than if the opposite is true.

Culturally and religiously a man should be the main provider. Again to them the inability of some men to accept the woman as the main provider does not prove gender inequality, or lack of reason on the part of the man. He would merely be aspiring to fulfill his natural duties. Middle aged women express a strong desire for change of attitude and practice. However, their caution and cognizance of such a transformation to be carried out within the parameters of the church's law and the bishop's vision from God, cannot be ignored.

Similarly, younger rural women favor change that will be within the dictates of the church's theme of peace. In addition, they displayed the same amount of faith and trust in the guidance of the bishop, in the same way as the elderly women. Although they very much would like to earn according to their skills, merit and experience, albeit earning more than men or husbands, these young women placed a higher amount of responsibility on themselves to maintain the balance and peace in the household more than on men. As one of them Yyr put it:

> *"If I earn more education and more money*
> *than my husband, I will be very careful that*
> *I do not use that to humiliate him. I will also not*
> *abrogate the responsibility as a woman, like doing dishes, lest*
> *he should think that earning more money gives me airs"*

On whether in the current non-sexist South Africa boys should be preferred over girls when decisions are made as to who should continue with schooling, their answers largely echoed the above. They still maintained that they will get married endogamously to educated men who will look after them. They still further remarked that this was in concert with the teachings of the church and God. Unlike the older women, these young rural women understand the concept of non-sexism as something that people outside the church define as unequal relationship between men and women. While they acknowledged that that might be so, as they are informed by their church's teachings they have to view it as relational division of labor, and not as a divisive cultural practice, even though they would welcome the change.

Younger women from urban areas on the other hand see the current state of affairs as a vehicle to transform these differences in practice. Being afforded the same educational opportunities as young men will benefit the country as well as the church. Earning an equivalent or more money than the man where they are more skilled would serve as an incentive for them to excel at work and in their education. The majority of these young women feel very strongly that men should not be bothered or be overly concerned when a woman earns more than they do. They understand the concept of non- sexism as a vehicle that will create equality and rectify imbalances in the schools as well as in the home and work place.[194]

The above view defies Durkheim's (1964) old explanation of socialization and social facts, respectively. He argues that education that socializes comes from without the individual and exists outside the individual consciousness. In addition, Durkheim contends the education gives the historical fashion in which a social being is constituted. These women's responses by their very contradiction of the socialization norms of the ZCC, demonstrated that resisting and contradicting the norm can also serve as a powerful form of socialization that comes consciously from within.

They therefore conceive of the concept of non-sexism as something that will change perceptions and attitudes, to the extent that it will not matter whether the man or the woman earns more. In addition family decisions about who should continue with schooling in cases where a shortage of resources exists, should depend on other factors, other than whether somebody is a girl or a boy. The views of these young women concurred with the those of ZCC members who have education beyond twelve grade, and are mostly employed as teachers and nursing assistants. The ZCC authorities seem to concur with the position that education forms an essential part of life, since they took upon themselves to establish means that will enhance their members education. How that manifests along gender lines will be examined in the next topic of discussion.

Women and the ZCC Literacy Campaign

Despite the fact that the ZCC schools have been in existence now for three decades, a substantial number of members still do not have "school education." I am employing the usage "school education" to deconstitute reference to people as "illiterate."[195] In 1980 Lukhaimane described the ZCC followers as "underprivileged, rural and illiterate." Numerous News papers and even ZCC members themselves echo the reference to members as both 'illiterate', 'rural' and 'underpriviledged.'

The high priest from Soshanguve maintains that "the majority of members in the ZCC have an average of six school years, with a high percentage of women with very little school education. One very well educated member who is also a medical doctor admits to the fact that most members have very little school education. The ZCC members themselves as well as the bishops have had concerns about the amount of school education its members possess. The 1988 September issue of their magazine the Messenger remarking on the campaign for literacy states in part:

> *"This campaign will fight adult illiteracy*
> *within the church and raise the level of*
> *education within the ZCC , thereby meeting the challenge that*
> *the ZCC has more than its fair share of people who cannot read*
> *or write"*
> (The ZCC Messenger, 1988, issue no 11 p13)

Thus responding to such criticism of its members the bursary funds, administrative staff management training and adult education centers were established The next discussion focuses on how women feature into these literacy efforts by the ZCC.

Women and the ZCC Bursary Funds and Merit Awards

The name of the fund, called Bishop Edward Lekganyane Bursary Fund, honors bishop Edward Lekganyane, the deceased father of the current bishop of the church. His courage of attending school at a very late stage to satisfy the apartheid regime requirement of ministers to at least have two years of schooling before the church can be a registered and recognized functioning body, played determining role in the choice of the name. The bishop appointed the committee of the fund that composes of six men. Any attempt to question the functioning and structure of the committee evokes rebuke. This became very evident when a final year law student, and a member of the church at one university questioned amongst others, the qualifications as well as the allocation of money. According to the student's estimation the current allocation would culminate in the exhaustion of funds after the first year of its life. Consistent with the perception of the bishop's infallibility, the student was thus in part told:

> "I still cannot believe that a long standing
> and allegedly dedicated member of the church can dare
> challenge a project which has been initiated and blessed by His
> Grace The Bishop." [196]

Even though the bishop chose the name , it was insisted that the [197]
> "the concept was born, nurtured and made
> into reality by men and women of foresight
> and love of their fellow human beings."
> (The Messenger, issue 2 November 1992)

Notwithstanding, I proceeded to ask how women felt about the fact that only men make up the deciding body of who should be awarded the bursary. The responses to this question suggest that older women in the rural areas do not feel qualified to even dare to voice objection to something that has been dictated by the bishop. They had faith that the holy spirit will guide the members of the committee to do the right thing. If women were needed as members the bishop, they maintained would have seen that before the committee was constituted. The fact that the bishop did not see the need reflected how unnecessary women's inclusion is.

Older women in the urban areas views slightly diverge from their rural counterparts. Although completely in agreement with the bishop's decision, they believed that women's presence in the committee would make a difference in the decision making. For instance, one offered, if there are more boys been given money and no girls, a woman would be more sensitive to that than a man, in her estimation. They echoed the rural women's belief that the need for women's presence, would if necessary have been made clear to the bishop.

For the first time the younger women from both the urban and rural consider the inclusion of some women in the bursary committee as needed. However the reasons given for the inclusion differ. Most young women from the urban areas perceive such incorporation as a fair non-sexist practice well overdue. On the other hand ambivalence on the part of the young rural women abounds. Some perceived that the inclusion will facilitate the men's responsibilities because they believe that women make excellent secretaries.

Thus affirming assertion by Parsons and Bales (1955) and Chodorow (1974) of the power of socialization in instilling beliefs. Other young rural women displaying discomfort and great ambivalence posit that the composition of such a secular committee should not necessarily be bound by religious dictates. Implicitly challenging the bishop's authority. An interesting observation in sharp contrast with views expressed by some of their counterpart with exposure to similar socialization processes. Such diversity of views demonstrates the fluidity, conflict and ambivalent nature of human personalities belonging to the same organization.

A factor which should caution social scientists against oversimplifying the psychoanalytical postulations of conditioning that comes out of socialization. Wrong (1961) notes that while internalization, a psychological aspect of socialization, may instill feelings that correspond to "feminine" psychic structure, it does not guarantee that the behavior will match the feelings. In line with Wrong's claim these young rural women, well vested with the supremacy of the bishop's directive within the church, more so than their urban counterparts, in a very rare move gave responses that do not conform to the expectations of the female ZCC.

The bursary fund has two sections. The first section called the merit award is a grant given to the three best twelve grade or matric students. Best translates into obtaining a minimum of four distinctions in the final examinations. The loan grant is partially a loan and partially a grant. Fifty percent of the grant will be payable when the bursar completes the education program for which the money was granted. The conditions of receiving any of the grants include, being a practicing member of the ZCC and continue to be so while still in receipt of the bursary. The bursary board requires that merit and need constitute the criteria used to distribute the money. In their words:

> *"Students who show academic merit but are disadvantaged by financial circumstances are the target group of the bursary fund, whereas sex, age of choice of academic stream are not considered"*

An examination of who has benefited from the fund most clearly shows that more young men than women benefit from the fund. In the 1988 distribution only four young women out of thirty recipients obtained the loan award. The trend still continues. Although I could not obtain the latest official statistics, during field research I hardly found any young woman who was a recent recipient. Or I did I not try hard enough? The merit award since its inception has been awarded to young male students only. The trend through the years has mirrored the 1980's. Since merit determines the selection of those awarded the merit grant, young women from the urban areas point to the attitudes and cultural practices as partially responsible for the pattern.

The culture expects girls to do more chores than boys. For instance girls have to clean the house everyday, cook and wash the dishes. In addition they have to do the laundry including the boys' laundry. Consequently, young women have less time to study because of cultural attitudes and expectations. Men and young men who engage in so called women house chores are still stigmatized, worse still adults in most households still hold similar views. These attitudes and perceptions account for young men doing much better than young women in school partially.   Young women from the rural areas are divided in their views on the reasons that accounts for the gender disparity in the distribution of funds. Some agree with the young urban women, while a few think that boys naturally possess more intelligence than girls. The latter way of thinking that clearly emanates from the teachings of the church, seems to influence the responses of rural older women. While they concur that cultural attitudes and expectations might be attributable to the persistent unequal distribution of funds, they nevertheless also allude to the fact that men possess more intelligence than women. Older urban women regard both cultural attitudes as well as the possibility that girls do not apply for the bursary as much as boys do as the causal factors of gender disparity in distribution of bursary awards.

The bursary committee makes up one of the church councils-- *lekgotla la kereke*. This body like all the other bodies commands absolute respect and deference to the person and office of the bishop. The impact of such respect and deference referred to as "a non negotiable first essential"[198] become apparent in the answers of both rural and urban older women. Reference to the holy guidance of the bishop and his wisdom that will transfer on to the decision making body, precede their responses.

In sum the transformation of any practice or law has to be mediated with the bishop's directive. The degree to which compliance with the bishop's instructions are carried out cannot be underestimated. Indeed the ZCC Adult Education Literacy Centers, the establishment of which was mandated by the bishop bears testimony of his influence.

Women and the Adult Education Literacy Centers

The bishop initially appointed inspectors JM Mamabolo and I Kutoane to serve as heads of the adult literacy campaign within the ZCC (ZCC Messenger 1992). They serve as chairman and secretary respectively. The bishop ordered that every branch of the church should establish an adult literacy center. As expected the branches heeded the call and centers were established, as illustrated in tables at the end of the document.[199] Men make up the governing structures as well as the functionary staff of all these centers, with the exception of just very few women teachers who teach sewing or needlework. However, women of varying ages from age twenty one upwards almost exclusively compose the student body. The curriculum still reflected the Bantu education structure with few additions. The additions include extra classes that train male ministers to conduct funerals and marriages in a uniform way.

Classes for women revolved around learning how to master basic writing and reading skills, as well as sewing, mothercraft, and home economics. That the above subjects promote servitude is efficiently articulated by C Wright (1989). In his article "an under the carpet view of the education crisis in Sub-Saharan Africa, " he writes about how education in many countries in Africa promotes the virtues of service to others than self and orients learners towards seeking employment rather than creating it.

Wright further argues that the latter paradigm entails values of selfless sacrifice, conformity and dependency.[200] I will assert that helping each other is a virtue to be admired and encouraged, however, if the purpose leans towards precluding people to participate in other structures that could develop more of their potential beyond domestically oriented duties, then I will part company with such a move. The school curriculum in ZCC schools, a mirror of Bantu education does just that, fitting into Wright's criticism about education in Sub-Saharan Africa.

As indicated above most of the students are women. Some centers show poor retention of students. The most notable exception to this pattern is the Rakopi Adult Education Center at Thabamoopo, a district of Lebowa. As the figure on tables shows the retention in this center for 1990 and 1991 is above 55%. The center continues to have even higher rate of retention. In most centers the pattern has been men students dropping out leaving the classes without male students at the end of the sessions. Given such a situation, I will then posit that the trend indicates that given the opportunity, access, and conducive cultural practices to educational and social development, women will seize the opportunity. As far as I am concerned that demonstrates the desire for women in the ZCC to advance, educationally and socially. It shows they value education. Since also the adult literacy centers came into being through the order of the bishop, it proves how influential he can be in encouraging the move towards non sexism.

The attitude of women to the fact that males constitute their administrators and trainers remained that of passive resignation. They feel that the appointed men have the qualifications to teach. In addition, since married men conduct the night classes it makes perfect sense that the wives look after the home and children. Again the practice translates into a clear division of labor and not an objectification of discordant representation of gender. The latter notwithstanding, they also submit that when women have acquired the skills to train, they will welcome them as trainers and managers, if the bishop and the church endorse such a practice.

The Administrative Staff Management Training

The administrative staff composition reflects a reproduction of the Bapedi leadership structures both nominally and substantively. *Kgoro*, made up of an inner council of related male kin, like I mentioned earlier, also benefits from the education campaign of the ZCC. To keep in touch with the larger world and to expose the council to the technological era, the bishop invited Damelin College to the headquarters in Moria for the purpose of enhancing their skills.[201] The initial invitation entailed an analysis study conducted by the Damelin staff to assess the efficiency of the systems that the ZCC had. In addition they had to recommend ways in which improvement can be achieved as well as to update in ways that will be in line with the larger technological world.

To this end the Damelin personnel interviewed the staff of *kgoro* as well as the bishop'about their record keeping, banking and cash flow practices. After the appraisal Damelin presented their report and the proposal for training and meeting educational needs of the ZCC kgoro staff. They proposed an in-service training program that will take place within a period of seven months. Personnel Management, Book-keeping, Accounting, Finance, Principles of Management, Business English and Law composed the entire curriculum. The training occurred two months after the proposal was presented to the bishop.[202]

Members attest to its visible benefits. Since *kgoro* is at the headquarters mostly people in the rural areas have exposure to its staff. Urban members come into contact with the staff on special occasions, like Easter. Even then it is extremely rare since on those instances millions visit the place. Women who come into contact with this male staff emphasized the bishop's efforts to improve the church. When I mentioned that Damelin trained men and not women, the general response was that you have to start somewhere. None of the women would be critical or question the constitution of the *kgoro* nor the decision of the bishop.

Summary

The discourse thus far sustains the claim of the existent discrepancies between the call for non-sexism in the current South Africa with the ZCC institutional structures and social cultural practice. The call for non-sexism in essence emanates from a construct of gender relations as hegemonies. The gender relations are not only perceived as hierarchical and unequal but also as a conflict between interest of men and women.[203] The diverging and converging influence of the interplay of the multiple structures of the precolonial, the ZCC, the colonial apartheid and the current, became evident in how the women conceptualize their reality.

To this end, some women in the ZCC part company with the construction of gender relations as symbolic polarities. Such a position proves both fallacious and divisive, in these elderly women's world. Actions like male priests opening by prayer services that are meant for women only do not essentialize men's superiority over women. Nor do they create a hegemoneous social hierarchy, on the contrary, it points to the division of labor with no reference to male power. Notwithstanding, ambivalence common to situations where people face different forms of structural ambiguity, marked these women's responses. Oakley (1974b:81) referring to this dilemma as "structural ambivalence" notes how such inconsistencies characterize women's positions in modern societies.

The mutually exclusive nature of structures from which women have to choose compound the situation, Oakley further posits, since the achievement of one can mean defeat of the other.[204]. Similar ambivalence prompted these women on several occasions to concede that they will welcome change when directed by the bishop. However, on the whole they rebuked the equation of gender roles to the apartheid racial discrimination. To them gender roles and institutional practices of men and women in the church reflect a non competitive duality, and not dichotomous hierarchies binarily ranked in opposition to each other.

The non-sexist call on the other hand, sounds like a potential explosive practice that will violate the basic *khotso* principle of the church and transform a system of peaceful co-existence into a system of rivalry. The fact that they could recall the practices from pre-colonial times and the bible, serves as an added reaffirmation of the authenticity of their construction of gender roles, thereby giving credence to Parson's (1954) claim, even today after so many years, of adult rigid conformity to tradition as a result of socialization.

To these women the nature of the transformation to conform to the redefinition of their perceptions will directly flow from the visionary guidance of their bishop. Consequently, one can conclude that they are not completely opposed to change or oblivious to some inequalities, but they exercise extreme caution not to violate the rules of the church. The middle age women and younger rural women's mediation of the conflict, displays transient alliances and loyalties. Their desire for transformation is expressed in subtle ways. Maintaining the peace in the church supersedes the desire for conformity with the call for non-sexism, without completely obliterating the presence of the wish for transformation. These women completely align themselves with the elder women in their loyalty to the power of the bishop's guidance. At diametric opposition with the latter are young urban women's views. They more than welcome the call for a non-sexist South Africa since their conceptualization of gender roles corresponds with that of the new government's.

What they perceive as a disjuncture between the two structures could be mediated by socialcultural practice of the ZCC brought in conformity with the non-sexist call. They see such a move creating a supportive alliance in compliance with the peace theme of the ZCC. Although they recognize and respect the bishop's influence in effecting change, they made very little if at all reference to his pivotal role.

The disjuncture in terms of perception of the division of labor amongst young and old, urban and rural can be traced to how the women frame the nature of men and women relationships. Urban and mostly younger women, perceive income inequality between the sexes as sexist and an unfair practice that needs transformation. The man's ego becomes a non issue, men have to adapt to women earning equal or more. These younger women give little or no consideration at all to the benefits that accrue from an educated husband or man. Their views agree with Gerson's (1985: 99) assertion that:

> *"income inequality between the sexes*
> *reinforces a traditional sexual division*
> *of labor and supports the priority of*
> *the male career on practical grounds".*

Older women on the other hand, choose to ignore the disparity in pay and concentrate on the peace that they enjoy.

The influence of the church's teachings extended to how these women perceive sexism as it plays out in education of young men and young women. The rural older and middle age women will still choose educating a young man to a young girl when circumstances dictate. Even in the context of a non sexist society, reaffirming their support for the structures of female domesticity. They see rewards in being married and disadvantage at being a spinster, *lefetwa*. They therefore encourage religious endogamous marriages for their daughters. Since this carries a lot of importance, I will argue that these women see marriage as an identity[205] essential for their survival.

Younger urban women will rather focus their attention on educating the society about the sexist nature of the nomenclature like *lefetwa* and not sacrifice their educational ambitions in favor of marriage. Spinsterhood, efficacy and self sufficiency seem more attractive to them than struggling to look for an educated prospective husband in the church. They advocate for choices about who should be educated in the face of hardship to be based on other factors besides the sex of an individual. Factors like who studies harder, who shows more interest in academics should play a major role.

While rural women and older urban women avoided referring to the impact of apartheid on education, urban woman did not. The latter pattern reflects the degree of loyalty and adherence to the ZCC values.

Rural and old women display a certain amount of rigidity, while urban young and middle aged women show more flexibility. Urban women want change. The middle aged want it to be achieved within the parameters of the *khotso* theme. Younger women see sexism as gross violation of the peace theme, and that peace between themselves and men will not be an authentic *khotso* until ZCC structures are brought into reconciliation with the dictates of non-sexism.

On the other hand women in the rural areas and older women in the urban areas, will most likely wait for the bishop to direct them. What I cannot ignore, in most of these women's responses, including urban middle old and middle aged women, but not urban younger, is the constant reference to the bible and the old traditional culture as a factor of endorsement in their beliefs. Durkheim (1964) recognizes the tremendous power invested in this, many years back. Describing the endurance and sustainability of such traditional beliefs and systems, he maintains that because of the ready made transmission from previous generations, such beliefs receive immediate and ready acceptance and adoption. Indeed, the ZCC women's responses make this old age insight true today as it was then.

Moreover, their collective and ancient nature invest them with a particular authority that education teaches that they should be recognized and respected. The latter phenomenon became very conspicuous in the ZCC women's perceptions and conclusions. Practices like polygamy, deference to males and authority, which they do not oppose, mirror to varying extents, the Bapedi traditional structures. Furthermore, the administrative composition and function of bodies like bursary funds, literacy centers, referred to as *lekgotla*, resemble the traditional administrative structures, not only nominally but substantively.

It becomes clear that traditional beliefs fashion the responses of elderly and rural women, especially. In addition the general operation of the church resonates the Bapedi tradition. The following chapter on how ZCC women as minorities in the educational institutions that do not belong to the church, demonstrates how the traditional practices of the ZCC impact strategies that young women adopt to deal with the conflict that affects their educational aspirations. The discourse will also show that the very historical practices influence how the community at large perceive ZCC members. Kanter (1977) argues that the dominant groups or groups in the majority often exaggerate the differences when the minority come into what they (majority) perceive as their space. He calls it boundary heightening.[206]

5

ZCC WOMEN AS MINORITIES IN EDUCATIONAL STRUCTURES OUTSIDE THE CHURCH

The position of ZCC women in educational structures that do not belong to the church reaffirms Kanter's (1977) notion of boundary heightening. The larger South African Black community magnified the differences and heightened the boundaries between themselves and the ZCC members. These actions precipitated the ZCC members' feelings of alienation in much the same way as Wilson (1971) and Ingram-Smith (1967) have argued. In their various discussions about religion and the transformation of society they contend that the basic insecurity for human beings can come primarily from the feeling that no one cares rather than from poverty.

Similarly, in external ZCC educational structures ZCC women experienced estrangement and abandonment because of being different to a point of despair. The ZCC's schools are all located in Lebowa and are minimal in proportion to the number of its members. The members compose part of the larger South African society and are scattered all over South Africa beyond the headquarters in Moria. Consequently the larger numbers of the members attend schools with an even larger number of non-ZCC members, making them minorities in terms of numbers, cultural frame of reference, and social orientation in these schools.

The two latter factors fostered clashing cognitive and perceptual constructions of what constitutes order. It further assured despondency and a volatile division between the ZCC members and the others. Most importantly others perceived the ZCC members as an aberration and questionable. This negative perception by others affected how the ZCC perceived themselves. It also impacted on the dual trust of both ZCC and other members of society. Based on this behavior which characteristically fits into how the dominant sometimes treat the minority or non dominant,[207] and also the fact that the ZCC students were fewer in number, this study classifies students belonging to the ZCC as minorities.

It is within this context of the ZCC women's minority status that Ogbu and Simons' (1994) tools of analysis are employed in a qualitative ethnographic manner to investigate several factors. These include: (a) The effects of the perception of the ZCC by others and themselves on their educational success, these are divided as follows: (i) the impact of discrimination and prejudice on ZCC women's decisions (ii) the extent to which the degree of trust affected relations with school authorities and peers (ii) cultural frame of reference and 'cultural models.'[208] Group identity and membership as operational factors in women's educational decisions. (iii) additional barriers and (iv) choices of alternative paths of developmental strategies.

The perception that impacted the ZCC women's education flows directly from dual cognitive distance between the ZCC members and the others. This distance in cognition precipitated the ZCC's lack of opposition against the apartheid regime. The latter played out through the intimate alliance that the ZCC and the apartheid regime enjoyed during the apartheid era. Consequently, **most** members of the South African Black community, especially in urban areas, negatively viewed the ZCC members. The view translated into concrete negative actions that caused ZCC members to experience isolation in various places, including schools.

Perceptions and Attitudes towards ZCC Students

Prejudice and Discrimination

In much the same way as Ogbu and Simons establish discrimination and prejudice as instrumental in minorities less optimistic view of their chances of success in education,[209] my research achieved the same results. Although, these two authors cite racial prejudice as salient and the prejudice in my study centers around religion, the idea of prejudice still stands and applies. Ogbu and Simons posit that African American students experience unfair treatment from the school authorities more than the other minorities. This unfair treatment in the students' opinions come from both the present and the past, and affects their lack of success.[210]

I found the latter also to be true in the ZCC women's case. The historical and continuing negative view of ZCC members as 'less intelligent'[211] followed them in the educational institutions. Ironically in the very places where they sought to improve and transform their view by others as 'illiterate'. Not only peers displayed prejudice and practiced discrimination against the ZCC students, **some** teachers did as well. This affected the ZCC women performance on two levels.

The women said teachers approached them with a preconceived attitude that they will never make it. Such an approach not only fostered inferiority and self doubt in **some** of the women, but served as a sure measure of discouragement. One woman Hyu2 postulated:

*"When educated people act like this", what is the use of getting education? I might as well drop out and do **some** other things."*

Other women reported that the cold disposition of **some** teachers made them reach decisions to quit school.[212] Once identified as a ZCC member **some** teachers exercised caution in how they dealt with them. The fear revolved around being identified as a symphatizer with a "deviant". This could be dangerous once the teachers were so labeled. The result could be isolation by the community or a target for attack when students went on a strike.

Some women said that they felt their ZCC membership adversely determined the grades they received.[213] Teachers also exercised a lot of caution not to be seen as friendly towards the "enemy." The practical manifestation of such resulted in blatant discrimination expressed through lower grading, humiliation through words or total discount of efforts. In extreme cases **some** teachers would ignore their very existence. Durkheim (1895) refers to such behavior or a phenomenon as induced by 'the power of external coercion,' a social fact that makes its presence felt by the application of sanctions. Recently, West (1975: 18) and Comaroff (1980: 188) although both observe the distinction between the 'orthodox' converts and the Zionists throughout South Africa, do not make any reference to the need others felt to punish the Zionists.

Thus **some** teachers like **some** students, regarded the ZCC members as violating the norm by belonging to the church. They responded by resisting offering any positive gesture to the efforts displayed by these women towards their education. The effects of such treatment culminated in pessimism much similar to that felt by US African American minorities about "future improvements in opportunity structure."[214] The perception of ZCC members as uneducated members of a church with strange beliefs that normal intelligent people would not engage in ran deep, the women reiterated.

Teachers treated them initially as incapable, and they had to work twice as hard to proof themselves and earn the respect that they deserved. Further, discrimination manifested in how **some** teachers treated them because of failure to complete homework. While others were not teased, ZCC students had to endure ridicule from being asked if they were singing, praying or giving *ditaelo* all night.

Such remarks, though sometimes true, elicited laughter from other students and caused extreme embarrassment. The degree of such discomfort played out in alienation that led to poor attendance or no attendance at all. ZCC members whose parents act as church leaders hold daily evening and sometimes night services and consultation for members.

These go on up to very late at night, since working or employed members mostly attended. Most of these because of the distance between the work place and home are not able to attend until eight at night.[215] The long services deprived all the neighbors enough sleep that complaints were lodged with the police. Needles to say the police as organs of the apartheid system often refused to intervene. The common answer referred to the harmlessness of the ZCC prayer meetings, which the police reported, when juxtaposed with the terrorist acts of those who fight against apartheid should be allowed.

Notwithstanding, using such instances as a source of ridicule discouraged **some** of the women to continue with school, and they constituted a barrier in the achievement of their education. Furthermore the discriminatory and prejudicial approach created ambivalence about the need to be educated. Sometimes it meant to alternatively stay on and not exert themselves, because even if they did it would not make a difference. Or they would just decide to drop out. Either way this would constitute the expectations of society about the ZCC,

> *"that will then not be a miracle,"* (one woman said, Zyu), *"so I dropped out."* (A different
> woman posited, Zyu2): *"I just came to school to pass time. I failed like everybody expected me to."*

In line with the utterance by these women, an assessment of how the students who belonged to the ZCC functioned and performed in these non-ZCC structures painted a bleak picture. There still appears to be a very great number of ZCC members who drop out. The chart on retention rates from one of the ZCC mesenger show a very low number of high school ZCC students. In spite of all the efforts by the ZCC to educate its members, the church has huge numbers of dropouts in the larger South Africa, compared to the larger South African Black society. In addition informants report that ZCC members tend to perform lower than the others in these schools. Further this study found that proportionally more women/girls than men/boys drop out.

The above reported interviews from women in Garankuwa, Atteridgeville and Mamelodi urban areas, suggest that how others perceived them as members of the church is central to their decisions. Such perceptions adversely affected these women's educational opportunities and also extended to affect how the ZCC students related to the teachers and their peers in the school system as the following discussion shows.

The Impact of Lack of Trust for School Officials on Women's Educational Decisions

Here again Ogbu and Simons' theory of the type of relationship between the minorities and the schools as a factor that affects the former's perception of schooling proved valuable. The ZCC (minorities) and non ZCC students' differed in their relations and perceptions.[216] Students belonging to the ZCC like the US involuntary minorities evaluated the schools very negatively and were also very distrustful of the school authorities. Uncertainties and contradictions between the differing functions and values provided by the school, home and religious structures, produced distrust that affected **some** of the women's relationships with the school personnel. Some women cited lack of trust for the school teachers and school administration as a deciding factor in abandoning their literacy development.

They viewed the authorities as immoral and lacking of integrity in their handling of the running of the schools. Examples cited included male teachers giving favors to and having relationships with school girls. Such willing women participants who even 'made eyes' at the teachers were favorites who could never go wrong. In addition they received good grades not because of their academic abilities, but because of other factors. Another example cited parallels Douglas' (1966) separation of the holy and unholy, the sacred and the profane. Women detested the drinking and cigarette smoking habits of teachers. It became hard for some of these women to receive an education from people who clearly indulged in what in their opinion, amounts to immorality. They became overly involved with doubting information that came from any teacher that they had seen engaging in what their values did not agree with. Paradoxically, others offered a view that diametrically opposed the above. The binary pressure from peers/teachers and parents that these women manipulated in order to please both also played a role.

Compliance with both and refrain from judgment proved valuable in their case. In the course of time though, they found it unbearable to balance the dictates of the church as guarded by the parents and the expectation of peers and teachers to behave differently.[217] Strategies to balance the two resulted in elaborate fabrication of their daily activities to both parties. They found their efforts consumed more by the need to develop manipulation strategies than by concentration on their studies. The extreme danger intrinsic in such dialectic non complementary way of life, forced them out of school. Maintaining the trust of their teachers/peers while trying to preserve their credibility as freedom fighters and not sell outs, found articulation in lives that diametrically opposed each other. They became very tired to juggle the tension and decided to just drop out.[218] It is true that a great majority of school children dropped out in the seventies and eighties because of the unrest. For the majority fear of police who had liberty to go to schools as they wished to detain student activists, prompted their leaving school. The latter factor rarely applied to ZCC members. Some of the women said they dropped out because of the constant teasing, taunting, and threats by others. The latter enhanced the distrust since they could not even depend on the school officials to be fair when they did decide to mediate in such conflicts. An incident that involved the bishop of the church making a donation to a white school proved detrimental in terms of ZCC students' relations with the school authorities and other students. The event directly and adversely impacted the trust. Some women alluded to this incident as a straw on a camel's back in their decision to finally leave school.[219]. School official refused to take action against students who meted out 'revenge' on ZCC students. Other women claimed that they even noticed teachers' unwillingness to just deal with them as students because of this event. A school bus carrying white school children fell into a body of water and culminated in the death of a number of white students. The bishop then donated huge amount of money to the school. The action enraged some, since the church and the bishop never contributed any money to further the struggle for liberation of Blacks. Some women configured this period as hard and unbearable as a ZCC and they decided to leave school. Others changed school districts. Identity then became an important factor during this period. Revealing or hiding identity became central to some women's decisions to continue or stay in school.

Cultural Frames of Reference and Identity

In the new environment others tried to hide their identity as ZCC members[220] by not wearing the badge and participating in all the political activities. However, for others this decision proved dangerous, because when the membership became known, they faced a long elaborate interrogation process where they had to proof their credibility as activists. The risk involved failure to convince the masses of their credibility. The ordeal resulted in their school performance suffering even more than before and culminated in them dropping out of school. Although women's views differed on this aspect, the commonly expressed view followed the theory of voluntary minorities as postulated in Ogbu and Simons' study.[221] Most women saw overcoming the barriers by hiding their identity as additive to their educational process in line with Ogbu and Simons' assertion. Insisting on displaying the cultural and group membership identity would prove subtractive as it would perpetuate the negative perception. Or at least feed more into it, since others thought the perception never goes away anyway..

The women reported that avoiding social aggregation and hiding and denying identity proved very effective in decreasing segregation. One woman Kyu, who successfully hid her identity reports that when one day one of the ZCC teachers who was a staff member at the school greeted her with *"khotsong,"* she felt so ashamed that she wished the *"earth could open and swallow her up."* She possessed a strong desire to stop future greetings of that manner but could not overcome the social norms, and in this case, constraints that discouraged confrontations with males and elders.

Her recourse lay in avoiding even remote contact with the teacher. She believed that a young man would have had the courage to confront the teacher and the response of the teacher to him would be receptive, she concluded. How did the teacher know that they are ZCC members? Teachers mostly identified ZCC students by their badges. The church requires that the badge be worn with pride so as to make the members stand out. Ambivalence prevailed with regard to this. On one hand the badge represents a "marker of group identity" to borrow Ogbu and Simons' terminology, while on the other hand it provokes attitude that culminate in discrimination. Most women thought it would have been best not to wear the badge until the whole society adopts a positive attitude towards ZCC members. One woman Jyu[222] on the contrary, pointed to the invisibility of other students' church affiliations, who do not bear markers that identify them. She remarked that the same should hold for the ZCC members to ensure uniformity and diminish the risk of attack. This woman advocated not wearing the badge at all times even during times of peace.

Other Miscellaneous Barriers

In addition to the above more definable aspects, other various barriers also functioned to force **some** ZCC women to drop out of school. The inability to mutually constitute their dual worlds in a way that made the tension tolerable, precipitated at least two women Hyu2 and Fyu[223] to deliberately fall pregnant. Equipped with the knowledge that the then South African school system forbade pregnant female students to attend school, these women set out to do just that.

Cognizant of the fact that the male students who impregnated them would be immune from the punishment of expulsion, since the school practice punished the pregnant girl and not the boy who impregnated the girl, they adopted the strategy. They however, regretted their decision now and attend one of the ZCC adult literacy centers to continue their education. At the time though the decision seemed better than enduring the ridicule and isolation.

In unison these women alluded to the education they acquired during this period. They agreed that their awareness to the system of apartheid was raised, and that they too suffer the effects of apartheid in their daily lives. In addition the dire need existed for the apartheid system to be fought. Further, they maintained that spiritual leaders also are fallible. However, I must mention that when the latter point came up the women who wished their identity to be kept and remain confidential, exercised caution by expressing that their statements should not be interpreted as a way of undermining the bishop and the teachings of the church.

As part of the larger South African reality the ZCC, they posited, needed to have joined in the struggle against apartheid. In fact in retrospect most of them reported that they left school because of the problems that directly came from the system of apartheid. It was because of apartheid that they had to hide their identity, be isolated, and suffer derision. I did ask them how they think the fact that they are females and not males played a role in their decision making as well as how they were/are perceived. They cited the sociocultural norms that encourage men to be confrontational and women not to be as something that serve as an inhibition in situations like the ones they experienced. This model, highly emphasized in the church's teachings, they report, should also be modified in the transformation period. Further, notwithstanding the high value they personally put on the respect for elders, a mechanism should be put in place where actions of elders could be questioned. The humanity of elders and their capacity to make mistakes should be acknowledged, the felt.

They concluded that the expectations to defer to elders applied without any or very little measure of flexibility where it concerned women. Most of them expressed the desire to be able to talk to the teacher's about their discriminatory practices towards ZCC students. They, nonetheless, would be even more restrained in the cases that involved male teachers. The deference to males, in their opinion is implicit in many of the teachings and affected their ability to contradict **some** actions by male teachers.

Poverty was also reiterated as a factor. The high cost of education that had to be provided by parents with very little education and lower salaries resulted in drop outs as well. The long distance that students had to travel to go to school proved to be an additional determinant. The cost of transportation required an expensive monthly pass. During bad months parents could not afford to buy such a pass and traveling the long distance from school was not a welcomed exercise by many. Women also referred to attitudes towards gender roles, repeating the same kind of concerns contained in chapter four. The chores that they performed after school took away from study time. Parents with very little school education also lacked the capacity to assist with difficult problems, even though they valued education and would like to see their offspring educated. Despite all of these obstacles women saw education as offering tremendous opportunities.

They agreed with the ANC government's Reconstruction and Development Program (RDP). The program includes changing the structures of schools to offer more opportunities to Blacks, like bearing the cost of text books, providing free transportation to schools etc. More importantly and pertinent to my theme of discourse the development includes the move towards non-sexism. They see the no-sexist movement as a tool that will change the perception necessary to transform gender roles.

Alternative Paths of Development: Opportunities

The above discouraging factors prompted women to look at alternative means of advancing. Some of the involuntary minorities in the US distrusted the school systems and looked to alternative paths of development.[224] The same pattern manifested in my investigation. The

ZCC women tended to look beyond the school systems to find alternative means of advancing their social and economic lives. Their value for education notwithstanding, they looked at selling food for school children during lunch as a viable opportunity that would ensure income.

Indeed, a lot of women engaged in such endeavors. The target group of school children consists of lower and higher primary education level. Several reasons accounted for the decreased danger of attack at this level as a stigmatized ZCC member. The reason could be the lack of or low degree of political awareness at primary schools as compared to high schools. The findings by the South African Market Research Association support the above suggestion. It indicated that while students who belong to other denominations tend to continue with their school education the ZCC students drop out.

This trend the survey suggested happens more in high schools than in primary schools. I will argue that more awareness of racial discrimination and efforts to fight apartheid occurred mostly at the level of high school. This will explain why the drop rate for ZCC students is lower at primary schools. It further elucidates on why these schools are a target. Selling food to younger school going students at these locations brought more money and posited less danger to ZCC members. This pattern also transferred to the attitude of school children at this level who did not find it offensive to buy food from ZCC members.

Being a maid constituted another alternative kind of employment. Some like Tyu, Nyu6 and Gyu[225] opted to go and work as maids. The desire to reconcile the contradictions inherent in the opposing principles of their dual cosmological social order, made them conclude that the resolution lies in the "embracing world" of white employers. That the white working environment contained extreme measures of subjugation and discrimination perpetrated by the white South African women, involved forms of underpayment, long working hours, subtle verbal abuse, as well as deprivation of seeing one's family seemed less important.[226]

Owning a taxi seemed another desirable option for a number of women, including Hyu, Myu7, Lyu, and Vyu. They did not have to drive the taxi themselves, but could hire somebody to do it. The community has a number of ZCC women who have successfully engaged in the business. The latter also involved transporting ZCC members to Pietersburg during important events. The marriage and funeral cultural practices that dictated that a huge number of people attend the services, also played an essential part in promoting the prosperity of owning a taxi. In such a context then their aspirations could be met and they would then have time and money to attend adult literacy centers.

Attending adult literacy centers also was an option for success, albeit in this case it represented a strategy that reproduced traditional gender roles.[227] Some of the women said that in addition to the other factors that culminated in their decision to abandon their education, their domestic orientation also counted as a reason.

They achieved a level of comfort in their relationships that encouraged marriage and not school as a practicable preference. The women stressed the fact that they were conscious active actors, who had adult literacy centers as a means of advancing later on in life.[228] In variance with these women' views one woman from Atteridgeville Tyu2[229] made a decision to drop out based on false information that she acquired from one member of the church. She at that time believed that having a child during teenage years benefited a woman's body than having it at 21. Whereas now she understands that to have a first child after 35 carries greater risks than if somebody does earlier, then she lacked the knowledge. She still has feelings of resentment toward the particular woman who misled her, but saw adult literacy centers as an alternative that will satisfy any ambition that she ever had of advancing her education.

In the group interviewed few women stayed on and completed their matric, that is, high school. Their strategies for survival included engaging in actions of fighting the apartheid. They would lead the masses in burning down government installation. This engagement not only advanced them as respected activists, but also culminated in **some** of them ending up in detention. Detention in the context of the struggle forged a sure guarantee of credibility as a budding activist.

Devoid of shame the act conjured respect from peers and community, much in the same way as Gandhi and King asserted that in such circumstances go willingly to jail and transform it from the dungeon of shame into a haven of human dignity symbol of freedom.[230] Such an individual was following in the steps of the great freedom fighters, like Mandela, Sisulu, Kathrada, Modise and others.

Other women renounced their identity as ZCC members and took pains to explain the difference in orientation between their parents and themselves. These women explained in great detail how their lives in secondary and high school comprised constant friction with parents on one hand, and comforting association with comrades, on the other. Parents felt the need to pray and administer *ditaelo* to no avail for these two women. Today however, their parents take pride in the fact that they are the only members of the family who have not only completed matric, but are also cited as examples of people in the ZCC who also fought in the struggle to liberate South Africa.

Most importantly most women alluded to the negative of the larger South African majority to the members of the ZCC. Women kept on referring to this attitude as stigma. In addition they lament the absence of a movement that will deal with the prevailing negative attitudes towards the ZCC.[231] The prevalence of this attitude of stigmatization **some** remarked, follows ZCC members to the work place, especially among the white-collar workers. This makes them wonder if getting education is worth it if the treatment and attitude of discrimination continue.

The general society still cannot reconcile what they perceive as a discrepancy between an educated person and an affiliation to a church of less intelligent people. The efficacy of ZCC members is still questioned in very subtle ways and the scorn continues. To remedy this **some** want the bishop to contribute funds to the education of Blacks outside the structures of the ZCC.[232] Given the concern expressed so frequently, examining the nature and the root of factors that caused this perception in detail becomes an essential, inevitable, and logical next topic of discussion.

Lack of Opposition, Negative Perception and Stigmatization

ZCC women felt they were stigmatized for belonging to the church. More specifically the ZCC's lack of opposition to the apartheid regime stands out as the primary causal factor of the stigma that precipitated isolation. The important role that this lack of opposition played in influencing women's decisions dictates the need to explore its degree. This will make sense of the continuing reproach that the members of the ZCC to this day still experience to a certain extent.

Although the ZCC claimed to separate church and politics actions to the contrary abound. In fact the discussion in this section shows that an intimate and extensive relationship between the ZCC and the apartheid government existed. The ZCC refrained from opposing the apartheid regime. The latter position not only negated the ZCC's administration's claim of no involvement in politics, but also precipitated the negative view of the ZCC by the South African Black community, especially. The community saw the stance as deserving of isolation and condemnation.

Whereas to the ZCC mixing politics and religion, the duality that should be separated, created chaos much as Douglas (1966) has observed and convincingly argued.[233] To the others mixing the two equaled the inevitability of a natural disaster like drought in the land, as Peteni (1976) has observed. As a result of this cognitive distance on various issues the ZCC women and members perceived others as lacking empathy and displaying total disregard for their situation. This deeply felt dejection, as we have seen in the preceding discussion, prompted important decisions that that the ZCC young women made about their education.

Firth (1964) a long time ago provided an enduring framework within which crisis would be assessed by scholars. [234] He describes social control as a crisis that occurs in personal experiences of individuals who find their actions and wishes in a discord with a structural principle and/or with the conduct or desires of others. The paradigm focuses on the dilemma and not on the resolution of the conflict. This predicament has the capacity to mobilize the community that holds variant views and motivates them to apply sanctions against the 'deviant.'

In line with Firth's argument the ZCC's members' actions in opposition to the majority, produced tension strong enough to have the community attempt to punish them. A factor very salient in the ZCC women's consciousness, as the following answers demonstrate:

> Question: *Why did you drop out of school?*
> Answers: *"The stigma--the stigma was too much It was a question of--do I want to go*
> *through this, or do something better*
> *for my health and life"*

Such statements became commonplace as one of the reasons why **some** women dropped out of school. These are answers from three women, Byu2, Kyu4 and Syu[235] who responded amongst others to the question, what accounts for the stigma?:

> *"Because I am a Zion--a Zion"*
> *"Being a Zion in the large society*
> *is like you are a leper, sisi, especially at this time that people say they want their freedom from thewhite man" "I am not white but I suffer, people chase me like I have their freedom-I am not a white man-they should chase a white man-I am only a praying Zion"*

These women dropped out of school because they experienced isolation emanating from the ZCC lack of opposition against the then government. Being a visible and known ZCC member carried the stigma as a collaborator, a sell out, and a potential police informer. The attempt to fit in by attending school meetings held by the student body, was eclipsed by intense feelings of danger and risk since they were looked at with suspicion. On other occasions they were outrightly told to leave the meetings. The male student members of the ZCC, **some** women posited possessed a greater amount of endurance.

In most cases they argued their pure intentions of participating in the struggle.[236] They would be successful in **some** cases, but **some** women said they chose not to engage in what they conceived as a further futile exercise of trying to convince people "*who lack the basic peace.*" One woman acknowledged that as ZCC members their views on "*who lacks the basic peace*" differs from their former fellow students, who perceived the white man in the same manner that they perceived their former fellow students.

Thus confronted with such circumstances it became hard to stay focused on their education. Suggestions to change to a different church have been made as an alternative that will ensure survival and safety.[237] In addition concentrated focus on education and success will be attained. The contempt contained in the voices of the respondents to this idea, made it clear that the ZCC provided a stable context with preordained comfortable life patterns outside the school environment. Precisely because of the latter, the idea would not even be viewed as a loss possibility or a path to been have taken. Dropping out of school comprised the only option, since even the grades were not so great, because of the stigma, these women argued.

The ZCC women's plight succinctly illustrates Barth's (1969) assertion that boundaries persist despite the flow of personnel across them. They still stood as distinct and experienced exclusion as a result of the preservation of the larger South African society's perception of them as a discrete category. Based on the dichotomous status of 'us' and 'them' the negative perception endured as the observance of the boundaries continued despite the social interaction in single milieu.[238] That their church refused to take a stand against the apartheid regime compounded the issue. The discussion that follows explores this lack of opposition and the degree of the alliance.

The Apartheid Government and ZCC Alliance

In Sundkler's (1949) formulation the Zionists and Ethiopian churches or "Native Separative Churches" (as the South African Government would have it), emerged in opposition to the missionaries. They are also a product of the politico-economic processes of colonial domination. Consequently these churches often posed a threat to the government. An attempt to minimize the threat culminated in three stages marked by different government policies: the period before 1910, characterized by the government's suppression of Zionists and Ethiopian Churches, the 1910-1925 period, which marked the beginning of government recognition, and the period of my particular interest, the post-1925 era.[239]

In order to curb the rapid growth of the so called "Native Separatist Churches," the government implemented the rules set down by the "Native Churches Commission" of 1924. Prerequisites for recognition included continuous existence for ten years and a minimal size of six congregations, each with a regular meeting place. The minister of each church, further, was required to have passed standard six (8th grade) and to have received two or three years of special training for the ministry in order to acquire a license.[240]

The church was expected to be conducted according to the accepted standards of ethical conduct and to be suitable for the exercise of the civil functions of their office. Overriding these requirements was the condition that each church should be judged on its own merit by the Native Affairs Commission. The government's recognition went with privileges. These included acquiring sites for church and school premises, the appointment of ministers as marriage officers, the granting of railway concessions to ministers when taking journeys related to their duties, and the exemption from Liquor Act #30 of 1928 (prohibition of the sale of liquor to Africans), which allowed ministers to serve wine to their congregations during holy communion.[241]

The Native Affairs Commissioner used the threat of refusing recognition to limit secession.[242] When attempts to register churches on their own by a large number of churches failed, it became fashionable to hire the services of attorneys. The founder of the ZCC, Engenase Lekganyane, however, initially tried through his white friends to gain recognition in 1925. When the request was politely rejected with the response "the government was not against any religious movement as long as law and order prevailed," Engenase employed the services of P. Roos, the legal adviser of the church, who managed to have the church officially registered in 1942.[243]

In spite of the government's benevolent attitude towards the ZCC, the Church was not exempt from the racially repressive laws of apartheid. One example is the restrictions of the 1913 Land Act. This act allotted 13% of the land to the 35 million Black majority and 87% to four million whites. Further the act affected, to a far greater extent the ZCC than other churches. Many of their applications for church and business sites have been turned down with a "still investigating the matter" reply, with no further response from the government. Even now the ZCC have very few church buildings, and rely on schools and houses to conduct church services.[244]

Lukhaimane argues that the policy of non-interference by the government forms the primary factor of the growth of the ZCC. Contrary to this assertion, I will argue that growth and increase in the number of the ZCC membership emanates primarily from the colonized Blacks' experience of alienation, deprivation and frustration, from which people hoped to be relieved through the faith healing function provided by the ZCC. However, I will further suggest that, the government non-interference, which reflects and depends on the ZCC's obedience, composes the secondary contributory factor in the growth of the church membership.

Most importantly I will posit, the retention of elements of African culture in the ZCC predominantly constituted a force of attraction for new members. Inherent in the syncretism subsists values that echo Bapedi social, political and religious systems. This conjuncture of the pre-colonial structures of the Bapedi and the ZCC simultaneous reproduction and transformation, attracted members. Unlike mission churches whose very nature proved to displace the African culture, the ZCC did not.

The Bapedi and the ZCC though related to each other, are deeply rooted in, and therefore arise from the larger South African reality. While the history of ZCC is a history of protest against deprivation of religious rights, the church never addressed the larger issue of deprivation of political rights of Black South Africans, an issue which, nevertheless, profoundly affected the church. This attitude is attributable for the South African government's favorable disposition, up to the last apartheid days of the ZCC. Since its inception the ZCC implicitly stressed obedience to the white South African government, and the controversial "homelands." Comaroff's (1980) assertion of "white ambivalence towards this church," misinterprets the prevalent favoritism members of this church enjoyed over others. This manifested in the workplace as white South African employers favored ZCC members. It further reflected in the mutually supportive dynamic by which various government officials were invited to address the church's conferences in Easter, reaffirming both the church's obedience and the government's recognition.

That the ZCC created a middle ground between a displaced traditional order and a modern world, cannot be refuted. However its remarkable durability and growth in numbers cannot be attributed to a successful resistance against the structures of apartheid. As far back as October 4, 1904, Jacobus Samuel Brander, together with other Black ministers of the Ethiopian Catholic Churches in Zion testified before the South African Native Affairs Commission, to further the oppression of Blacks. Their affirmative answer to the white Commissioner when he posed the following question to them vividly illustrates their position:

> "Do you in church preach loyalty to the
> Government and obedience to the white   man?"[245]

The essence of such a question posed many years ago found perpetuation in the declarations of many apartheid government officials who would visit the ZCC church throughout the years. Dr. de Wet Nel and Dr. Eisselen, two of the apartheid ministers, visited the church during the times of Edward Lekganyane, the deceased father of the present bishop, Barnabas. Most strikingly Botha's visit of April 7 1985 evoked retorts never heard before. Botha, the then president of the apartheid regime, after being granted and receiving the freedom of Moria by the bishop, Barnabas, proclaimed:

> "The Bible also has the a message for the
> government and the governed of the world.
> Thus we read in Romans thirteen that
> every person be subject to the governing
> authorities. There is no authority except from God.
> Rulers are not a terror to good conduct, but to bad conduct. Do
> what is good   and you will receive the approval of the
> ruler. He is God servant for your good"

Similar to his predecessors president Botha's clear intent to ascertain the level of loyalty of the ZCC to the government as well as to encourage its adherence to the apartheid laws became evident. Flowing in the same direction as his ancestors were citation from the Bible as well as the apostle Paul's dictum, "servant be obedient to your master" were evoked to support obedience to inhumane systems, so did Botha's statement and message to the ZCC. In resounding resonance of his predecessors so did Barnabas proclaim his and his church's unequivocal lack of opposition against the regime by the following words:

> *"This is our duty and mine--we shall with help assist in making South Africa a shining example to the rest of the world, an example which shines brightly to the world as our lapel stars shines in the summer sun*
> *an example to be followed.* "[246]

In spite of the clear evidence of alliance, members and the church have by and large denied that the church had any interest in politics. In most cases members and priests would refer to themselves as peaceful and therefore not concerned with matters of opposition of the government since that constitutes conflict. Such statements would be made privately, never before April 1985 did the ZCC publicly respond to criticism for collaborating with the apartheid system. The church however, seemed to be affected by the increasing pressure, that for the first time publicly it issued a declaration confirming its "non-political stance". The statement read in part:

> *"In view of the wide publicity given to the events at Moria over the Easter weekend and various subsequent reactions, the Zion Christian Church reaffirms that it has no political bias or ambition, but is committed to the preaching of the Gospel and the promotion of peace and love among all South African"*
> (Pretoria News Newspaper 12
> April 1985)

Contained in the declaration was the implicit reaffirmation by the church of its stance not to oppose the apartheid regime. The church reiterated its adherence to the biblical injunction of the "respect of those set in authority" over them. The honor that the ZCC felt and the welcome it extended to Botha and his wife, the statement continued to say, should be seen against the above background. The sentiment continued throughout the years to align with the regime and condemn those who fought against it.

Some members never shied away from condemning the African National Congress, the present government in power in South Africa, led by Mandela, as terrorists. Seemingly oblivious to the vicious practical nature of the apartheid system and the many millions it killed, members continued to condemn freedom fighters, like the Nobel Laureate for Peace recipient Desmond Tutu, Mandela and Allan Boesak. One of the head minister epitomized the above practice in 1987 in the United Kingdom during the filming of BBC Scotland university debate series "A House Divided." This minister characterized the ANC as the faceless element of radicalism sitting in Lusaka[247] trying to curb freedom in South Africa. He continued to refer to the ANC as terrorists who attacked their own people, and accused Bishop Desmond Tutu of spearheading the disinvestment campaign.[248]

Other elders who were priests and respected members of the church then, constantly preached against the actions of movements against the apartheid government like the United Democratic Front and AZAPO. They viewed them as terrorists who deserved to be cursed. To their preaching members responded in agreement. In like fashion the ZCC bishop would visit the apartheid regime created homelands to speak in support of them and to condemn, albeit implicitly, the actions of the ANC and other liberation movements.

Visits to the Bophuthatswana, Venda, and Transkei homelands occurred several times. Such actions spelled out unequivocal support of the homelands that were produced specifically to deny Black South Africans citizenship and a rightful place in their country.[249] The homeland leaders themselves were carefully chosen by the apartheid officials, mainly from those with royal blood who would not go against its policies. The intent of creating the homelands was to hopefully silence the protest against the systems since Blacks would feel like they have self determination. These pieces of scattered dry and the poorest of South African land, where Blacks were relegated represented a further carefully orchestrated design to perpetuate apartheid.

In addition the homeland policies delayed the struggle for liberation, since homeland leaders went along with the apartheid policies. Thus the ZCC and the homeland leaders were in alliance for apartheid and against the ANC and other liberation efforts. This kind of attitude persisted until the early nineties. During this time **some** of the important figures in the ZCC started changing their rhetoric to resemble that of liberation theologists in South Africa. One prominent member came up with the rhetoric in 1992 never heard before in the ZCC, he stated:

"peace is when nobody cheats on his fellow

human being, when no race has the best of
everything, when no race dominates and
imposes its will on another race. Peace
in South Africa, when all are well
represented in the government of the
day. Peace in South Africa is when laws
of the country are fair to all. Peace
in South Africa is when the employer
commits himself to fair labor practice
and does not exploit employees"[250]

This member continued to say that a church of the people should advocate liberation for all its citizens. Indeed, when in 1992 I queried one of the head priests about the role of the church in the liberation struggle, he told me that Mandela was the chosen leader by God's will.

Later on the church invited three political figures, Mr. Mandela, De- Klerk and Buthelezi to the famous Easter meetings. The three of them addressed the congregation of millions. Mandela stole the show as he enjoyed resounding standing ovations on numerous times. Ironically the other two who represented the structures that the church formally supported were received less warmly.

The response to Buthelezi who together with the church in the past opposed sanctions[251] against South African apartheid system was marked with rejection expressed through discountenance. But until then the church stood in opposition of anybody who fought against apartheid, a move welcomed by the overwhelming majority of white South Africans. The sincerity of the church's commitment to change is doubted by many and the stigma remains.

The members identified by the badge enjoyed a lot of favoritism from white South Africans. Employers would chose to hire them over the others because of their unlikelihood to engage in strikes, walk outs and "go slow". These actions made up many of the mechanisms which Black people employed to fight injustices. Workers would either strike, walk out or carry out their duties very slowly, so that management should lose in terms of production. It was common knowledge that the ZCC members in consonance with its church's instructions will not engage in such actions.

Likewise in schools students would engage in a number of protests against the apartheid system. Peaceful demonstrations, stay away and walk outs made up methods through which students fought the system. Thus the ZCC student body in these schools had to face such challenges just like their parents had to in the work place.

Cosmologically the ZCC's faced asymmetrical representation that created tension that needed mediation in their everyday life. The resolution of the tension depended on individuation rather than aggregation, since the ZCC structural organization demanded compliance with the apartheid regime. Individuals and their individual families had to find ways of mediating and negotiating the tension. The church made no attempt nor any visible conscious awareness of the fact that an interplay and/or an interrelationship between its faith healing mission and the total political reality in South Africa existed. The absence of such awareness rendered the ZCC thoroughly apolitical and established it as a retrogressive force in the struggle for liberation.

This subscription by the ZCC to the pie in the sky theology and not the theology of liberation, put its members in opposition to the liberation movement as well as the other forces that sought to substantially transform the apartheid system. Unfortunately such a decision by the church also proves to have unfavorable consequences on women education and social development.

Summary

The above discussion convincingly demonstrates accommodation and tolerance by ZCC of the apartheid regime, while favorable to the administrators and bishop, proved harmful for women. Pretending to maintain the dichotomy of church and state, namely, the strict separation between spirituality and the hierarchy of the temporal world, in actuality the ZCC was perhaps in inadvertently was in cohorts with the apartheid officials.

The association represented an obvious distasteful reality to the majority, yet a matter of complete oblivion to most ZCC members. The origin of the "stigma" a phenomenon that came to play such an important part in women's decisions about their education, can be traced to this alliance. The collaboration, when played out, forms behavior that parallels as much as it diverges from Durkhiem's (1915) view of ritual in religious practices as separate entities, that is, the sacred and the profane. Ketzers writes about ritual

> "--a highly structured and standardized
> sequence enacted at certain places and
> times that are endowed with symbolic meaning. "it"----is
> repetitive, and therefore often redundant, but these very factors
> serve as

important means of channeling emotion, guiding
cognition, and organizing social groups. (Kertzer 1988: 9)

He interprets Durkheim's perception of the sacred and the profane as
societal arrangements emanating from people's emotionally charged
interdependence, and not to a metaphysical being.

Comparable to Kertzer's definition and interpretation of
Durkheim the ZCC administration ritualized its members' social and
psychological behavior to strictly observe and separate religion (sacred)
from politics (profane). Yet, in a paradoxical twist that diverges from the
above dictate, the church administrators themselves functioned in a way
that the sacred and the profane mixed. The direct consequence of that
action mirrors Douglas' (1966) analysis of such a phenomenon as chaos
that results from polluting the sacred with the profane. Ironically, the
very disorder that the church sought to avoid in the first place by
ritualizing the membership to behave differently prevailed.

Similar conflict of perceptions manifested as a further point of
disharmony in the schools, between ZCC students, teachers and non-
ZCC students. Teachers' perceptions of involvement in the struggle for
liberation agreed with the majority of students. This mutual alliance
created a huge cognitive dissonance between the ZCC members who
were in the minority, and the school population. Festinger (1957)
explains cognitive dissonance as inconsistency among cognition. He
posits that the psychological discomfort that accompanies people holding
dissonant beliefs motivates them to reduce the disharmony by avoiding
situations that will increase the conflict. Correspondingly, the teachers in
the schools held beliefs that were mutually consistent with the majority
of students. This cognitive consonance found articulation in how **some**
teachers perceived and treated the ZCC students.

The treatment, both differential and discriminatory matched
those of the majority of students. This treatment very much in line with
the experiences of the involuntary minorities in the US schools[252]
prompted the ZCC students to come up with different cultural models
and educational strategies. By aligning with the majority, the teachers
avoided further rifts in the school community, because the ZCC students
comprised the minority. Women's growing awareness of and reaction to
this adverse impact by structures of oppression, (ironically not the
apartheid), was to abandon school rather than contest the treatment. The
latter to a greater extent mirrors the ZCC teachings, the preference to
suffer rather than controvert those in authority.

Other barriers additionally presented structural contradictions
that necessitated decisions based on individuation rather than

aggregation. Thus **some** chose to become activists, while others chose pregnancy and white employment with its own elements of oppression. The choice of women who opted for the latter path can be explained in various ways. Either they failed to realize or wanted to ignore the even more structured constitutive oppressive nature of the white employers. Or they could tolerate ill-treatment from somebody different than them. The mediation of these conflicts in the women's lives prompted them to look for other alternatives of succeeding in society. Consequently owning taxis, selling food, continuing education through adult literacy centers, became options that they would otherwise have not considered. These varied responses, akin to Giddens' (1979:131) contention that the contradictions in the social practices make more sense than the function they satisfy, reflect the uncertainties inherent in the various structures these women faced. In turn, these structural ambiguities inject logic into and make sense of these women's different reactions.

Reactions that embody both psychological ambivalence and adjustment strategies. For example those who chose as strategies to engage in business or enroll in adult literacy centers act as a force for structural and ideological change. While those who opted for the strategy of dropping out and choosing white employment, as a form of benevolent oppression, not only reproduce subjugation, but also fail to improve their status as women. In line with their church's teaching they possessed neither the leverage nor the incentive to transform the structure of their work place. They would not for instance, demand better pay, thus this strategy reproduces yet similar forms of disadvantages for women. Other women however, decided that they would enhance their development by being prophets in the church.

They make reference to the fact that their destiny have been determined by the church. Indeed the power and resilience of such beliefs that find authority from the very fact that they are ancient and have been transmitted as ready made from previous generations cannot be minimized as Durkheim has proven.[253] The degree of the effects of the church's teachings cannot be minimized. They extended beyond the home into the work place and other informal structures. The next chapter will illustrate this impact as it discusses the informal transmission of non sexist messages.

6

The Effects of Informal Transmission of Non-Sexist Message on ZCC Women

Makgoba (1995:58) writing on education transformation in South Africa conceives of transformation as a process distinct from reformation. In other words, Makgoba asserts transformation yields a "blue print" as an end product, and not a modified representation of the old. He further notes that the transformation process "is underlined by race, gender, and cultural dimensions" whose effects will be felt by every institution in South Africa. In his words "transformation is here to stay, we can delay but not stop or avoid it." (Makgoba: 1993:58) The ZCC as a constituent of the larger South African sociocultural order, will thus not be immune to the process of change. Similarly, the lives of the ZCC women will be impacted by the transformation. Various mediums serve as educational forums to push forward the process of change in South Africa. Trade unions make up one such powerful mode in its role of advocating for a non-sexist society.

Some ZCC women logically also form part of the union movements and through such participation cannot escape additional educational exposure to information that informs their view of a sexist South Africa. Before 1994 the ZCC members avoided participating in structures that seemed to oppose the apartheid regime. Union movements in South Africa have historically assumed the stance of opposing racism in the work place as well. Congress of South African Unions (COSATU) during the apartheid era galantly fought against the regime. Its leaders then like Cyril Ramaphosa, were very well known political activists. The unions themselves were targets of attack by the organs of the then government.

The discussion on lack of opposition to apartheid in the previous chapter, illustrates the position of the ZCC towards apartheid. Consequently, most ZCC members refused to join the unions. The authorities of the church, much like the those of the apartheid governmnet accurately saw the unions as supportive of the struggle against apartheid. With the collapse of apartheid, the New Constitution of South Africa guarantees everyone the right to fair labor practices. Pertinent to this discussion, Section 23 of the Bill of Rights reads as follows:

> *(1) "Everyone has the right to fair labour*
> *practices."*
> *(2) Every worker has the right:*
> *(a) to form and join a trade union.*
> *(b) to participate in the activities and*
> *programmes of a trade union; and*
> *(c) to strike."*

In the context of the new South Africa, the ZCC officials as far as I know, have not expressed any misgivings about participation in the unions. This explains in part why quite a number of ZCC members are now members of the unions. The ZCC women logically also form part of the union movements and through such participation cannot escape additional educational exposure to information that informs their view of a sexist South Africa.

This chapter focuses on the impact of education acquired informally on the ZCC women's perception of a non sexist South Africa. It starts by a brief historical account of the union movements in South Africa with a special focus on women's role in these unions. This in turn prepares the discussion that follows on the ZCC women involvement in the unions. Their engagement occurs as a trilateral process that requires ingenuity in handling spaces with differing interests or similar interests not yet reconciled.

Intrinsic in such a process is an observable tension. The latter tension is created by the contradiction of the hegemonic gender order and by the social public practice that directly opposes the underlying principles of the domestic. Of course we remember that the domestic derives most of its gender axiology from the ZCC teachings.

Women and the Black Trade Unions in South Africa

South African women's involvement in the union dates as far back as their employment in the white working space. Like women elsewhere in the southern countries, they[254] bear reproductive responsibilities through domestic or family support labor.[255] Consequently their numbers in labor movements count substantially lower than that of men. In addition cultural expectations of gender roles also account for reduced number of women participation in such unions. I am referring to the division of labor practice that commonly assigns women to the domestic and men to the public, like so many anthropologists have argued.[256] With this logic men will number more than women in most work place structures, thus making their numbers more.

The contribution of the apartheid laws to the disproportionate representation of men and women in the trade unions also plays a role. The Industrial Coalition Act of 1924 and the Wage Act of 1925 granted full recognition to white South African unions while denying Blacks the right to participate in recognized trade unions. The acts excluded Black workers from the category of "employee" as defined in the Industrial Coalition Act. Blacks had no say about their wages and working conditions at all.[257] In spite of these horrid conditions throughout the years several Black trade unions came into being.

Laws such as the 1950 Suppression of Communist Act, the 1953 Bantu Labour Act, as amended in 1959 sought at best to defeat and at worst to eliminate the operation of the Black trade unions. These draconian legislation inter alia, meant that: a) a trade union official perceived as a communist could be ordered to resign, b) an engagement by any union member in an activity that the government arbitrarily disapproves of could result in detention or banishment, c) an African who takes part in a strike will be committing an illegal act, and d) processing a stop order payment for an African to pay trade union dues constituted an illegal act.[258]

Further the migrant labor and urban rights apartheid legislation reinforced the deterrent of association with trade unions by undercutting residential rights of Africans and exposing them to "deportation" to homelands and prospects of permanent unemployment.[259] Such conditions meant to dissuade involvement, ironically, functioned to produce class-consciousness and encourage rather than inhibit involvement in trade unions. This social fact also extended to women workers, and encouraged them to participate in unions. South African women's participation can be traced to the 1920's in the Industrial and Commercial Workers Union and Women Workers General Union. The leadership structures in these unions more then than now, portrayed gender hegemonious pattern in favor of men. Men such as Solly Sachs, held leadership positions with women as cadres. The 1930's union activities combined political and economic issues as vehicles to unionize workers. This mechanism embraced by women garment workers in alliance with communist party affiliations succeeded in unionized female sweet and tobacco workers, milliners, as well as food and canning workers.[260]

The rise to prominent leadership in the Food and Canning Worker's Union, of Black and colored[261] women like Francis Baard and Mary Mafekeng stands out as a remarkable achievement of the strategy. The extension of these women's leadership to the organization called Federation of South African Women,[262] through which approximately 25,000 women matched to Pretoria to protest against the government law that mandated women to carry passes in 1956, deserves to be mentioned. Women's visibility in unions persisted especially with the introduction by the government in the mid 1960 of the male female wage differential. From the period 1965 the disparity between men and women pay has fluctuated from women receiving 80% to 75% of men's salary. The employment of Black women in the less skilled and lowest paid jobs, as well as the fact that supervisors compose of males, with little chance of advancement for women, served as a further motivation for women's participation.[263]

In this period too, women in unions like the National Union of Clothing Workers rose to leadership positions. Lucy Mvubelo and Sara Chitja served as first Black women shop stewardess. They played a meaningful role of continuing strikes inspite of the repression by the employers and the apartheid government. Their influence most felt in the 1973-80 intensified level of industrial protest massive stay home which followed the 76 uprising workers, culminated in increased numbers of women involvement in different unions.

During this era when more than a fair share of Black South African workers willingly withdrew their labor to register political grievances, the apartheid regime appointed Wiehahn Commission 1979. The regime worried about the failure of its strategy to curb the mushrooming Black trade unions. The Wiehahn Commission would hopefully investigate and resolve the problems that the union presented as a threat to the stability of the apartheid. It recommended that Africans should be granted trade union rights but imposed other restriction, for example, the government was advised to continue imposing legal restrictions on the Black unions.

The Commission's constraints notwithstanding, women took full part in the revival of the unions, including unionizing previously difficult domestic workers. Women's prominence and efficacy prompted concession from men of their female co-worker's commitment. One official of the Textile Workers Industrial Union remarked on the political consciousness of African women.[264] In a statement that reflects attitudes that the call for non sexism seeks to abolish, a male shop steward praised women for "having fought like men." [265]

Motivations for women's involvement mirrored those of their male counterparts. Similarities of interest/concern included; rigidly controlled working conditions, low wages in a time of rapid inflation, lack of adequate procedure for airing grievances, the densely packed hostels. The differences also abound. White management relied on male dominance to ensure industrial discipline. Berger (1986) reports that through the marginal supervisory privilege granted to males by white management, Black males could either allow or forbid women from using the bathroom or sitting down during menstrual cramps. Women were expected to reciprocate with sexual favors. Perhaps actions like the latter explain why some time during the history of the unions when Lucy Mvubelo tried to foster unity between all men and all women unions, she received this response: "Lucy you want to bring in the men? Men are dominating us enough at home. We don't want to be dominated by men" (Mvubelo, NUCW general secretary, as quoted by Berger, I 1986). Westmore and Townsend (1975:26) also report that women complained of the lack of respect from male co-workers. Males ill treat them and touch them on embarrassing parts. Reporting such incidents yielded negative reaction towards women from white management that always sided with Black males.

Women also implicitly and explicitly experience intrusion into their private lives. The mandatory requirement by the management for women to take a pregnancy prevention pill daily under a nurse's supervision, robs them of privacy and control of their destiny. Those who survive the compulsory pregnancy test endure further invasion perpetrated by the doctor who continuously search for impending signs of motherhood. A pregnant woman not only loses her job immediately but also run the risk of permanent unemployment. Losing a job through pregnancy carried a stigma, since companies would most likely refuse to hire such a "high risk" person. Conditions such as the above occur in the work place and contain elements that fit the definition of sexism. Education about non-sexism in the unions forms one of the priorities of the present government. Messages of a how a non sexist society should be like, find articulation in the experiential fabric of union life, through various educational programs. The ZCC women as a component of the South African women working population, face the difficulties that other women face in the work place. Some of them become members of the unions, not out of choice but out of necessity.

The next discussion explores the ZCC women's responses to structural predicaments imposed by the work place and the church. The discussion centers on how these ZCC women mediate the education that they receive from the unions about non-sexism with their experiences and perceptions of their spiritual cosmos.

ZCC Women's Education on Sexism in Workers Unions

*"Women are not only coming around the corner,
they are coming out".*

The above statement was said by the deputy chairperson of one of the Unions, a non ZCC member in a meeting attended by ZCC union members. These women have been municipal workers for some time now. They are urban from Atteridgeville, Garankuwa, and Mabopane area. They belong to various unions including the South African Municipal Workers Union (hence forth SAMWU). Their ages range from thirty five to fifty nine. In the apartheid years they observed the dictates of their church and avoided participation in unions, but since the advent of the new South Africa, they have been active members of the unions.[266]

The rhetoric about the advancement of women occupies the central stage in the meetings. The assertiveness of women cannot escape an observant eye. The Women's Committees make up very strongholds of grooming women to become leaders. In the words of one of the Provinces deputy chairperson: *"As women we would gather strength through these committees to stand up and be brave."* Thus with the semantic structure of the unions in disharmony with that of the ZCC, the women have to mediate the inherent dialectic conflict through a transformation that required a reconstitution of their view of the dual world that make their reality.

Compartmentalizing their world into two dichotomous entities became a necessity. They could not continue to remain passive listeners in environments where working situations were appalling. They could not expect the others to fight for them, either. Being actively engaged in their self determination and articulation took primacy over the church's wishes. Partitioning their lives also translates into complete avoidance of fighting church structures. The church will take its course and decide when it chooses to follow the path of the country's non sexist movement. In the meantime they will continue to contribute through avenues beyond the church that lend themselves to transformation.

To avoid a lot of confusion and answering questions that reflect elements emanating from the "'stigma'" some women take their badges off and keep private their membership to the ZCC. When those questions sometimes arise in private conversations, they take it upon themselves to assert their intention to keep and treat the two world as separable. Indeed I could not help but notice the determination and assertiveness that these women have acquired from the unions. In other words, the process of empowering women to abandon practices, like inhibitions in questioning authority, benefits ZCC women on a different level. The process also empowers them to fight the 'stigma' legacy, against their fellow Blacks.

The ZCC membership of certain two women who belong to central committee, is a matter of public knowledge. However, they contend, in a workers union, unlike amongst intellectuals people pay less attention to stigmatization, and the level of school education. Qu2 contends:

> "Here with my limited school education,
> and a known ZCC member I am
> respected as a woman leader, at least
> by most people from the urban areas."

These women agreed with their deputy chairperson, Pahlani Mkhabela's[267] words,

> "If you are a leader it is not a matter of going
> for higher education, just use the brains you
> have and lead people in the right direction.
> Don't mislead people and beware of intellectuals."
> (Workers News, July 1997, p39).

Because they regard the choice to hide ZCC membership as private and up to an individual, they refrain from making any judgments on those who hide their ZCC membership.

Further discussion revealed that the women's world consist of further apportionments. Their work world and domestic world engendered for some, a further need to create a different space. Those whose husbands were not in places of employment where unions exist, mediated the tension and inherent conflict through strategies that required a much more concerted effort of manipulation than those whose husband were. While for both the careful construction of domestic spheres reflected partial conformity with male dominance, for the former the potential for the sexual struggle was greater, if they failed to do so.

Interest could easily clash, at such the mediation of conflicting desires required even well planned strategies. For instance, one woman, Ku2[268] called for limited meetings that take place within set hours strictly adhered to as well as a provincial program for the whole year. This could make it easier for women to attend meetings and be active. She asserts

> *"we have to give enough time of notice out of respect for our husbands husbands sometimes do not agree when things are put forward on the spur of the moment by a woman."*

In other words, in variance with their actions of challenging patriarchy through the unions, they did not contest the patriarchal domestic structures. Their strategy included debating a place within them that made their husbands amenable and very tolerant of the fact that they had to go and attend union meetings, as leaders of even men. Such an amicable approach, they believe, will in due course hopefully transform their husband's attitudes towards sexism. An aggressive approach will result in alienation and end in defeating the purpose of the movement.

They valued their involvement in the unions and needed to keep working through this medium. Issues like maternity leave, 'downsizing,' or 'rightsizing' that affected their lives required their continual participation, they conclude. In the meetings as members of the committee they are instrumental in encouraging women to voice their opinion and become a formidable force to be reckoned with. They encourage women not to be weak and happy to fill token positions, the arena gives them a lot of power and sense of fulfillment.

It would then be a shame if they inadvertently antagonized their spouses, by treating them like employers who are essentially abusive by virtue of their exploitation of workers, or like comrades in the unions with whom they do not share the same intimacy. All these relationship are different. Knowing how to mediate the trichotomous reality works well for them. They believe that the church will take the responsibility of changing its members, and then their husbands will follow.

The positions of women whose husbands are in the workplace and involved in unions parallel as much as it diverges from a woman's whose husband were not.[269] With varying degree both had to support the traditional apparent male supremacy and adopt the domestically oriented stance. That is, in their domestic spheres they both had to participate and actively support deferring to their spouses to avoid disturbing the material balance of exchanges. On the other hand, unlike their counterparts, these structural contradictions furnished advantages.

Exposure granted by involvement in union structures contributed to the rapid development. Men who were thus exposed accepted the changing reality of gender relations faster than those who have not. Union structures provide education that raises men's level of awareness about why women say they suffer triple oppression. In addition seeing other men in the unions advocating for women's equality on a daily basis, proves very helpful. The latter notwithstanding, the women still maintain that conflict was manifest where they found themselves in the same committees as their husbands.

In such cases the calculus of power lay in their ability to negotiate the spheres of influence around formal marital defined parameters. The latter composes a process of great strategic significance that demand active conscious conversion of potential rivalry into supportive alliance. For example, these women have to exercise caution that the views they express concur with their spouses. They contend that this move to non-sexism should be approached with great caution.

Some men might be agreeable to the movement in the work place, but still harbor misgivings in the domestic sphere. In the work place men feel less control, but the domestic makes up their domain, and the constrains of many years of socialization interferes with their complete conception of the idea. In cases where they hold a different opinion, they choose to keep quiet rather than engage in a debate, hopefully as it happens most of the time, another person will express exactly what they had wanted to say. This ensured progress and eliminated the possibility of delays by husband and wives discord. Refusing to serve on the same committee as your spouse proves to be the best strategy the women contend. However, in the face of the empowerment of women, it becomes hard to do so, especially since SAMWU had just adopted a constitution that gives women more opportunity to become worker leaders through a quota system. Since they supported and vigorously took part in its adoption the possibility existed for them to be chosen as leaders.

Consequently, avoiding tension in the marriage becomes obligatory. The acquisition of such, then lies at the level of practice, where the disjuncture of two conflicting worlds of ideology gets resolved by conformity to patriarchy in one, and opposition to it in the other. These newly configured social fields though ambiguous, for the present ensured aggregation and progress. The women feel that if a woman chooses such a path, it becomes her burden to maintain the balance of participation and peace with a spouse.

Maintaining peace with spouses extended to choices of the revelation or concealment of ZCC membership. The women found it necessary to come to the decisions about whether their membership should be kept private or public. Two women say their husbands would not even entertain hiding their identity as ZCC members. I have observed these women in meetings and they come across as very assertive, but they could not assert their wishes in the same way when it came to this kind of disagreement with their spouses.

Such choices posed by antagonistic interest, may suggest to others like Parson (1956) a phenomenon of "false consciousness." I will argue that on the contrary these women are involved in a conscious dialectic social practice of reproduction and transformation, as they "acquiesce and yet protest their predicament" to borrow Comarof's words (1980: 1) Their conceived interest takes primacy in their choices. Jackson (1984) argues perceived interests are ideological responses to obscure, ambiguous, and indistinct circumstances very rarely objective.

Related to Jackson's analysis these women identified and defined their respective interests. That is, fight sexism in the public sphere and refrain from doing the same in the domestic and thereby preserve their marriage interest. By both affirming and protesting patriarchal arrangements in different spheres they gain more than they loose. Referring to such perceptions as false undermines these women's ability to accurately determine the existing potential of gaining ground in the fight against sexism in both the public and in the domestic eventually in different ways.

They conceive of the public and the domestic as on one level socially individuated, but as ultimately mutually constitutive; because the laws of the land will guarantee that the move to sexism be implemented where necessary. At this stage then will the symbiotic relationship be apparent. Therefore these women's perception cannot be described as false, at best their dichotomous acquiescence and protest symbolizes an active conscious effort to protect their double interest, albeit in acceptance of patriarchy on one level. They cannot be accused of passivity.

Education on Sexism in Workers Unions of Women in the Rural Area

SAMWU and all the other workers union have rural ZCC women as members. These women work as municipal workers, for water services, as refuse collectors, and very few do clerical work. Like the women in the urban areas, these women ages range from thirty five to late fifties and early sixties.[270] Distinctly different in disposition from their urban counterparts these women seemed alarmed that I have identified them as members of the union. However, they were willing to participate in my interviews.

Socially structured institutional conditions compelled the women to join unions, a complete divergence from the church's practice and expectations. Perhaps I should elaborate. Members of the unions engage in strikes and at times end up being arrested and have to appear in court. Recently, the bishop registered his disgust in seeing ZCC members in courts. He called for them not to engage in activities that will culminate in them having to confront the authorities in court.[271] These women however, found themselves members of SAMWU because of inevitabilities. They are all married and have children, and their pay vary from R147 to R165 per week. Ironically, the women clerical workers' form part of those in the R147 per week bracket.[272] None of them have benefits. In addition they are contract workers and at the will of their employers. Such conditions left them no option but to join the union.

The majority of these women's participation in the union involved paying membership dues and attending meetings as listeners. They deeply maintained values that they acquired in the church, and as such avoided getting confrontational and assertive especially when it came to matters of women's empowerment. The centrality of *khotso* to their existence restricted their participation in the struggle for positions with men. They perceive some of the proceedings as bickering and unnecessary, this they contend, go against the valued element of peace.

While they fully understand the argument about triple oppression of women and the demands of SAMWU's and other union's constitutions to increase women leaders in the union, their focus has primarily to do with ending unfair labor practices by employers. Locating their interest as such minimizes the amount of contradictions that they have to mediate in their lives. They applaud those women who have the capacity to fight for women's rights within the union. Most of these women not only keep their identity as ZCC members hidden, but also had to explain their membership to their husbands as something that the job required. Subjected to a thorough analysis, there was an element of truth in that. The horrible conditions made it necessary to join the union. Even in the face of conflicting ideologies of the church and the new South Africa's move to non-sexism, these women would not erode the traditional arrangements of ZCC expectations in terms of men and women relations.

Whereas the urban women exhibited dual dichotomous dispositions, these rural women's behavior displayed consistency in both the work place and the home. Their inhibitions result in behavior that affirms female subordination, and yet provide a context within which they objectify and address the need of transforming their appalling working conditions. These constraints ironically allow them to do both, that is, maintain peace and fight. Attending every union meeting held outside working hours, that is, on Saturdays, proved an impossibility for some of these women. They preferred to give primacy to their domestic demands, and avoid the risk of arguments with their spouses. However, some reported notable support from men who valued the unions since they were also part of SAMWU. In such cases mutual agreement beyond coercion culminated in a complementary and negotiated agreement.

Structural constrains in this case, like patterns of socialization, seem to disappear in the face of exposure. Like their urban counterparts these women, who consider themselves fortunate in having activist husbands, attribute such a transformed attitude as a product of education that goes on in unions about the oppression of women. Getting involved in the unions has not only educated them but has also raised their own level of awareness in terms of the need for a non-sexist society.

Women whose husbands were not in the unions, which is the majority of these rural women, preferred to keep their ZCC identity concealed from union members if they could help it. This parallels the beliefs and actions of their urban counterparts. A few who have husbands in unions left that decisions to their husbands. All but one expressed the view that their husbands do not hide their ZCC membership. In concert with their urban counterparts, the women report less stigmatization in the midst of workers or laborers.

Resknin B, and Padavic (1994) define internalized sexism as a phenomenon that plays out as men and women participating in behavior that perpetuates gender hegemony. In juxtaposition with their urban counterparts, the rural women tend to show higher degrees of internalized sexism. Their lack of assertiveness becomes conspicuous, as well as their deference to males in the unions. The women compared the new social order to the apartheid order. Seeing that the current government have laws guaranteed by the South African

The Constitution encourages participation in labor movements, what they are doing does not constitute a violation of the ZCC mandate. Certainly, their participation forms a complete compliance with the laws of those in power, an act which in the apartheid era amounted to treason. In this way the new government mandate plays a role in helping to formulate the concept of a non-sexist South Africa. They argue that they now see the need for the society to move in that direction. Like most of their urban counterparts, however, they do not wish to address that at the domestic level. The church should assume that responsibility, they contend.

Urban ZCC Women's Education on Sexism in Professional Unions

The women forming this part of the study are from the urban areas of Atteridgeville, Garankuwa, and Mabopane. Some of them have already participated in the study and a others have not. Choices that reflect interaction of socially structured opportunities and constrains, as well as active attempts to respond to these structures, mark how these women mediate the ideology of non-sexism with their reality. An assessment of available options led some of them to conclude that engagement in unions was necessary, despite the incompatibility with the ideological structures of the ZCC. Additionally, the working conditions reduce the risk of being stigmatized.

These women's choices diverge from Matina Horners' (1972) "motive to avoid success," syndrome, although in this case success refers to achieving emancipation from patriarchy, and not necessarily economic success. However, these women opted for a process that constituted their reality as a "simultaneous process of reproduction and transformation," (Comaroff 1980, p41) not because of psychological handicap peculiar to the female sex. Structural circumstances dictated the need for them to mediate the education of the church and unions about non sexism in a way that excluded choice between love and work.

The value they place on their marriage suggests they will have something to lose by opting to succeed in achieving the defeat of patriarchy in their dual social fields. To the degree that they evaluated their preferences correctly, their choices to preserve personal happiness by perpetuating sexism in one world and fighting it in the other made complete sense in the context. The approach, however, still fails to resolve the practice of sexism.

That those women perceived the prevailing hegemonies in gender relations as sexist became obvious. However, their strategies of mediating the contradictions, diverged from the younger women's. These women have been members of the church for many years ranging from fifteen to thirty five. They also have ZCC spouses. Their attempt to resolve structural predicaments can best be described as the creative benevolent violation of the ZCC, a practice that seeks to avoid enstragement in the process of, "reconstituting the divided self."[273]

Their spouses know of their union membership. As I mentioned before, the empowerment of women and practices of non-sexism permeate the semantic structure of the unions. Almost on a daily bases these women face rhetoric that stands in opposition to the one that has formed the foundation of their socialization. In discussions with their husbands about the union activities, some avoid topics of women's empowerment, unless their spouses bring it up.

Even then, the discourse, carefully structured, avoids tones that could be interpreted as undermining the male's position. At such the efficacy of reporting in the third person has proven most fruitful. Like Bmu4 posits:

> *"the say that women should be the*
> *leaders of the unions too. And*
> *they adopted the quota system in*
> *their constitution."*

One exception is a woman who forms part of the committees as well, and I have observed her strongly advocate for women's rights.

In fact in an open meeting of men and women shopstewards talked about the fact that women's triple oppression should be acknowledged. Further that the emancipation of women should constitute one of the essential elements in building a democratic society, and that the blame falls on the society, history, culture, tradition, men and policy. Such powerful statements that display a tremendous amount of ideological consciousness and awareness, cannot possibly be suppressed at the level of domestic practice?

The nature of the work place, as well as the Constitution of the country serve as supportive measures in that area. Personal relationships, however, do not enjoy such support from the constitution. It is not easy the woman responded, but one has to weigh the cost of either losing a spouse or a job. Since she needed both the strategy requires that she present herself as non threatening as possible in the domestic sphere. Change has the ability to disturb familiar, comfortable assumptions, even positive change can appear as threatening and dangerous.

One woman, Fyu[274] whose initial strategy involved transferring the actions and attitudes of the work place in terms of demanding non sexist practice to the domestic, caused her spouse to tell her to "go get married to the Constitution." She was also told that Mandela might the president of the country but he was definitely not the president of that particular household. Her marriage meant a lot and she resorted to a strategy of seeming disinterest in the transformation of the home and vigorous interest in the work place.

Other women turn the discussion into that of human rights instead of women' s rights. In both cases women mentioned how they go to great lengths to avoid appearing to possess the desire to transform their husbands. Internally, they do, but since they know that their husbands believe more in religious teaching, they will hope that the church will follow the rest of the South African society in the path of non sexism. If and when it does then they strongly believe their men will change.[275] Those having husbands in the unions enjoyed the advantage of not having to wait for the church. Outside ZCC structures already play a role in educating their husbands. Noteworthy is the developing pattern of the decisions about the ZCC badge by husbands in the unions. Couples with husbands report that their spouses encourage public knowledge of their ZCC affiliation. As such wearing a badge as a proud symbol of identity is common among such members of the union. Maybe this reflects the different socialization between men and women within the ZCC. The older members with no husbands preferred concealment of ZCC identity.

However, in cases where they are identified, they are able to now confront the complainers. The unions endowed them with the ability to confront people on their generalization of opinions about ZCC members. Some even say they point to the fact that some people can forgive atrocious actions perpetrated by some whites during the apartheid era, but still harbor bitterness towards ZCC members. This produces results.

Few of these older women faced overt opposition expressed through traditional husbands intervening directly to frustrate their union involvement to preserve some valued aspects of their lives. These women report that husbands would complain even when they were just a couple of minutes late after having attended a union meeting. Reference would be made to the fact that they neglect their domestic responsibilities, like cooking on time in favor of the union. For the sake of peace some of these women peripherized their union involvement by just paying their dues and keeping away from attending meetings.

Strategies and reasons for younger women's involvement in unions differed from the older women's. The desire to close the gap of the disparity in pay between gender and race of people with equal qualifications motivated women in Atteridgeville to join the union promptly. Unlike in Mabopane and Garankuwa, the apartheid laws still affected the former in this regard. The latter two fell under the jurisdiction of the Bophuthatswana Homeland, where the president abolished the law. The new government inherited the homelands as well as the other apartheid structures, as they were.

The process of restructuring and development entailed priorities that sometimes translated into going along with some of the unfair practices of the past in some areas. Some of these women wanted to play a role in defining this area as a priority that needed immediate attention. They perceived the new dispensation as offering avenues to transform the previously non productive structures into structure of expanded opportunities.

These unmarried younger women in their middle and late twenties, cherish the view expressed in non-sexist movements-- that women's self reliance is pivotal and women should realize that men will not always be there to care for them. The obvious inherent contradictions of the view with the church's value of marriage, created a syncretic context that carried messages of protest and resistance to patriarchy. Unlike the women in SAMWU, these women mediation of the discordance became a discourse of alienation.

The enstragement contained both overt and covert metaphors of rejection of what they also perceived a sexism in the church. Their stance, in vivid contrast to the ZCC orthodoxy, was not only known but culminated in the acquisition of labels as rebels. Their only recourse in countering that, lay in their faithful attendance of church services and participation in other activities. The mediation also include keeping their views to themselves and refraining from seeking converts from inside the church to their conception of no-sexism. The latter I will argue constitutes a form of continuance of sexism, which differs in degree compared to the benevolent yet serious compliance that results from strategies of older women.

Another Domain: ZCC Union Mothers and their
Children

The married women in the unions also have children. They could not escape having conversations with their children, girls and boys about non sexism. Elderly women from both the urban and rural areas tended to avoid the issue. They contend that the church and the schools provide enough information on the basis of which decision can be made. They often expressed confidence in the exemplary lives they have led and exposed their children to in terms of how they related to their spouses and men in general. The above mentioned too constitutes knowledge base from which their children will draw. Others report that they witnessed their children have conversation with their fathers about the topic, they however, chose to keep out of it. They still maintained that the movement carries a lot of risk that could cause a division among the couples. In other words these women would opt for love and peace in a marriage rather than have educational and social mobility jeopardize the former, when faced with the hard choice.

The former represented a greater benefit than the latter. Since they have proven success in compartmentalizing their domestic and public sphere they convey the same message to their children, very much aware of the fact that the children might chose a different strategy. They insisted that they would leave the domestic orientation to the church and the bishop. The professional younger and middle aged urban women in the unions, maintain that the abundance of the information in the media has opened a dialogue between their husbands and children. Most of them like the elderly women avoid participating. Some reported husband stressing the teachings of the church to their children legitimized by traditional culture. Others report that they have observed slight change in their husbands attitude towards the call for non sexism.

They heard their husbands telling their daughters that everybody should have access to education and that when a man passes away a woman should be in a position to take care of the children. In the current times education comprises the mechanism that will make that possible. All these women talk about opportunities that they have when they are alone with their children, daughters in particular. They use the opportunity to relay to them to use wisdom in making choices and maintaining peace. Some reported that their daughters thought of them as too submissive to men and to authority. However, what stood out was the fact that the women were willing to engage their daughters about the topic of non sexism in the absence of their husbands.

The Media and Non Sexism

The decision making context of the ZCC women in dealing with the concept of non-sexism, their education and social reality, also benefit from the media messages that the new government use as propaganda. The benefit finds articulation in both the affirmative and the negative. For primarily those in the urban areas with TV's and Radio exposure, non-sexism as a concept of the contemporary and future relevance is unavoidable. In addition various literature and newspapers contribute to raising consciousness regarding women's issues. These media though sometimes delivering mixed messages, played a role in shaping some women's perceptions. The current government, in line with the call for non-sexism, appointed a Gender Equality Commission to further the wishes of the people as articulated in the constitution for an establishment of a non sexist society.

The commission until recently was headed by a respectable veteran activist, Ms Thenjiwe Mtintsho, a former Black Consciousness and current ANC member. Ms. Mtintsho possesses a wealth of experience in women's issues and issues of equality in general. She had to leave her post because she was appointed as a member of the executive committee of the ANC.[276] The commission continues to play a very assertive role in promoting the cause of a non sexist South Africa. Some of the messages from the commission have stated that the course for non sexism should be fought through communication. One posited that "communication is the missile of tomorrow." The commission has encouraged close relationship with media production and media workers.

Education through news letters, newspapers, higher levels of technological equipment, as well as the non formal low tech means of production. Also present are action slogans with words that would engender change in gender in equality. Some of the women in the ZCC commenting on how they are constantly bombarded by the message of non sexism reiterated quotes from the commission's communication. These women maintain that in as much as they want to separate their spiritual beliefs about gender relations from the current movement, it proves difficult. The difficulty lies in the fact that in an environment where the focus centers on the topic of men and women relationships as well as the equality for women, they cannot avoid receiving the information. They refer to the debate about affirmative action which amongst others gives primacy to the advancement of Black women in particular.

The whole country contends that they have been at the bottom of the ladder throughout 342 years of subjugation. They hear it on the radio, read about it in the newspapers and magazines, they hear politicians speaking about it, and they see and hear about it on TV. Elderly urban women who reluctantly concurred with the latter affirmation, still stressed to me that they would feel comfortable if the bishop can reaffirm their beliefs through a vision that would determine how men and women relationships should change. Union members contended that the media does contribute to their construction of sexism as different from that of the church. They claim they acquire more knowledge and views about the construct from the media. However, they do not allow the information to influence the strategies that they have mentioned above of separating the home and the work place. They also notice how on occasion men will bring the topic up. This indicates the influence of the media and the climate in the country about non sexism.

Rural elderly and some middle aged women also admit to the influence of the information from the media. Fortunately, some of them said their husbands also listen to the radio and receive the same information. Most of them say they do not act on the information, but do think about it. They are still committed to and have total confidence in the visionary power of the bishop to guide the move towards a non-sexist society. Women with more than twelfth grade education, urban middle aged, and the young and urban see the effects of the media as part of an inevitable transformation in terms of how women are perceived. The information they maintain will definitely influence them to want to advance their education and position in society as well as that of their children.

The huge amount of information that surrounded the preparation for Beijing conference became very salient in the discussion about the media. Most women brought it to my attention that men at home cannot avoid the topic of equality for women. Everybody they said talks about the coming Beijing conference. The talk and the amount of money, energy and time put into that endeavor reflected the extent of the seriousness of the issue. Other women referred to the need to be careful as they reported their men feeling threatened by the amount of attention focused on women.

Some women reported that their men have held conversations with them where they complained about so and so's wife behavior which has changed drastically after she attended the Beijing Conference. That is constructed as sign enough to warn women not to alienate men in the fight against sexism.

Summary

The above discussion demonstrates that South African women's history of involvement in the unions involves working against unfair working conditions, racial domination as well as male domination. The current transformation period has accelerated women's commitment in fighting against sexism, since like Makgoba (1993) observed, reversing the current trend of current change in South Africa is impossible. The ZCC women also form part of the South African women and therefore cannot all escape participating.

However, for them more than for anybody else, as far as this study is concerned, they have to contend with their church's teachings and beliefs. Firth (1969) speaks of religious beliefs as a mode of action that can at times be active weapons in the process of adjustment. Adjustment or change entails an incessant process whereby individuals attempt to create order in relation with the physical, the social, own systems of thought, sets of emotions, desires and impulses.

ZCC women's experiences in the unions expose them to new facts which both diverge from and challenge their ZCC religious teachings. The latter situation creates tension that demands mediation and change at individual, group, communal and personal levels. The circumstances however, seem to obligate adjustment more at the personal level. The mediation of their experiences and perceptions with the spiritual, the valued, the expected, and the real occur as self-contradictions.

Consequently, outside these ZCC structures, the impact on their formulation of a non sexist society cannot be spoken of as a single voice of collective consciousness. On the contrary, such a discourse becomes an expression of individualized cognition, as individual members struggle to harmonize the ensuing social arrangements and dictates with their religious convictions. Their active participation though contradictory, bears a message of repudiation against certain values and concepts practiced in their church. Although failing to significantly mitigate the manifest inequalities of gender, the women's involvement translates into symbolic rejection of patriarchy and sexism.

This involvement introduces a mode of practice which when compared with forms of their religious background furnish a position that stands in vivid contrast to ZCC orthodoxy. The emergent experiential fabric of their daily life manifest as an elaborate order of signs that objectify elements of both resistance to and replication of sexism. For example, both in the rural and urban areas women construct their divided self by also splitting their home and work lives. The faith and hope in the bishop's visionary power remain intact. They hope the vision will appear to the bishop who will then issue a mandate that will transform views and practices of their husbands to conform with the non sexism call. These women faced a complex divided cosmos that through a process of reproduction and transformation generated tension that needed mediation and resolution. Their concern centered around mediation without seeking final resolution. Thus to mediate the conflict they fostered the balance between the domestic and the work place, by refraining from addressing the issues of gender equality in the former domain. They wore their badges only at the direction of their husbands. They valiantly fought sexism in the public work place, while deferring to the men in the home.

The above strategies proved profitable in the double sense. It allowed peace to reign in the domestic and women to advance the course of non sexism in the public. Deference to male dominance in the home culminated in simultaneous support to defeat male dominance in the work place. Unconsciously ZCC males participated in the fight against patriarchy through the ingenious conscious strategies of their spouses. Thus, confirming Gerson (1985) assertion that unconscious motivation is not confined to psychodynamic process, structural as well as psychological processes mold behavior in ways that actors barely recognize.

7

Conclusion

Introduction

Although this study provided insights into much more than its explicit topic, it still sustained the initial claim. That is, it examined how women in the Zion Christian Church perceive and construct the concept of non sexism and patriarchy. The study further analyzed how these women mediate specific individual and collective construct with their education and social reality within the context of South Africa.

I argued that the non-sexist ideological construct of the ANC stands in sharp contrast with the ZCC lived experience. These contradictions between the ideology of the one and the social practice of the other pose problems. For one, they render the ZCC as one of the many South African vehicles of patriarchy. Accordingly, the ZCC contains elements that fall within the purview of what constitutes sexism. Such a milieu of conflicting ideology and human practice embodies tension.

Obviously that manifest tension needs to be resolved in the sociocultural process of the movement towards a non-sexist South Africa. More importantly these disharmonious perceptions in the country as a whole, and within the ZCC in particular produced even more concerns. They created and perpetuated the limitation of women's participation in educational and other forms of advancement. My account in examining this starts to develop in chapter four, after three chapters that lay the ground for the discourse.

The ZCC as a Component of the Larger African Initiated Churches

My theoretical framework defines the ZCC as a Christian movement that originated from reaction to colonialism and Christianity. The framework further sees the ZCC as a part of the larger movements that developed covertly and overtly in Africa. The missionaries who were mediums of Christianity, treated Africans in ways that created isolation. Colonialism integrated autonomous African polities into unitary imperial systems, and thus turned Africans into a powerless people, lacking in special privileges.

Africans also lacked significant degree of control over their own land and their own labor. The same historical dynamic that peripherized Africans, also contributed to the formation of new social classes. These modes of awareness were as subtle and diverse as they were overt.. They were also as premeditated as they were inadvertent and covert.[277] More importantly, they gave birth to a mutually exclusive social field that stood in binary opposition to each other. The conscious, purposeful and apparent domain constructed the believers and non-believers; the literate and the illiterates; the rural and the urban.

The less conscious, unintended and subtle field, on the other hand yielded social divisions distinguishable by attire, lingua franca,[278] work ethic, and as "Black yeomanry" to quote Comaroff and Comaroff (1991:311). The field also created hegemonies that led to the development of African Christianity different from the Christianity of European oppressors. Thus the churches currently called African Initiated Churches came into being.[279] The missionaries insistence to instill in their converts northern values and a distaste especially for traditional values and African culture, resulted in a dilemma for Africans.

Omoyi (1905) a very long time ago made an enduring observation when she contended that "there is no doubt that the rejection of a western style and western dominated Christianity was the major cause of schism in Africa."[280] While Africans appreciated and could fully associate with the discipline of church membership, access to schooling and acquisition of jobs, they lacked full loyalty precisely because they were not convinced about the inferiority of their cultural and religious values.[281] The fact that some of these values were recognized and sanctioned by either the old or new testament, e.g. revelation through dreams, polygamy, complex ritual in the old testament, healing, and the expulsion of evil spirits in the new testament vindicated their claim.[282]

A less pronounced but similar colonialists' discriminatory attitude by some missionaries and white Christians towards their Black counterparts compounded the conflict. Africans protested the missionaries' treatment of indigenous Africans that semantically and ideologically conflicted with the message of the bible. The missionaries preached "love your neighbor" and equality to all people, but behaved in ways that demonstrated by virtue of discrimination and unequal treatment, their dislike for Africans. This led some scholars like Ramose (1988) to conceive of the introduction of Christianity to Africa as a quantitative superfluity. Ramose argues that what Christianity purported to deliver, Africans already knew how to do. They related communally with their neighbors in ways that reflected love and care. In addition they knew how to pray. To that extent it was irrelevant to Africa. Through collaboration with the colonialists the marginalization of Africans in many institutions became possible.

African Christians then sought to rehabilitate African culture and the African way of life within the context of their new faith. They expressed an active reaction against the domination that was also reflected in the mission churches. To assert their right and reclaim their rightful place, the break with these churches was inevitable. Africans then initiated churches that differed in liturgy and practice from the missionaries. Indeed the emergence of AICs culminated in the famous rhetoric "whites came with a bible on one hand a gun on the other."[283] Or better still "whites told us to close our eyes and pray, when they said amen, and we opened our eyes the land was gone."

The discourse also illustrates that some of these churches played a central role in effecting social, political and economic change in most parts of Africa. Further women in these churches generally outnumber men in terms of membership.[284] In addition, the study illustrates the ephemeral position of women in the AICs. The study also shows that the power women attain comes from sponsorship by a male. Further Julles-Rosette (1975) and the others demonstrate that women's positions in these churches become articulated as protégés whose symbolic power derives from males.[285] The study has illustrated that the ZCC follows the same pattern.

However, I maintained, that in as far as this study specifically focuses on the ZCC's role in the transformation of sexism and patriarchy as per government mandate in South Africa, it is the first of its kind. I further posited that by virtue of the presence of elements that can be defined as patriarchal in the ZCC, a discrepancy exists between the non sexist ideology and the ZCC's institutional structures and sociocultural practice. I argued that the presence of these patriarchal elements arises from an interplay of sociocultural order and practice on one hand, and the articulation of systems dominant and subordinate on the other.[286]

Multiple Conjuncture of Structures

The study has determined that Colonial, Judo-Christianity, apartheid and the traditional Bapedi make up this confluence of unequal proportion. The latter puts this study in the context of several key concerns in modern social theory. This includes the interdependence of anthropology and history in the analysis of social issues. Pertinently, through an exploration of the mutual constitutive relationship of the Bapedi, the group from which the church originated, and the ZCC, I identified and exposed patriarchal and sexist tenets within the church. I did this first by examining membership and the role of the prophetesses. This investigation further revealed a complex process of interdependence with complementary and contradictory reproduction of men and women unequal relationships. The articulation of these two organizations with external forces, specifically, the missionaries and colonialist on one hand, and apartheid on the other, created new paradoxical ideologies and experiential social fields for the ZCC and Bapedi.

These recent social domains of the two reflect the existence of altered forms of patriarchy as still maintained and perpetuated. The social structures of both the Bapedi and the ZCC, for example, suggest a valorization of patriarchy over matriarchy. The latter finds expression through practices such as sororate, levirate, patrilineality, patrilocality, polygamous marriages, and the birth of a son as punctuating the completion of marriage.

Similarly the leadership and religious structures of both, the study demonstrates, personify persistent male ascendancy. Only males make up inner councils and decision making bodies with no history of a woman occupying the highest leadership position. Mutual expressions that imply the God given invisibility and relegation of women to the margin predominate, e.g., "if led by a woman it falls into a pit" God is perceived as male in both. The presentation of instruction and informal education with a focus on aspects of the bible and culture that emphasizes male dominance is very salient. The implication is that where and when God is male, then male is God. Both institutions refer to impurity, but in case of women, their biological make up over which they have no control renders them impure. I argued that to the extent that the logic follows the structural binary association of women with nature and men with culture[287] the practice falls within the definition of sexism as posited by the ANC. Related to the latter, is what I contend forms the most telling form of sexism in the ZCC, the requirement of a woman to reach menopause before they can be prophetess.

The practice parallels that of peripheral *Mapale* in Bapedi structures, who have to conform to the same requirement, while the male *Ngaka* does not have to. The rational inference, I argued, centers around equating lack of menstruation with purity. This then means by virtue of their inability to menstruate, men enjoy the state of purity most of their lives, a factor that entitles them to priesthood and other unfair advantages over women. Thus having proven existing historical patriarchal ideology and lived experience in the ZCC, I situate the church within the purview of structures defined as sexist, in the current South Africa. The church has to contend with a charge of being one of the patriarchal institutions that requires transformation in the new non-racial and non-sexist South Africa. The seriousness of the demand as an important and envisaged reality found resonance in the newly adopted South African Constitution, the study established.

Additionally the new bill on affirmative action, which states that South African Black women have been at the very bottom of the ladder of opportunities, and therefore should be given priority, also exposes the extent of the gravity, of the call to non-sexism.[288] The ZCC women compose part of the larger South African reality, consequently, they have faced and continue to face similar obstacles like the rest of Black women in South Africa.[289] One of those problems is the transformation of a sexist South Africa into a non-sexist society. The obligation translates into addressing cultural elements, ideology, and practices that engender women's exclusion and prevent them from participating in national structures as qualified leaders. Education and experience through exposure and participation in decision making bodies, comprise criteria necessary to guarantee women's participation and competency.

Construction and Mediation: Non Sexism, Education and Social Advancement

Massive re-education that will raise people's level of awareness to the ideology, nomenclature, beliefs, practices has to be undertaken to even come closer to achieving the goal of non-sexism.[290] I argued that the ZCC as a powerful influential patriarchal institution cannot escape the charge. I do not think most of the institutions in South Africa can. Its education in religious instruction throughout the years, has been a reaffirmation of males' position over women. This has existed in the ZCC as a practice sanctioned, accepted and authorized by God and communicated through the various bishops.

The latter forms a social fact that culminated in the majority of the members lacking school education. The discussion has also determined that men in the ZCC are more educated than the women. [291]- In fact the disparity is huge. Other factors like the apartheid migratory labor laws, population registration act, also contribute to the lack of school education amongst members. [292] Despite the latter factors, the study ascertained that the ZCC sends explicit and implicit educational messages that promote male dominance.

The degree of lack of school education among ZCC members in general and ZCC women in particular, prompted the general and seemingly indelible labeling of members of the church as illiterate, even by members themselves. I asserted that in order for a call of a non sexist society to be successful women's education, both attainment and lack of in the ZCC needs to be addressed. Such an endeavor I argued, should commence with how women perceive and construct the concept of a non-sexist South Africa, and how they will mediate their construction with their social and educational reality. The ANC might have its ideology, but it cannot and must not do it for them.

That discourse, contained in chapter four, revealed divergent and convergent pathways. In the context of contradictory circumstances, and the process full of ambiguity and conflict, a uniform outcome proved impossible. Pain, confusion, determination, despair, oscillation between certainties and uncertainties, divided loyalties, rigid compliance with the church, total abandonment of religious beliefs marked the process as these women negotiated a space to define and control their situations. The latter process places this study within the purview of yet another important modern social theory-theory of conflict. Still applicable in the modern times, Glukman (1963)[293] and Malinowski (1926)[294] theories from a very long time ago, lend resonance to my analysis. They hold seemingly opposing views about conflict. Malinowski sees conflict as divisive except where it is ritualized. Gluckman on the other hand, sees conflict as a mode that both integrates groups and produces social balance. [295] The significance of the two theories to my analysis becomes clear only when considered as simultaneously descriptive, rather than as mutually exclusive, and that will become clear as I continue with this discussion.

The study established that generally, religious instruction and the peace theme *khotso* formed sources of knowledge production and cultural logic that informed the epistemological foundation from which women framed their conception of patriarchy and sexism. That a discordance between the concept of non-sexism and the religio-cultural practices of the ZCC exists the women did not contest. However, their responses to this hegemony produced a degree of opposition and resistance, as well as compliance and acceptance typical to many hegemonic relationships.[296]

Akin to Malinowski's (1926) assertion, elderly ZCC rural women's conception translates into non-sexism as a potentially divisive call that will engender rivalry and unnecessary competition between men and women. This is so, since in their opinion, the call to non-sexism has adopted the redefinition of the division of labor as dichotomous hierarchies binarily ranked in opposition to each other. A definition not only inaccurate, but also clearly a breach of *khotso* as the central theme of their religious belief, they asserted.

These women's constructs conduct legitimacy and authority by virtue of its being ancient and transmitted to them through education in the church.[297] Subjected to further analysis, their constructions contain a number of important implications in understanding men and women's relations. Sexual division of labor does not necessarily create inequality in men and women's relationships. Indeed, several scholars have analyzed pre-colonial Africa and pre-industrial Europe and concluded that the separate men and women's labor spheres were devoid of subordination.[298]

However, people like Boserup (1970) have convincingly demonstrated that sex differentiation, in modern times, tends to devaluate women, their education and work. In addition, a strict assignment of different tasks to different sexes functions to preserve the sex inequality that marginalizes the importance of women to get education. The focus by religions of the world on aspects that devalue women and their activities compounds the situation. There are numerous instances, but suffice it here for me to cite, Leviticus 27:3-7 that ascribes to female servants three fifths the value of the male servants. In the context of the ZCC the impact of such verses of the bible as authority on education, and the construct of sexism as a just natural division of labor, is directly related to how these women make their decisions about who to educate. Precisely because of the value placed on men's work, young women drop out at the request of the parents and the coercive power of the cultural dictates,[299] to give opportunity to their brothers who receive more value from the culture in varied ways.

The women's perception of this phenomenon as non sexist, notwithstanding, the fact remains their construct and perceptions are bound to reproduce patterns of behavior that work against advancing

ZCC young women's education. That the women claim or profess not to feel any disadvantage from this, I can only attribute to socialization through the education that they receive in the church. Durkheim (1895) and later Comaroff (1980) realizes the power of such socialization that culminates in internalized tendencies. The latter have a propensity to make humans interpret hierarchical relations of inequality as natural.

Therefore, for a non-sexist society to be achieved the ZCC women should take cognizance of the fact that sexual inequality is preserved by the fact that men and women do different tasks, and not by the task performed by each sex.[300] The construct of these older rural women, while valid, and authenticated in their minds by its longevity, perpetuates tenets of sexism as defined by the ANC. In contrast to the rural elderly women, the middle aged and younger rural women carefully take a different position, that of oscillating alliances and subtle embrace for change. The latter position in Gluckman's (1963) way of thinking fosters a social balance that will eliminate extremes. Thus the integration of the fundamental insights of the Malinowskian and Gluckman's approaches benefits this study as tools of analysis. It offers a full explanation of the varied women's responses to conflict, providing kinship of opposites in a subtle fashion.

The middle age and younger rural women are nevertheless in concert with rural elders on some issues. All of them display loyalty to the power of the bishop's visionary superiority that will determine the course, if ever, of non-sexism. In addition both strongly perceive the maintenance of peace in the church as primary to the call of no-sexism. The younger urban women on the other hand advocate for the mediation of the disjuncture through a process that will bring the ZCC in conformity with non-sexism. They do not perceive such a move as a potential violation of peace. In fact they interpret the current state of men and women relationship in the church as a violation of the peace theme.

Generally all these women recognize some inequalities. While the urban young clearly call for change, the others, exercise caution and would prefer the change to occur within the parameters of the fundamental principle of ZCC *khotso*. Women of all ages rural and urban profess their value for education. It became very clear that in the face of dilemmas about the education of young men and women, that of the former will take primacy. The decisions while informed by socialization[301] like I mentioned above, and implied messages from the church like a woman should acquire just enough education to complement and not compete her man, were nevertheless, also products of other external factors. Structural coercion[302] - like the apartheid system laws, dictated some of the choices made in favor of boys. Constrained and opportunities in these women's immediate social environments, like the influx control and migratory labor system laws, limited the range of possible options and channeled motivation to chose advancing men and not women's education. Of course socialization knowledge base injected a reaffirmation of logic in their decisions, as sensible choices.

Socialization processes as described by Parsons a long time ago (1955) and recently Gerson (1985) link the societies functional needs and people's personality, as a point of departure in understanding gender socialization. Sensible choices can be arrived at either consciously or unconsciously. In the ZCC elderly women's case, the inability to articulate the impact of the apartheid laws on their choices, suggests either oblivion to or the location of the awareness of the apartheid system as the unconscious, like Parson has argued. Lack of money, expensive education, disparity in remuneration on the basis of gender, are all impacts of apartheid laws. Even though these women cite these as motivating factors in their preference for the education of young male over young women, they seemed either reluctant or to lack the ability to recognize and link the integrated and mutually influential forces of their structural and cultural orders.

That contextually the women's decisions make sense, does not guarantee an inevitable awareness of the structural forces impinging on them or the overall logic of their choices. Sadly the role of socialization becomes evident at the unconscious level of younger and middle age rural women who themselves believe that enough education for a young woman to "complement and not compete" a man seems a path to take. The latter message obviously derives from the church's teaching.

The discourse illustrates the concern of the ZCC officials about the lack of school education for their members. The church, through the bishops' mandate, thus established education initiatives in the form of adult literacy centers throughout South Africa, schools in the church's capital of Morija in Lebowa, bursary and merit funds, and management training. These enterprises, unfortunately, fail to address the unequal access to education and representation of women in the ZCC educational structures. They operate in a manner that echoes the hegemonic social hierarchy model of the larger sexist ZCC structures. The distribution of bursaries for in stance, is differential in favor of young male students.

Women's responses to the latter circumstances also reflect their construct of sexism and patriarchy, they continue to reflect ambivalence, and follow the same pattern along young/old and urban/rural divide. The elder women from both the urban and rural and some middle aged from both areas, maintained their stance of constructing the differential manifestation as a non competitive duality, which needed no change unless the bishop says so. The other women, conceded that they will welcome change effected within the parameters of the peace theme. Urban younger women still wished for immediate change and made no reference to the bishop. The conflicting semantic and ideological views of the church and the non sexist call will be mediated by bringing the views of the church in compliance with the new South African reality. The rural younger women on the other hand and some middle aged rural women's mediation of the conflict found articulation by an oscillation of loyalties between the two entities.

Based on the above findings I argued that most of these women are not completely opposed to change, nor are they oblivious to sexism in their church, but feel the need to give primacy to peace. In the context of social theory a mandate from the bishop inspired by supernatural visionary abilities will help mediate and resolve the conflict in a manner acceptable to the women.

The predicament that faces the ZCC women goes beyond the ZCC school structures. The discussion in chapter five established that outside the ZCC structures women and men of school going age, especially in secondary and high schools, are stigmatized. In detail the study traced the origin of the negative perception as emerging from the ZCC lack of opposition against the apartheid regime. To its members, however, the church stressed the necessity of separating the sacred from the profane.[303] I argued that the lack of opposition against and affiliation with the regime while conducive and profitable to the agenda of the ZCC officials, harms women in their educational aspirations. The church expected its members to observe strict separation between spirituality and the hierarchy of the temporal world. On the other hand its officials functioned in a manner that mixed the sacred and the profane. Such actions precluded the ZCC students from participating in the struggle. The latter created an environment where ZCC members suffer isolation and stigmatization from other students. A point of disharmony shared by teachers. This shared cognitive consonance between the majority of students and teachers, resulted in differential treatment of ZCC students. It also culminated in ZCC young women students decisions to drop out, rather than controvert those in authority, especially when they are males.

The women's mediation of this tension then plays out as a dialectic that concurrently generates reinforcement and tension, reproduction and transformation.[304] That is, the refusal to confront male authority reproduces and reinforces sexism by its virtue of intimidating women to confront males. It further affirms the stereotype of ZCC members expected behavior of leaving school early and contributing to their perception as "illiterates." At the same time dropping out signify transformation, the process which by its very character creates tension.

Hurdles presented by structural contradictions, in addition to the above, made a uniform outcome emanating from the mediation of the conflict, impossible. The mediation of the dilemma and contradictory circumstances involved negotiation in a process full of ambiguity and conflict, and at times necessitated decisions based on individuation rather than aggregation. From their different responses and mediation emerged varied life paths. We therefore see "outrageous"[305] activists, women who fall pregnant deliberately, women choosing to work and endure the oppressive white employment, taxi owners, women selling food to school children, women who aspire to be prophetess in the church, and finally women continuing education through adult literacy centers.

These diverse reactions that embody acquiescence and protest, reproduction and transformation act as a complex force that induce structural and ideological change as it simultaneously reproduces subjugation and fails to improve the ZCC women status. The study illustrated that the current situation in South Africa offers education about non sexism in the work place as well. Exposure to such education affects ZCC men and women and requires mediation as the concept still continues to conflict with that of their religious instruction. The discourse demonstrated that the unions expose ZCC men and women to new information about non sexism that both diverges from and challenges their ZCC religious teachings. This information, I maintained, creates tension and provokes delicate adjustment and mediation at different levels, including the personal.

The mediation of the women's experiences and perceptions with the spiritual, the valued and the real occur as paradoxes with decisions based on individualized cognition. Working ZCC women from both the rural and urban areas, professionals and non professionals participate in various unions. The latter signify a significant departure from the practice of the ZCC members during the apartheid era, where participation in the union amounted to involvement in politics. I should acknowledge that some members hide their membership for various reasons, including the fact that since the new government came into power the ZCC has not announced its stance in politics.

Ambivalence abounds as to whether participation now constitutes an appropriate church practice or not. Despite the latter some women participate in the unions. I have argued that their active participation though contradictory, reflects repudiation against certain values and concepts practiced in their church. Although still perpetuating manifest inequalities of gender the women's involvement metaphorically subtly bespeaks of the rejection of sexism. In a process of simultaneous reproduction and transformation, as Comaroff (1980) will have it, their involvement objectifies elements of both resistance to and replication of sexism. For example, both in the rural and urban these women react to the disharmonious semantic, ideological, and experiential reality, by compartmentalizing their lives in varied ways.

The study showed that the commonalties include leaving changes within the domestic sphere to the church and bishop, avoiding confrontation with spouses on issues of gender equality, leaving the decisions of whether to wear badges or not to the men, fighting sexism vigorously in the public work place, while yielding to the men in the home. The latter complex form of reproduction and transformation, I maintained generate tension that needed mediation.

Women's deference to their husbands wishes obliterated rivalry and created benevolent alliances. In the final analysis this enhanced the men's support for women's involvement in the unions, and by extension though unconsciously, I argued, the course of a non-sexist South Africa. The benefit of the education about non sexism that is offered in the union structures proves invaluable to both men and women. Those whose husbands participate in the unions experience less resistance from their husbands to perform the union duties.

The Bishop, No-Sexism, Social Theory, and Change

The study further, demonstrated the faith that the majority have in the power of the bishop. He constantly gives orders about several important issues. The orders are immediately obeyed. Indeed, the elders and important officials proclaim that implementing and obeying what the bishop demands constitute "an absolute essential." Also women in my study referred to the importance of guidance from him. I am very much cognizant of the fact that the bishop being a man such a suggestion might be conceived as conflicting with the ideological basic principle of non-sexism, at best. At worst it can translate into a perpetuation of sexism by the ZCC women. Will a man really fully understand the impact of sexism, let alone define how it should be eliminated? Why would women in the ZCC want the course of non-sexism to be defined by the very man whose ideology and cultural practice yield sexism? That is not for the ANC or me to decide. A substantial number of the women in my study do not see a discrepancy in asking for his guidance. The very fact that they expressed a desire to be guided by his directive affirms their construct and view of sexism and patriarchy.

The view might not be palatable to the ANC and me, but it belongs to the ZCC women. Conversely, for these women such a directive would make up an important component of the social process of transformation from the ZCC's side. Please note that this study recognizes that the ZCC forms but a small portion of the South African society. The women's reality and not the ANC's ideology will determine whether change within the church happens or not. A durable change that will be hard to reverse, will be a change that occurs with the contribution of all in the ZCC. Most importantly the ZCC themselves must see the need to move towards a non sexist society. If the ZCC is committed to the course of non sexism, which will include the educational and social development of ZCC women, will asking the bishop to give such a directive be a bad idea?. I am not suggesting that such a mandate will produce divine magical results, if it happens.

In the context of social theory, I see such a mandate comprising an enduring part of the mediation and the social process towards an objective of a non-sexist society. What I see as really pivotal is the need to bridge the perceptual distance of what constitutes sexism. Would it even be bad to ask Mandela with the amount of respect and influence he commands to play that role? He visited Moria for a related purpose before first real democratic elections, as such this will not be an anomaly, or would it?

FOOTNOTES AND NOTES

[1] I am employing the word minimal school education and not "illiterate." Most of my informant resented the word.
Indeed, I found out that even though
they have not attended school, they were very
knowledgeable.

[2] Anthropological literature has referred to this practice as
ancestor worship. I am referring to the practice as the

living dead in line with African scholars like Mbiti (1969).
Besides the believe in Badimo is
Centered around life after death

3   Cf. J and J Comaroff 1991: 219. They discuss in detail
how the missionaries interpreted the concept of Badimo as
demons.

4   I am employing the word king here very much aware that
the Comaroffs use the word chief, to keep up with current
debates in South Africa. In the 'new' South
Africa an effort is made to restore through nomenclature
among others the position and prestige that were displaced
by the taxonomy used by colonialist
Most of the kings were called chiefs.

5   Please note that even other families who belonged to the
missionary churches
and still practiced the living dead religion were never
negatively viewed.

6   A special tree planted for the purpose of conducting
offerings to the living dead.

7   The north and south characterization follows the debate that
marked the United Nations in the 1970's. While at that
time the intention was to move away from
the political and economic valuation of other countries as
inferior, people claimed confusion with regard to New
Zealand and Australia. The latter were regarded as
northern therefore part of the west. This study recognizes,
that New Zealand, Australia like the Americas and South
Africa etc. have indigenous, imposed western, and other
ways of knowing, being and thinking. Common to
all is the invasion by westerners that resulted in imposition
of foreign values.The north in this study refers to "western-
Euro" and the south to indigenous and different from the
Western-Euro.

8   Cf. Sundkler (1948), Oosthuizen (1968) Barret (1968)
Pauw (1963) and West
(1975)

9   An extrapolation of mine since Sundkler IS talking about
male leaders and not women.

10 I find this depiction as strong, unfair and indicative of
double standard adopted by some scholars in their
comparison of African and western phenomena of
Christianity. I elaborate further on this later on in the text
under the purpose of the study.

11 These anthropologists explore various churches in Africa
including the Harrist movements in Ivory Coast, and
Ghana, the Church of the Messiah in Ghana,
Maranke's church in the former Zaire etc.

12 Wallis, R 1982(b) "The Social Construction of Charisma."
Social Campus 29, 1:25-39. West, M. 1975 *Bishops and
Prophets in a Black City*. Claremont, Cape Town: David

Phillip Publishers. 1964 *Max Weber: The Theories*
Johnson, B 1992 "On Founders and Followers: Some
Factors in the Development of New Religious
Movements." *Sociological Analysis* 53:S1-S13.

[13] West 1975 op. cit.

[14] Perrin-Jassy 1971.

[15] Mma-Nku means mother Nku. She started the church and
has managed to sustain it with a female oriented leadership
that echoes the Lobedu of the Northern Transvaal
leadership. Men in the church play a marginal role. Mma-
Nku's success in running the church is well known.

[16] These two authors were discussing cultural specific focus
of gender relations in general. King's argument
focuses on religion reflects their influence

[17] Sered, S. S. 1994 (a) Ideology, Anatomy and Sisterhood:
An Analysis of the Secular Consequences of Women's
Rights. In *Gender and Society*. Vol 8 No 4. 1994 (b)
*Priestess, Mother, Sacred, Sister: Religions Dominated by
Women*. Oxford: Oxford University Press. Comaroff, J.
1980 *Body of Power Spirit of Resistance*. Chicago:
Chicago University Press.

[18] Hoehler-Fatton describes how in the Roho church women
led church initiatives and exercised charismatic authority.

[19] Bradenbach, P. 1977 The Woman on the Beach and the
Man in the Forest. In *The New Religions of Africa*. Edited
by Jules Rosette. New Jersey: Albex Publishing
Corporation.Barrett, D.B. 1968 Schism and Renewal in
Africa: An Analysis of Six Thousand Contemporary
Religious Movements. Nairobi: Oxford University Press
And Walker. S. The Message as the Medium. In
Bond, G., Walton, J. and Walker, S. 1979 *African
Christianity: Patterns of Change and Continuity*. New
York: Academic Press, Inc.

[20] The complexity is also present in labor settings and family
relations.

[21] 1987 *The New Religious Movements in Nigeria*. 193-5
New York: Edwin Mellen Press.Lehman, D. 1963 Women
in the African Independent Churches
In Hayward, V.(ed) *African Independent Church
Movements* 65-69. Edinburgh House Press. Taylor and
Lehman 1961: 248-268.

[22] Johannes Dimpe and his wife who is the prophetess
provided the information.

[23] The information provided by the high priest' with the
assigned coded name Mr Ju and his second wife with the
assugned coded name of Dr2.
the information provided by the same informants as above.
Others too like Mmu shared the same opinion.
The discussion on the history of the church in chapter two
details the reasons.

[26] Lukhaimane, E. 1980 *The History of the Zion Christian Church*. Unpublished Masters Thesis. Pietersburg: University of The North.

[27] See *The Apartheid Regime: Political Power and Radical Domination*.. Edited by Price, R. and Roseberg C. 1980 University of California Berkeley: Institute of International Studies 1980. Meli, F *A History of the ANC: South Africa Belongs to us*.. Harare: Zimbabwe Publishing House.

[28] *Workers News*, November 1994 The Magazine of South African Municipal Workers Union. *Sechaba: ANC Magazine* Vol 24, August 1990: Women Fight for Freedom.

[29] op. cit. cf. also *Women and Class in Africa*. Edited Robertson C and Berger I. 1986 Great Britain: Holmes and Meir.

[30] Kiger, E. J. (1948) *The Realm of a Rain Queen*. London.

[31] Sechaba: ANC Magazine August (1990) op. cit.

[32] Comaroff, J. 1980 *Body of Power Spirit of Resistance*. Chicago: Chicago University Press.

[33] Lukhaimane 1980, op. cit Kruger, M.A. 1971 *Die Zio n Christian Church- 'n Religieuse Bantoebeweging in 'n ty d van Ontwrigting*. Unpublishe Masters Thesis, University of Potchefstroom.

[34] Kruger 1971 *Die Zion Christian Church:. In Religieuse Bantobeweging in die tyd van Onbtwrigting*. Unpublished Masters Thesis. University of Potchefstroom.

[35] *Women and Class In Africa* 1986 Robertson, C and Berger, I. eds. New York: Africana Publishing Company.

[36] Cf. *Persistent Inequalities*, edited by Tinker. New York: Oxford University Press. Cf. also McCormack 1981 "Development with Equity for Women." In *Womenand World Change*. Black, N., and Cotter, A.B. Albany : SUNNY Press and 1982 "Control of Land, Labor and Capital in Rural Southern Sierra Leone." In *Women and Work in Africa* edited by Bay, E.G. Afonja, S. 1986 *Social Change in Nigeria. New York*: Holmes and Miers Publishing and 1990 "Changing Patterns of Gender Stratification in West Africa." In Persistent Inequalities edited by Tinker, I. New York: Oxford University Press. Boserup, E. 1970 *Women's Role in Economic Development*. New York: St. Mary's Press.

[38] Benston M. "The Political Economy of Women's Liberation" *Monthly Review* 1969, September 13:25. Parson, T. 1967 *The Social System*. London: Cohen and West. Parson T and Bales, R. 1955 *Family Socialization and Interaction Process*. Glencoe, Ill: Free Press. Resknin B, and Padavic, 1994 *Women and*

Men at Work. Thousand Oaks: Pine Forge Press.

[40] Gerson, K. 1985 *Hard Choices*. Berkeley: University of California Press.

[41] Sundkler 1960 op. cit.

[42] Barrett, D.B. 1968 *Schism and Renewal in Africa: A Analysis of Six Thousand Contemporary Religious Movements*. Nairobi: Oxford University Press. 1970 AD 2000: 350 Million Christians in Africa. In *International Review of Missions*. Nairobi: Oxford University Press.

[43] Sundkler ibid

[44] Barret J, et al 1985 *South African Women on the Move*. London: Zed Books Ltd.

[45] This becomes clear through the discussion of the history of the church in chapter two.

[46] Comaroff 1980 op cit., Pauw (1960, 1963, 1975), Linington 1924, Martin 1964.

[47] A code name.

[48] Comaroff 1980 op cit.

[49] Jules-Rosette, B. 1975 (a) *African Apostoles: Ritual and Conversion in the Church of John Maranke*. Ithaca: Cornell University Press. and Sundkler, B. 1948 *Bantu Prophets in South Africa*. London: Oxford University Press 1961 *Bantu Prophets in South Africa* 2nd edition. London: Oxford University Press for the International African Institute. 1976 *Zulu Zion and SomeSwazi Zionists* London: Oxford University.

[50] Some people participated in the study but were not keen to answer questions. Some would justnod in agreement and not give a verbal answer. The charts show the social identity of those informants who directly responded.and gave me information in general.

[51] Again in the interest of protecting my informants, I am not being specific about whether the alphabet if from the first or last name.

[52] Please note that I do not cite every informant in the text. Consequently the code name that appear are not going to be necessarily in numerical order.

[53] Ogbu, J.U. and Simons, H.D. 1994 *Cultural Models of School Achievement: A Quantitative Test of Ogbu's Theory*. University of California at Berkeley.

[54] Ogbu and Simons ibid.

[55] Schapera I *The Tswana* London: International Institute: 1953

[56] Van Warmelo *Bantu Speaking People of South Africa* ed by Hammond Tooke ibid.

[57] Monnig 1969 ibid.

[58] Van Warmelo, op. cit., also West and Morris p32 op. cit., Sundkler 1969 op. cit. p49

[59] Biko, B.S. *I Write What I Like*. San Francisco: Harper and Row 1986 pp. 54-60.

60   Hunt op. cit. pp. 295-318

61   Mönnig: 1969, Hunt: (1931), Hammond-Tooke (1953 and Nthabu (1989)

62   Lukhaimane: 1980, Kruger (1971) and Ramose (1987).

63   Lukhaimane, op. cit.

64   A code name.

65   Mr. Lu also confirmed the information. (a code name)

66   Lukhaimane 1980 op. cit.

67   Mr. L u in fact provided me with a book which I still have, that has lost some pages, but has a detailed History of the ZCC written in Sepedi. The written account also dismisses the claim In fact some of the illustrations in this study come from that book. I cannot cite the title,the year and the publisher since those pages are missing.

68   Lukhaimane 1980 op. cit.

69   ibid.

70   Lukhaimane 1980

71   All code names

72   *The Star News Paper* Johannesburg, April 19, 1985.

73   Cf. Lukhaimane 1980 op. cit.

74   ibid., Kruger 1971 op. cit. also information collected from ethnographic research.

75   Lukhaimane: 1980 op. cit.

76   The Internet

77   See Sundkler 1976, Pauw 1963 and West 1975.

78   These included in code names: Lu, Mu, Mu2, Kr, Dr, and Dr2

79   Nthabu (1989) ibid.

80   Nthabu op.cit.

81   Cmr, Amr, Dmu, Smu, Smu2, Cmu and Cmu2

82   I observed several processes where members have been on probation and finally accepted into the church.

83   These included in coded names: Ar, Br, Mu3, Lu2, Lu

84   The information was obtained from participant observation. Information from: included in code names: Cmr, Amr, Dmu, Smu, Smu2, Cmu and Cmu2 amongst others.

86   Ibid.

87   These included in coded names: Cmr2, Gmr2, Fu, Fu2, Ku, Kmu.

88   These included in coded names: Ar, Br, Mu3, Lu2, Lu, Dmu, and Zu amongst   others

89   These included in coded names: Smu, Smu2, and Lu amongst others.

90   Mostly women from the rural areas and urban older and middle aged women expressed the sentiment.

91   Observed in the field. Other scholars like Comarof and

Daneel noted similar practices.

[92] Nthabu (1989) and Jules-Rosette (1977)

[93] Nthabu 1989 op. cit.

[94] Souls of the bishops who have died.

[95] Nthabu ibid.

[96] Nthabu ibid.

[97] From field observation

[98] Smu, Smu2, and Lu

[99] From participant observation. Women were extensively quizzed and judged before ordained.

[100] *Ditaelo* refer to directives inspired and conferred by the holy spirit on male ministers to prepare and administer medicine prescribed by the prophetesses to cure and rectify afflictions.

[101] A code name of a prophetess who is married to a high priest.

[102] Explained in full in the next section that juxtaposes the ZCC with Bapedi structures.

[103] From field research data.

These were mainly older women rural and urban and some middle aged women
from both urban and rural.

[105] This will become clear in chapter five of this study.

[106] As chapter four will reflect women from schools in urban areas provided the information.

[107] Oosthuizen, B 1968 *Post Christianity in Africa: A Theological and Anthropological Study* Stellenbosch: Peabo Publishing Company.

[108] A cultural practice where a man marries his deceased brother's widow.

[109] Mönnig, H.O. 1967 *The Pedi* Pretoria: Van Schaik Limited. More information can also be obtained from Nthabu 1989

[110] The north and south characterization follows the debate that marked the United Nations in the 1970's as I have previously explained.

[111] Cultural practice that manifested in three ways: (I) a woman marrying her deceased
sisters husband (ii) sisters getting married to one man because one of the sisters is unable to conceive (iii) sisters getting married to one man simply because all the parties prefer it that way in the context of polygamy.

[112] Mönnig, ibid.

[113] Oosthuizen, 1986 .op. cit

[114] Monnig, 1969 op. cit.

[115] ibid.

[116] 1951. Bantu Authorities Act, no 68.

[117] This was in a coded name Xu.

[118] These included in code names Wr, Mr2, Rr, Gr, Jr2, Jmr,

and Tr amongst others.
119 Nthabu 1989 op. cit.
120 Ogbu J Current Anthropology 1977
121 Mönnig, op. cit.
122 Oosthuizen, 1980 op. cit.
123 ibid.
124 Nthabu 1989, op. cit.
125 These included: Mu2, Dr2, Dmu, Ar and Jmr amongst others.
126 Nthabu ibid. Cf. also Lukhaimane 1980 op. cit.
127 Mönnig 1969 op. cit. Cf. also Hammond-Tooke, W.D. 1953 *The Bantu Speaking People of South Africa.* London: Routledge and Kegan.
128 ibid.
129 Nthabu 1989 op. cit
130 Hanekom, C 1965 *Krisis en Kultur: Geloofteopsvatinge en Seremonise binne 'n Swart Kerk.* Pretoria: Van Schaiks Limited. and 1965 *Die Huidige Stand van die Tradisionele Godsdienspatroon by die Mamabolo.* Unpublished D.Phil. Thesis, Pretoria.
131 ibid.
132 Nthabu op. cit.
133 Coded names for Reverends Lu3, and Mr2, Mu. and Lu.
134 ibid.
135 ibid.
136 Nthabu 1989 op. cit.
137 Nthabu 1989 op cit.
138 ibid.
139 Monnig, 1969 op. cit.
140 ibid.
141 Monnig, 1969 op. cit..
142 Nthabu 1989, op. cit..
143 Monnig, 1969 op. cit. and Oosthuizen 1968 op cit.
144 Lukhaimane 1980 op. cit.
145 Ibid.
146 Coded name. Other men and women expressed the same opinion of the phenomenon. Priests also shared the sentiment.
147 Lukhaimane 1980 op. cit.
148 Nthabu 1989 op. cit..
149 Durkheim 1964 op. cit., de Miranda and Clignet 1976 op. cit.
150 Cf. also S. de Beauvior *The Second Sex* London Penguin 1971, M.D. Caulfield 1983 "Equality, Sex and Mode of

Production" in Berreman *Social Inequality* New York: Academic Press 1983), Chodorow, N. *The Reproduction of Mothering* Berkeley: The University of California Press 1978) Ortner, S. Is Female to Nature as Nature Is to

Culture" in *Women Culture and Society* eds. Rosaldo and Lamphere. Stanford: Stanford University Press 1974 Sacks, K. 1981 *Sexual Meaning*. Cambridge: Cambridge University Press 1976.

[151] Resknin B and Padavic 1994 *Women and Men at Work*. Thousand Oaks: Pine Forge Press

[152] Bergman, B 1986 The Economic Emergence of Women. New York: Basic Books, also argues that this segregation code is used to reverse the training slots leading to higher level jobs for men.
Sacks, K 1979 *Sisters and Wives*. Connecticut: Greenwood Press Incorporation also
refutes the concept of universal oppression of women based on their biological make up. She uses the Nuer as an example of how wealth endows the women in this society with autonomy. A woman wealthier than her husband holds her property and assumes the dual status of husband and wife.

[154] These included:. Lu3,. Rr2, Rr, .Mmu, Mu, Bu3, Bu, Br, Nmr, Nr and Zr.

[155] These included in coded names: Mmu, Jmr, Dmr, Gmr, Pmr, Pmu, Pmu2 and Cmu2 amongstothers

[156] These included in coded names: Lu, Kr, Dmu, Cmu, Pmu, Bu, Ar, and Zu amongst others.

[157] Parsons, T. 1950 "Psychoanalysis and the Social Structure." *Psychoanalytic Quarterly* 19: 371-184. and Parson T and R Bales *Family, Socialization and Interaction Process* Glencoe, Illinois: Free Press 1955.

[158] Cf. *Women and Men at Work*. Edited by Reskin, B and Padavic, I. California: A
Sage Publication Company.Cf. also The New Testament (1 Timothy 2:11-2)

[159] A coded name.

[160] These included:. Lu3, Ar, Cr, Xr, Rr2, Rr, .Mmu, Mu, Bu3, Bu, Br, Nmr, Nr and Zr.Gmu,
Gmr, Kr and Lr amongst others.

[161] A coded name.

[162] For a further understanding see: Omoyajowo (1984) and Julles-Rosette (1977) observe that within the newer AIC across Africa, a woman's power increases after her childbearing period has ended. Daneel 1970, 1971 asserts that Shona custom already contained precedence of an old "neuter" medium figure through whom God spoke, thereby removing all of her sexual characteristics. Glukman (1956)describes Zulu traditional agricultural rites in which women dressed in men's clothing and imitated male familial and work tasks, as a symbol of power and potential change.

[163] Walker 1975, op. cit and Hackett, R.I.J. 1987 *The Ne*

Religious Movements in Nigeria. NewYork: Edwin
Mellen Press. Weber, M. 1947 *The Theory of
Economic and Social Organization*, edited by. Parson T.
New York: Oxford University Press pp. 358-373. 139

ZCC Messenger, Easter 1992, Issue No 22 P10. The wives
of some priests who hold positions of priestesses are goood
examples.

164   These were women from Garankuwa, Mamelodi and
Mabopane areas.

166   A coded name.

167   The viewed shared by women from both urban and rural
including those coded as Zu, Zr,
Wr and Lu

168   Bishop's Tutu attendance at the conference was reported on
the *Internet* and in the South
African *Star News Paper*, July 19 1998

169   Nthabu (1989) Ramose (1988)

170   These included in code names Myu, Jyu, Yyu, Jyu2,
amongst others.

171   A coded name

172   Younger women mostly from Zone Four Garankuwa. But
also some from Atteridgeville

173   These were in coded names Mr Mu and Mr Lu. Mr. Lu.
holds a graduate degree from the US. Hiswife is also
highly educated and is a manager/matron of Garankuwa
Hospital

174   Mönnig, H.O. 1967 *The Pedi* Pretoria: Van Schaik
Limited.

175   A code name.

176   These included in coded names, Kmu, Wu, Wr, Wr2, Lu,
Mr, Mr2, Mmr, Sr, Smu
amongst others.

177   In coded names these included: Cyu, Cyu3, Cyu2, Kyu,
Fyu, Myu amongst others.

178   Star, T. 1991 *The Natural Inferiority of Women.* New
York: Poseidon. I must add here that despite the fact that
ministers, at least most of them lac school
education, some of them are surprisingly familiar with the
western ways of thinking that reinforce the ubordinate
status of women. Hence in addition to the above quote by
John Knox, I alsovery often was referred to the sayings of
people like Clement of Alexandria, Augustine, Aquinas.
The pronunciation of the names and sometimes the
association of the quotes with the right person
were confused. But during field research quotes like:
"You cannot challenge the fact that a woman has to live
under man's influence and has no authority over her lord
were thrown at me to remind me that even western
educated men knew.

179   Information from participant observation in church
        meetings.

180   These included in coded names Wr, Mr, Mmr, Ymr2, and
        Ymr amongst others.

181   These included in coded names: Younger rural--Cyr, Ayr,
        Dyr, Fyr, Kyr amongst others
        Middle aged rural included: Omr, Omr2, Vmr, Vmr2,
        Vmr3, and Qr amongst others.

182   In coded names the 10, 11 and 12 year olds are Syr, Syr2,
        Myr3.

183   In coded names the younger women in the urban areas
        include: Ayu, Dyu, Lyu, Myu6,
        Jyu. The 12, 15 and 17 year olds in coded names were:
        Myu2, Myu3, and Dyu2,
        respectively.

184   I hesitate to give a translation of these names in English as
        they can result misrepresentation. Suffice it for me to posit
        that the words letekatse and sefebe are derogatory. I
        explained lefetwa as meaning a person who has been
        passed with no reference to gender.

185   E. Unterhalter 1989 "Contradictions in Bantu Education".
        In *Sechaba, official organ of the African National
        Congress* Vol 23 No. 2.

186   R. Clignet Women, Education and Labour Force
        Participation: Social Change and Sex
        Differentiation in the Cameroun and Ivory Coast. and de
        Miranda G. Women's Labor ForceParticipation in
        Developing Society: The Case of Brazil. In *Women and
        National Development*. Edited by Wellesley Editorial
        Committee 1977 The University of Chicago Press.

187   It should be noted that even though South Africa attained
        its independence, the structural changes are marked by
        resistance from white population and political parties. The
        Government of National Unity process of consultation and
        the resistance ensures that the impact of apartheid is still
        felt and in place.

188   For more information cf. West, M. The Urban African
        Population of South Africa., 1980 In R Price and C Roseerg
        1980 op. Cit   Also see information in Boatamo Nthabu
        (now Mosupyoe's 1989)

189   Although I am writing in the past tense things are still very
        much the same. The transformation process is still at its
        initial stages with still a lot of resistance from whites

190   Robertson, C and Berger, I. 1986 op. cit.

191   A coded name.

192   These included in coded names Umu, Gmu, Mmu, and Lr
        amongst others.

193   A coded name.

194   The younger urban included in coded names Dyu, Byu,

Byu2, and Kyu. The Younger
rural included in coded names Tyr, Myr3, Nyr, and Gyr
amongst others.

195 Using this word proved to be very detrimental to
people perceived me. I had to
change.

196 *The ZCC Messenger* 1991 reaffirms my experience.

197 Lukhaimane 1980 the name of the school is Stoffberg, next
to the University of North.

198 *Morongwa* ZCC Magazine 1985 issue 2 November.

199 ibid.

200 Wright, C. 1989 Precursors to adjustment, Revitalization,
and Expansion: an under the carpet view of the education
crisis in Sub-Saharan Africa. In *Zimbabwe Journal of
Educational Research.* Volume 1 no 1.

201 Damelin College is one of the largest adult training
colleges in South Africa, renowned for its efficacy and
deliverance of great number of graduates, it is well
respected world wide.

202 Information also from Morongwa p13 1991.

203 Resknin B, and Padavic, I. *Women and Men at Work.*
Thousand Oaks: Pine Forge Press.

204 Coser. R. Authority and Structural Ambivalence in the
Middle Class Family." In The Family: Its Structures and
Function ed by R. Coser New York: St. Martin's Press
1974.

205 Daniel A.R. and Weingarten, K. (1978) "Parenthood Now
or Later". Wesley, Massach: Welseley Center for Research
on Women.

206 Kanter 1977 Men and *Women of the Corporation.* New
York: Basic Books.

207 The minority here follows the notion of the non dominant
group. This study recognizes that the white South African
were in the minority and yet dominated the Black majority
through oppression

208 Ogbu ibid.

209 It is important to note that in addition to just discrimination
Ogbu and Simons also refer to racial prejudice with
regards to African Americans as minorities in the US. In
the case of my study religious prejudice against the ZCC
became very apparent.

210 Ogbu and Simons Document Resume Final Report: CSW
1994 p10.

211 Lukhaimane 1980 op. cit.

212 These included in code names Ryu, Ryu2, Dyu, Myu5
amongst others.

213 These included in coded names: Wyu, Ryu, Lyu amongst
others.

214 Ogbu and Simons 1994 ibid.

215 The apartheid laws of population control declared any area

that was less than 75 miles away fromthe white area as a
Black spot in a white area and people were forcibly
removed. The result was and still is Blacks lived quite a
substantial distance from their place of employment, since
whites are the employers. In addition, the transportation is
very poor and crowded. Missing a bus or a train because it
was full happen often.

[216]   Although Ogbu and Simon's make a distinction between
the voluntary and involuntary minorities, this study
borrows the idea and applies it to the ZCC and the non
ZCC members.

[217]   Coser. R. Authority and Structural Ambivalence in the
[218]   Middle Class Family." In The Family: Its Structures and
Function ed by R. Coser New York: St. Martin's Press
1974

[218]   Giddens, A. New Rules of Sociological Methods: A
Positive Critique of Interpretive Sociologies. New York:
Basic Books 1976

[219]   These included in coded names Wyu, Zyu, and Myu5
amongst others.

[220]   These included in coded names Myu6, Lyu4, Vyu, Kyu4
and Xyu amongst others.

[221]   Ogbu and Simons predicted that voluntary minorities
would interpret cultural differences as barriers to be
overcome by learning the cultural practices of the school,
that would then be additive to their education. Involuntary
minorities on the other hand would see the differences as
markers of group identity and resist learning them, this
would be a subtractive process.

[222]   A coded name.
[223]   Coded names.
[224]   Ogbu and Simons 1994 op. cit.
[225]   Coded names
[226]   These particular women expressed the view that they saw
that as less important.

[227]   These included in code names Syu, Fyu5, Fyu3, Pyu
amongst others.

[228]   This seem to fit in with Giligan's 1982 theory that women
tend to stress a morality of intimacyand
interconnectedness over morality of autonomy

[229]   A coded name.
[230]   Ghandi and Video Speeches of Martin Luther King.
[231]   C.f. Crossroads July/August 1994.
[232]   The Star News Paper 1983, estimated that the Bishop gave
as much as R100, 000 to the white school.

[233]   Mary Douglas 1966 in her book Purity and Danger notes
that in **some** societies
order will prevail by not mixing what should be kept apart,
and the rules of Leviticus are invoked to prove the victory
of order over chaos. Mixing that should be kept separate

causes pollution. In the same way, the ZCC cited the
rules of Leviticus to validate many of their teachings. On
the other hand theview of the others about involvement in
the struggle epitomizes what Peteni 1976 in his book *Hill
of Fools.*, talking about the Xhosa young men perception
of their involvement in the faction fights as unavoidable as
the occurrence of a hail storm or natural disasters that
people do not have control over.

234 Jules-Rosette (1979:114) discusses external political
attacks that resulted in almost the destruction of a
movement that was regarded as a menace. The
Kimbanguist and Kitala movements suffered in a similar
fashion.

235 A coded names.

236 Parson's 1958 op. cit. Structural socialization theories
attribute this to different ways in which society conditions
girls and boys.

237 This implies I was not the first person to have asked if that
would have been an option.

238 Barth, F. 1969 *Ethnic Groups and Boundaries.* Boston:
Little Brown.

239 Lukhaimane 1980 op. cit.

240 ibid.

241 Kruger 1971 op. cit., Lukhaimane 1980 op. cit. And
Sundkler 1949 op. cit.

242 Oosthuizen 1968

243 Lukhaimane 1980

244 From fieldwork observation

245 Ramose 1988 op. cit.

246 ZCC Messenger op. cit.

247 Lusaka was the head quarters of the ANC in exile located
in Tanzania. It consisted of modern sophisticated
buildings. The money came from world wide
organizations and countries that opposes the system of
apartheid.

248 *Pretoria News Foreign Service.* 1987, 11, 11 London:

249 *The ZCC Messenger* September 1988 contains a report of
the ZCC bishop visit to the
Transkei homeland.

250 *ZCC Messenger* 1992.

251 Sanctions proved to be one of the effective tools that
defeated apartheid regime. The ANC and other liberation
movements called for the world to impose sanctions
against South Africa Buthelezi and ministers of the ZCC
church like Mokwena opposed sanctions

252 Ogbu and Simons op. cit.

253 Durkheim 1895 op. cit.

254 I employ the classification southern versus northern in line
with the debate that marked the United Nations in the
1970's to move away from the first and third world

valuation of other countries as politically and economically inferior. Northern refers to "Western Euro" while Southern refers to Indigenous

[255] Elson D. and Pearson. R. 1981 "Nimble Fingers Make Cheap Workers: An Analyze of Women's Employment in the Third World." In *Feminist Review* 7: 87-107.
Rowbatham, S. *Women Resistance and Revolution: A History of the Modern World*.
New York: Pantheneon. Berger I "Sources of Class Consciousness: South African
Women in Recent Labor Struggles." In *Women and Class in Africa*. C. Robertson
and I Berger eds. 1986 New York: Africana Publishing Company.

[256] Cf. Rosaldo 1974 op. cit, Ortner 1984 op. cit.

[257] Bonner P. Black Trade Unions in South Africa since World War II. in *The Apartheid Regime*. Price R, Roseberg C eds. Institute Of International Studies: University of California, Berkeley.

[258] Horrel M. *South African Trade Unionism: A Study of a Divided Working Class*. Johannesburg: South African Institute of Race Relations, 1961 *South African Workers: their Organization and Patterns of Employment*: Johannesburg: South African Institute of Race Relations, 1969.

[259] Price and Roseberg 1986 op. cit.

[260] Robertson and Berger 1986 op. cit.

[261] Colored here referring to the apartheid race classification of the South African population of Black and/or Khoisan with White.

[262] Federation of South African Women is powerful women's organization and not a union, that has fought valiantly for women's rights.

[263] Robertson and Berger 1986 op. cit.

[264] Hemson, D. 1978: 32 "Trade Unionism and the Struggle for Liberation in South Africa." *Capital and Class* 6: 1-41. 1978:32

[265] NLRC 1980:38

[266] These include in coded names: Qu, Qu2, Ru4, Ku4, Xu3, and Du4 amongst others.

[267] Real name that also appears in the publication.

[268] A coded name

[269] These included: in coded names Cmu3, Zmru, Mmu2 amongst others.

[270] They include in code names Wr3, Wr2, Omr Omr2, Vmr, Vmr2, Vmr3 amongst others

[271] ZCC Messenger 1992

[272] The South African Currency, called Rand and designated by the letter R, has to be divided by six to get the US equivalency in dollars.

273 Comaroff 1980 op. cit.

274 A coded name.

275 Gerson 1985 op. cit.

276 Thenjiwe worked with Steven Biko and the others in the
Black Consciousness movement. She and Mapetla
Mohapi who was killed in detention by the police
worked as reporters for Donald Woods. At such, this
remarkable woman in addition to the many talents that she
has, also has vast knowledge of how the media
can impact change. Then she reported on the Black news
for Woods 'News Paper. She is portrayed in the movie
Cry Freedom and in my opinion one of the unsung heroes
who deserve a respectable place in South African and
world History

277 Comaroff and Comaroff 1991, 1997, op. cit.

278 Cf. Comaroff (1980)

279 Biko 1987, op. cit., Bhere 1979 op. cit., Hacket 1987, op.
cit and Jules -Rosette 1987 op. cit.

280 Omoyi, B.A. 1905 *A Defense of the Ethiopian Movements*.
Edinburgh.

281 Ngubane 1977 op. cit.

282 Ngubane op. cit., Ramose op. cit.

283 Bradenbach, P. 1977 op. cit, Rosette, J. op. cit. Barrett,
D.B. op. cit.Walker. S. 1979 op. cit., Bond, G., Walton, J.
and Walker, S. 1979 op. cit.

284 Barrett 1968 op. cit, Lewis 1971 op. cit. Murphee 1971

285 Ngubane 1979 op. cit., Ramose 1988 op. cit., Kruger 1971
op. cit. Comaroff 1980 op. cit.

286 Comaroff 1980 op. cit.

287 de Beauvour 1952 op. cit, Ortner 1974 op. cit.

288 ANC News Letter

289 Ibid.

290 The ANC has embarked on a massive educational
campaign, not limited to the schoolsto enlighten people
about what constitutes sexism. As the discourse in this
study continues we will see how this campaign takes place
in the unions.

291 Firth 1969 op. cit.

292 Price and Roseberg 1980 op. cit.

293 Gluckman 1964 p.p. 207-234 discusses conflict with
reference to the South African situation. He borrows the
idea from Malinowski in his analysis. He posits that the
racial differences in South Africa and the discrimination
will be gaped by the fact that shared and parallel aims in
education and religion..

294 Malinowski 1926(b) 101-5 discusses the Trobriand
Islanders.

295 C.f. Simmel 1932, Neihbur 1951, and Durkheim who
maintain that religion is a source of social integration at

the time when either threatened or actual social dissolution is feared or experienced.

[296] Williams 1977: 108ff

[297] Durkheim 1895 op. cit.

[298] Robertson and Berger 1986 op. cit., Scott, J. and Tilly A 1975 "Women's Work and the Family in the Century Europe." In *Comparative Studies in Societies and History* 17:36-64

[299] Durkheim 1895 op. cit p6 succinctly posits that all education is a continuos effort to impose ways of feeling and acting which people especially children could not have arrived at spontaneously. The constraints ceases to be felt as time goes on, giving rise to habits and internal tendencies that renders the restriction unnecessary without obliterating it since it is the source from which these habits are derived

[300] Reskin and Padavic 1994 op. cit.

[301] Parson 1955 op. cit.

[302] Gerson 1985 op. cit.

[302] Douglas op. cit and Wilson op. cit

[302] Sahlins, M. 1976 *Culture and Practical Reason*. University of Chicago Press. 1981 Historical Metaphors and Mythical Realities: *Structure in the Early History of the Sandwich Island Kingdom*. Ann Arbor: University of Michigan Press

[302] The study recognizes that the view of activism as outrageous is matter of opinion.

Bibliography

Afonja, S.
1986 *Social Change in Nigeria. New York*: Holmes
and Miers Publishing
_____. 1990 "Changing Patterns of Gender
Stratification in West Africa." In Persistent
Inequalities edited by Tinker, I. New York: Oxford
University Press.

Anderson, A.H.
1957 African Pentecostalsim in a South African
Urban Environment: A Missiological
Evaluation. Pretoria:
1958 University of South Africa

Anderson, E.
1958 *Messianic Popular Movements in the Lower
Congo.* Uppsala: Aimquist and Wiksel.

Antwerp, C.M.
1938 *Die Separatistiese Kerklike Beweging onder
die Bantu van Suid Afrika.* Unpublished Manuscript.

Apter, D.
1987 *Rethinking Development.* California: Sage
Publication.

Aquina, Sr. M.
1967(a) Christainity in a Rhodesian Tribal Land.
African Social Research, 1: 1-40
_____. 1967(b) The People of the Spirit: An
Independent Church in Rhodesia. *Africa*, 37: 203-
219.
_____. 1969 Zionists in Rhodesia. *Africa* 39 (2)

Baeta, C.G.
1959 *Prophetism in Ghana: The Study of Some
Spiritual Churches.* London: SCM
1960 Press.
_____. 1968 *Christianity in Tropical Africa.*
London: International African Institute.

Balandier, G.
1965 Messanism and Nationalism in Black Africa.
*In Africa: Social Problems of Change and
Conflict* edited by van Den Berge, P. San Francisco:
Chandler.

Banton, M
> 1967 *Anthropological Approaches to the Study of Religion*. London: Tavistock

Bantu Authorities Act, no 68, 1951

Bardhan, K.
> 1986 "Stratification of Women's Work in Rural India: Determinats, Effects and Strategies. " In *Social and Economic Development in India: A Reassessment*. New Delhi: Sage Publications.

Barrett, D.B.
> 1968 *Schism and Renewal in Africa: An Analysis of Six Thousand Contemporary Religious Movements*. Nairobi: Oxford University Press.
> ____. 1970 AD 2000: 350 Million Christians in Africa. In *International Review of Misssions*. Nairobi: Oxford University Press.

Barret J, et al
> 1985 *South African Women on the Move*. London: Zed Books Ltd.

Barth, J.A.
> 1979 "Introduction." In *Ethnic Group and Boundaries*, edited by Barth, F. Bergen-Oslo: Universitetforgalet.

Bay, E.
> 1982 *Women and Work in Africa*. Colo.: Westview Press.

Beattie, J. M. and Middleton, J.
> 1969 *Spirit Mediums and Society in Africa*. London: Routledge and Kegan Paul.

de Beauvoir, S.
> 1953 *The Second Sex*. Harmondsworth: Penguin.

Bell, D. and Klein R
> 1996 *Radically Speaking: Feminism Reclaimed*, eds. Australia: Spinifex Press.

Bellah, R.
> 1970 *Beyond Belief: Essays on Religion*. New York: Harper.

Bellman, B. L.
> 1977 The Social Organization of Knowledge in the Kpelle Ritual. In *The New Religions of Africa*, edited by Jules-Rosette, B. New Jersey: Albex Publishing Corporation.

Beneria, L. and Sen, G.
> 1979 "Reproduction, Production and the Sexual
> Division of Labor." *Cambridge Journal of
> Economics* 3:203-25

Bennholdt-Thomsen, V.
> 1988 "Investment in the Poor" In *Women the Last
> Colony* Mies, M., Bennholdt-Thomsen V., and von
> Werlhof, C. eds

Bennet, L.
> 1983 *Dangerous Wives and Scared Sisters: Social
> and Symbolic Roles of High Caste Women in Nepal.*
> New York: Colombia University Press.

Benston M. 1969
> "The Political Economy of Women's Liberation"
> *Monthly Review* 1969, September: 13:25

Berom-Larsson, M.
> 1982 "Women and Technology in the Industrialized
> Countries." In *Scientific Technological Change and
> the Role of Women in Development* D'Onofrio-
> Flores, P. and Pfafflin, S. eds. Boulder: Westview
> Press.

Berger, I. (1976) 'Rebels or Status Seekers/ Women as Spirits
> Medium in East Africa, in Esat Africa. In N.J.
> Hafkin and E.G. Bay (eds) *Women in Africa.*
> Stanford: Stanford University Press

Bergman, B 1986 The Economic Emergence of Women
> New York: Basic Books

Berglund, A.I.
> 1986 *Rituals of an African Zionist Church.*
> University of the Witwatersrand: African
> Studies Program
> 1987 Occasional Paper 3.
> _____. 1971 Church and Culture Change in a Zulu
> Tribal Community. In *Church and Culture Change
> in Africa* edited by Bosch, D.J. Pretoria: Lux Mundi
> (3)

Berreman, G.
> 1972 "Social Categories and Social Interaction in
> Urban India." *American Anthropologist*, 74 (3)
> (June).
> _____. 1983 *Social Inequality*, (ed). New York:
> Academic Press.
> 1983 "Social Inequality: A Cross-Cultural
> Perspective." In *Social Inequality* New York:
> Academic Press.

1983 "The Evolutionary Status of Caste in Peasant India." In *Social Anthropology of Peasantry* edited by Mencher, J. Bombay: Somaiya Publications.

Beyerhaus, P.
1969 An Approach to the African Independent Movement. *Ministry* 9.

Bhere, M.
1979 *Christianity and Traditional Religion in Western Zimbabwe 1859-1923.* Great Britain: Western Printing Services Ltd.

Biko, S. B.
1986 *I Write What I Like.* San Fransisco: Harper and Row Publishers.

Bledsoe, C.
1961 "Women's Marital Strategies Among the Kpelle of Liberia. " *Journal of*
1962 *Anthropological Research* 32:372-389

Bond, G., Walton, J. and Walker, S.
1979 *African Christianity: Patterns of Change and Continuity.* New York: Academic Press, Inc.

Bosch, D. J.
1973 Onhafhanklike Beweging. In *Study Guide: Missiology aand Science of Religion.* Pretoria: Unisa.

Boserup, E.
1970 *Women's Role in Economic Development.* New York: St. Mary's Press.
____. 1981 *Population And Technological Change.* Chicago: University of Chicago Press.

Bourqus, S. & Warren, K.
1990 "Access is not Enough." In *Persistent Inequalities*, edited by Tinker, I. New York: Oxford University Press

Bradenbach, P.
1977 The Woman on the Beach and the Man in the Forest. In *The New Religions of Africa.* edited by Jules Rosette. New Jersey: Albex Publishing Corporation.

Bucher, H.
1980 *Spirits and Power-An Analysis of Shona Cosmology.* Cape Town: Oxford University Press.

174

Burja, J.
19 "Urging Women to Redouble their Efforts." In *Class, Gender and Capitalist Transformation in Africa*. London: Tavistock.

Buvinic, M., Lycette, M. & Mcgreevey, W. P.
1983 *Women and Poverty in the Third World*. Baltimore: John's Hopkins University Press.

Breidenbach, P.S.
1973 *Sumsum Edumwa, the Spiritual Work: Forms of Symbolic Action and Communication in Ghanian Movements*. Northwest: University Press.

Brookes, E.H.
1956 *The History of Native Policy in South Africa*. Pretoria: Van Schaiks Limited.
____. 1967 *The Color Problems of South Africa*. J Johannesburg: Johannesburg Publishers.

Cairnos, J.
1974 *After Polygyny was Made a Sin*. London: Routledge and Kegan Paul.

Carr, M.
1954 *Appropriate Technology for African Women*. Addis Ababa: Economic Commission for Africa, United Nations.

Carrillo, R.
"Feminist Perspectives on Women in Development. " In *Persistent Inequalities*, edited by Tinker, I. New York: Oxford University Press.

Caulfield, M.D.
1974 "Imperialism, the Family and Cultures of Resistance." *Socialist Revolutions* 4 (20): 67-85
____. 1983 "Equality, Sex, and Mode of Production." In *Social Inequality*, edited by Berreman, G.,New York: Academic Press.

Chodorow, N.
1978 *The Reproduction of Mothering*. Berkeley: The University of California Press.

Cohen, S.
1955 *Folk Devils and Moral Panics*. New York: African Publishing Corporation.

Cohn, N.
1978 *The Pursuit of Millennium*. London: Secker and Warburg.

Colson, E. 1969 Spirits Possession Among the Tonga of
Zambia. In *Mediums and Society in Africa*.
Beattie J.M. and Middleton, J. Spirit eds. London:
Routledge and Kegan Paul.

Collins, P.
1988 "The Emerging Theory and Pedagogy of Black
Women's Studies." *Feminist Issues*, 6

Comaroff, J.
1956 *Body of Power Spirit of Resistance*. Chicago:
Chicago University Press

Comaroff, J and J
1991 *of Revelation and Revolution: Christianity
Colonialism and Consciousness in South Africa*,
Volume One Chicago: The University of Chicago
Press
___1997 *of Revelation and Revolution: Christianity
Colonialism and Consciousness in South Africa*,
Volume Two. Chicago: The University of Chicago
Press

Constitution of the Republic of South Africa.
As adopted on 8 May 1996 and amended on 11
October 1996 by the Constitutional Assembly. South
Africa: ANC Government Printers.

Coser. R.
Authority and Structural Ambivalence in the Middle
Class Family." In *The Family: Its Structures and
Function* ed by R. Coser New York: St. Martin's
Press

CrossRoads
1994 July/August No 43 *Building the New South
Africa*

Curtin, P.D.
1971 Jihad in West Africa: Early Phase and
Interrelations in Mauritania and Senegal. *Journal of
African History* 13 (4): 647-658.

Dachs, A.J.
1972 Missionary Imperialism: The Case of
Bechuanaland. *Journal of
African Hstory* 12, 1, 11-24.

Daneel, M.L.
1970 (a) *Zionism and Faith Healing in Rhodesia.*
The Hague: Mouton. vol 1
____.1970 (b) *The God of the Matopo Hills.*
Leiden: Africa Study Center.

____.1971 (a) *Old and New in Southern Shona Independent Churches*. The Hague: Mouton, Vol 1

____.1971 (b) Shona Independent Churches and Ancestor Worship. In *African Initiatives in Religion* edited by Barrett, D.B. Nairobi: Nairobi Press

____.1974 *Old and New in Southern Shona Independent Churches, 2*. The Hague: Mouton.

____. 1975 Shona Independent Churches in Rural Society. In *Christianity South of the Zambez* edited by Dachs, A.J. Gwelo.

____. 1980 The Missionary Outreach of African Independent Churches. *Missionalia*, Vol 8 No 3.

____.1982 (a) *Swart "Messianisme"-Verwording of Kontestualise Intreede*. Unisa

____. 1982 (b) Fission Dynamics in African Independent Churches. In *Denominasionalism: Its Sources and Implications* edited by Voster, W.S. Pretoria: Unisa

____. 1983 Communication and Liberation in African Independent Churches. *Missionalia*, 2 (2), (August)

____1987 *Old and New in Southern Shona Independent Churches: Leadership and Fission Dynamics* 3. The Hague:Mouton.

Dangarembga, T
1988 *Nervous Condition*. England: Women's Press
DanielsA.R. and Weingarten, K.
1978 "Parenthood Now or Later". Welesley, Maassach: Welesely Center for Research on Women
Davis, A
1981 *Women, Race and Class*. New York: Vintage Books
Douglas, M.
1966 Purity and Dance: *An Analysis of the Concept of Pollution and Taboo*. New York: Praeger.
Draper, P.
1975 "!Kung Women" Contrasts in Sexual Egalitarianism in Foraging and Sedentary Contexts." In *Towards Anthropology of Women*, edited by Reiter, R New York: Monthly Review Press.
Dube,
J. 1936 u*Shembe*. South Africa: Pietermaritzburg.

177

Durkheim, E.
1965/1976 *The Elementary Forms of Religious Life.*
New York: Free Press.
Dwyer, D. & Bruce J. eds.
1988 *A Home Divided: Women and Income in the Third World.* Stanford: Stanford University Press.
Eck, D. and Jain, D.
1986 *Speaking of Faith: Cross Cultural Perspectives on Women, Religion and Social Change.* New Dehli: Indraprastha Press
Ekejiuba, F.I.
1977 "Introduction" In *Women and National Development: The Complexities of Change. Chicago*: The University of Chicago Press.
Elliot, C. & Kelly, G.P.
1977 "Theories of Development: An Assessment" In *Women and National Development*: The Complexities
1978 of Change. Chicago: The University of Chicago Press.
_____. 1982 "New Directions for Research." In *Women's Education in the Third World: Comparative Perspectives*, Elliot, C. and Kelly, G.P. eds. 331-343 Albany: SUNNY Press.
Emett, D.
1956 Prophets and Their Societies. *Journal of the Royal Anthropological Institute*, 86.
Engels, F.
1884 *The Origins of the Family, Private Property and the State.* New York: Pathfinder.
Erchack, G.
1974 The Position of Women Among the Kpelle of Liberia. *American Anthropologists*, 76(2,): 344-345.
Evans-Pritchard, E.E.
1956 *Nuer Religion.* London: Oxford University Press.
_____.1965 "The Position of Women in Primitive Societies." In *The Position of Women in Primitive Societies and Other Societies.* New York: The Free Press.
Fabian, J.
1971 *Jamaa: A Charismatic Movement in Katanga.* Evanston: Northwest University Press.

_____.1974 Genres in Emerging Tradition: An Anthropological Approach to Religious Communication. In *Changing Patterns in the Scientific Study of Religion,* edited by Eister A.W. New York: Willey.

Farrant, J.

1966 *Mashonaland Martyr: Bernard Mizeki and the Pioneer Church.* Cape Town: Oxford University Press.

Fernandez, J.W.

1975 The Ethnic Communion: Inter Ethnic Recruitment in African Religious Movements. *Journal of African Studies* 2, 131-177.

_____.1978 African Religious Movements: *Annual Review of Anthropology,* 7: 198-234.

_____1982 *Bwiti: An Ethnography of Religious Imagination in Africa.* Princeton: Princeton University Press.

Field, M.

1937 *Religion and Medicine Among the Gha People.* London: Oxford University Press.

_____. 1960 *Search for Security: An Ethno-Psychiatric Study of Rural Ghana.* London:Faber and Faber.

Firth, R

1973 *Symbols: Public and Private.* Ithaca: Cornell University

Fortes, M and Dieterlin, G.

1965 (a) *African systems of Thought.* London: International African Institute.

_____1965 (b) Some Reflections of Ancestor Worship in Africa. In *African Systems of Thought*

Foster,-Carter, A.

1978 The Modes of Production Controversy. *New Left Review,* 107:47-77

Fox, R.C., De Cramer, W. and Ribeaucourt, J.M.

1989 The Second Independence: A Case Study of the Kwilu Rebellion of the Congo. In *Comparative Studies in Society and History,* 8, 78-110.

Framer, L.

1944 *We Saw the Holy City.* London: Epsworth.

Friedl, E

1967 "The Position of Women: Appearance and Reality." *Anthropological Quarterly* 40: 97-108.

Fry, P.
    1976 *Spirits of Protests: Spirits Medium and the
    Articulation of Consensus Among the Zezuru of
    Southern Rhodesia (Zimbabwe)*. London:
    Cambridge University Press.

Geertz, C.
    1966 Religion and Cultural Systems. In
    Anthropological Approaches to theStudy of Religion
    edited by Banton, M. London: Tavistock.

Gerson, G.
    1985 *Hard Chpoice*. Berkley: University of
Caliofrnia Press.

Gerth, H and Mills, W.
    1953 *Character and Social Structure: The
        Psychology of Social Institutions*. New York:
    Harcourt, Brace and World.

Giddens, A.
    1976 *New Rules of Sociological Methods: A Positive
    Critique of Interpretive*
    Sociologies. New York: Basic Books

Gluckman, M.
    1956 *Custom and Conflict in Africa*. Oxford:
    Blackwell. 1972 Moral Crisis: Magical and Secular
    Solutions. In *The Allocation of Responsibility* edited
    by Gluckman, M. Manchester: University Press.

Goody, J.
    1962 *Death, Property and the Ancestors*. London:
    Tavistock.

Groves, C.P.
    1954 The Planning of Christianity in Africa. *Africa*
    2. London: Lutterworth Press.

Gusfield, J.R.
    1973 *Utopian Myths and Movements in the Modern
    Societies.* Morritown N.J.: General Learning
    Corporation.

Hackett, R.I.J.
    1987 *The New Religious Movements in Nigeria.*
    New York: Edwin Mellen Press.

Haliburton, G.M.
    1971 *The Prophet Harris*. London: Longman.

Hall, S. Jefferson, T and Robert, B.
    1976 *Resistant Through Ritual*. London: Hutchison.

Hammond-Tooke, W.D.
    1953 *The Bantu Speaking People of South Africa*.
    London: Routledge and Kegan.

Hanekom, C

 1965 *Krisis en Kultur: Geloofteopsvatinge en
Seremonise binne 'n Swart Kerk.* Pretoria: Van
Schaiks Limited.

 ____.1965 *Die Huidige Stand van die Tradisionele
Godsdienspatroon by die Mamabolo.* Unpublished
D.Phil. Thesis, Pretoria.

Harlan, G.W.

 *John Alexander Dowie and His Christian Catholic
Apostolic Church in Zion.* Evansville Wisconsin:
Press of R. M. Antes.

Hartman, H.

 1975 "Capitalism, Patriarchy and Job Segregation by
Sex."*Signs: Journal of Women inCulture
and Society* 1(Spring): 137-169

Hastings, A.

 1971 *Missions and Ministry.* London: Hutchison.

Haule, C.

 1969 *Bantu Witchcraft and Christain Morality: The
Encounter of Bantu Uchawi and Christian Morality.*
Schoeneck: Beckenried.

Hayford, J.E.

 1915 *William Waddy Harris: The West African
Reformer.* London: Phillips.

Hayward, B.P.

 1977 *Displays of Membership: Participation and
Change in Lusaka Independent Churches.*
Unpublished Doctoral Dissertation, UC Sandiego.

Hess, M.M.

 1954 Political systems and African Church Polity.

 1955 *Practical Anthropology,* (iv) 5.

Hewitt, G.

 1990 *The Problem of Success: A History of the
Church Missionary Society.* London: SCM
Press.

Holleman, J.F.

 1952 *Shona Customary Law.* Manchester:
University Press.

 ____.1961 Some Shona Tribes in Southern
Rhodesia. In Colson, E. and.

Matina Horners

 1972 "Towards an Understanding of Achievemnet-
Related Conflicts in Women."

 Journal of Social Issues. 28: 157-75

Hunt, D.R.

    1931 The Development of the Bapedi. *Bantu Studies*
Vol V 1931 4

    276

Huntington, S.

    1975 "Issues in Women's Role in Economic
Development Critique and Alternatives." *Journal of
Marriage and the Family* 37 (4) 100-12. International
Labor Office,

    1984 *Rural Development and Women in Africa.*
Geneva: International Labor Development.

Jabavu, D.D.T.

    1942 *An African Independent Church.* Lovedale

Jules-Rosette, B.

    1976   (a) *African Apostoles: Ritual and Conversion
in the Church of John Maranke.* Ithaca:
Cornell University Press.

    ____. 1975 (b) Marapodi: An Idependent Religious
Community in Transition. *African Studies Review*,
45, 2, 150-165.

    ____. 1975 (c) Song and Spirit: The Use of Songs in
the Management of the Ritual Settings.
Africa, 45(2), 150-165.

    ____. 1976 The Conversion Experience. *Journal of
Religion in Africa*, 7: 132- 164.

    ____. 1977 Grass Roots Ecumenism: Religious and
Social Cooperation in Two Urban African
Churches.*African Social Research*, 23: 185-216.

    ____. 1978 Prophecy and Leadership in an African
Church: A Case Study in Continuity And
Change. In *African Christianity: Patterns of
Religious Change and Continuity* Bond, G., Walker
S. and Johnson W. eds. New York: Academic Press
Inc.

James, J.

    1996 "Experience Reflection, Judgement and Action:
Teaching Theory, Talking Community" in
Radically Speaking: Feminism Reclaimed Bell, D.
and Klein R, 37-44 eds. Australia: Spinifex Press.

Jaquette, J.

    1982 "Women and Modernization Theory." *World
Politics* 34(2): 267-284.

    ____. 1990 "Gender and Justice in Economic
Development." In *Persistent Inequalities*, edited
by Tinker, I. New York: Oxford University Press.

Kalu, O.U.
    1980 *The History of Christianity in West Africa.*
    Hong Kong: Sing Cheung Printing Company.
Kanter, R.
    1977 Men and Women of the Corporation. New
York: Basic Books
Kelly, G.P. & Elliot, C.
    1982 *Women's Education in the Third World:*
    Comparative Perspectives. Albany: SUNNY Press.
Kiernan, J.P.
    1974 Where Zionist Draw the Line: A Study of
    Religious Exclusiveness in An African Township.
    African Studies, 33 (2) 79-90
    ____. 1976 The Work of Zion: An Analysis of An
    African Zionist Ritual. *Africa*, 46 (4): 340-355.
    ____. 1977 Poor and Puritan: An Attempt to View
    Zionism As a Collective Response to Urban Poverty.
    African Studies, 36 (1): 31-43.
Kileff, C. and Killef M.
    1977 The Masowe Vapostori of Seki. In *the New*
            Religions of Africa, edited by Julles-Rossette,B
    .New Jersey: Ablex Publishing Corporation.
Kilton, M.
    1971(a) *Kpele Lala: Ga Religious Songs and*
    Symbols. Cambridge: Havard University Press.
    ____. 1971 (b) Ambivalence and Power: Mediums
    in Ga Traditional Religion. *Journal of*
    Religion in Africa. Ritual Potrait of a Ga Medium.
    In *the New Religions of Africa*, edited by
    Julles-Rossette, B. New Jersey: Ablex Publishing
    Corporation.
Kiger, E.J.
    1948 *The Realm of a Rain Queen.* London
Kruger, M.A.
    1991 *Die Zion Christain Church- 'n Religieuse*
            Bantoebeweging in 'n tyd van Ontwrigting.
            Unpublished Masters Thesis, University of
            Potchefstroom.
Kusterer, K
    1990 "The Imminent Demise of Patriarchy." In
            *Persistent Inequalities.*edited by Tinker, I.
            New York: Oxford University Press.
Lan, D. 1991
    Guns and Rains. London: Heineman

Lanterani, V.
  1963 *Religious of the Oppressed*. New York:
  Mentor.
Leacock, E.
  1979 *Introduction to F. Engels the Origin of the
  Family, Private Property and the State*, edited by
  Leacock,
  E.B., 7-67 New York: International Press
  ____ 1978 "Women's Status in Egalitarian Society:
  Implications of Social Evolution." *Current
  Anthropology*.19 (2): 147-175
Leacock, E and Safa, I.
  1986 *Women's Work. Development and Division of
  Labor by Gender*. South Hardley, Massachusetts:
  Bergin and Garvey Publishers Inc.
Lee, R.B.
  1979 *The Dobe !Kung*. Cambridge: Cambridge
  University Press.
Lee, S.G.
  1969 Spirit Possession among the Zulu. In *Spirits
  Mediumship and Society in Africa* Beatie, J. and
  Middleton, J. eds. London: Routledge and Kegan
  Paul.
Levi-Strauss, C
  1969 *The Elementary Structure of Kinship*. Boston:
  Beacon Press.
Lewis, I. M.
  1971 *Ecstatic Religion: An Anthropological Study
  of Spirit Possession and Shamanism*. England:
  Penguin.
Linington, P.A.
  1924 *A Summary of the Reports of Certain
  PreUnion Commission on Native Affairs: Church
  Separatists Movements*. Pretoria: Van Schaik.
Linton, R.
  1943 Nativistic Movements. *American
  Anthropologist*, 45: 230-240.
Lim, L.
  1990 "Women's Work in Export Factories: The
  Politics of a Cause." In *Persistent Inequalities*,
  edited by Tinker, I. New York: Oxford University
  Press.
Loza, S.
  1957 "Roles of Women and Their Impact on
    Fertility: An Egyptian Case Study."

Unpublished Masters Thesis .

Loutif, M.

    1980 *Rural Women: Unequal Partners in*
    Development. Geneva: ILO.

Lukhaimane, E.

    1980 *The History of the Zion Christian Church.*
    Unpublished Masters Thesis. Pietersburg: University
    of The North.

Mac Cormack, C.

    1977 (a) "Biological Events and Cultural Control."
    In Women's *Education in the Third World:*
    Comparative Perspectives, Elliot, C.and Kelly
    G.P.eds, 331-343 Albany: SUNNY Press.

    ____. 1977 (b) The Public of A Secrete Society. In
    the New Religions of Africa, edited
    by Julles-Rossette, B. New Jersey: Ablex Publishing
    Corporation.

    ____. 1981 "Development with Equity for Women."
    In *Women and World Change.* Black, N., and Cotter
    A.B. Albany : SUNNY Press

    ____. 1982 "Control of Land, Labor and Capital in
    Rural Southern Sierra Leone." In
    Women and Work in Africa edited by Bay, E.G.

Mac Cormack, C. & Strathern, M.

    1980 *Nature Culture and Gender.* Cambridge:
    Cambridge University Press.

MacKnight, J.D.

    1967 Extra Descent Group Ancestor Cults in African
    Society. *Africa*, 37 (1):1-21.

MAcKinnon, C.A.

    1996 "From Practice to Theory, or What is a White
    Woman Anyway." In *Radically Speaking:*
    Feminism Reclaimed Bell, D. and Klein R eds, 45-
    55. Australia: Spinifex Press.

MAcKintosh, P.

    1990 White Privilege: "Unpacking the Invisible
    Knapsack." In *Working Papers 189 White Privilege*
    and Male Privilege: A Personal Account of Coming
    to See Correspondence Through Work in Women's
    Studies.

Madala, A.

    1965 *Amayo Amafutshane.* Cape Town: Oxford
    University Press.

185

Magubane, B.
   1965   A Critical Analysis of the Indices Used in
   the Study of Social Change in the Study of Colinial
   Africa.*Current Anthropology* 12, Introduction, 22
   415-445. 1979 *African Independent Churches.*
   Hammanskraal: St. Peters Seminary.
   Mail and Guardian 1996 September Khumalo, S.
   "You tout Dr. Mamphela Ramphela--"
   Mosala, I. "Letting Down Steve Biko" Ramphela, M.
   "Can Steven Biko Arbitrate From the Grave."
Makhathini, D.L.
   1965 *Ancestors, Umoya, Angels in Missiology
   Institute: Our Approach to the Independent Church
   Movement in South Africa.* Mapumolo: Lutheran
   Theological College.
Malinowski, B.
   1922 *Argonauts of Western Pacific.* London:
   Routledge and Kegan Paul
   _____1957 *The Sexual Life of Savages in N.W.
   Melanesia.* London: Routledge and Kegan Paul
   _____1961 *Sex and Repression in Savage Society.*
   London: Routledge and Kegan Paul
   _____1978 *Crime and Custon in Savage Society.*
   London: Routledge and Kegan Paul
Maranke, J.
   1953 *The New Witnesses of the Apostoles.* Rhodesia
   (Zimbabwe): Bocha.
Martin, M.
   1964 *The Biblical Concept of Messianism and
   Messianism in Southern Africa.* Pietersburg: Morija.
   ____. 1968 Prophetism in the Congo- Origin and
   Development of An African Independent
   Church. *Ministry: Theological Review of Africa*, 8(4)
   ____. 1971The Mai Chaza Church in Rhodesia. In
   African Initiatives in Religion edited by Barret, D.B.
   Kenya: East African Publishing House.
   _____1975 *Kimbangu-An African Prophet and his
   Church.* London: Oxford Press.
Marwick, M.
   1970 *Witchcraft and Socery: Selected Readings.*
   London: Penguin.

Marx, K.

    1964 *The Communist Manifesto.* New York:
Russel.

    ____. 1967 *Capital: A Critique of Political Economy*, 3 Vols. New York: International Publishers.

Massiah, J.

    1958 "Defining Women's Work in the Commonwealth Caribbean." In *Persistent*

    1959 *Inequalities*, edited by Tinker. I. New York: Oxford University Press.

Mayer, M.

    1961 *Townsmen and Tribesmen.* Cape Town:
Oxford University Press.

Mazumdar, V.

    1985 *The Emergence of Women's Questions in India and the Role of Women in Development Countries.*
New Dehli: Center for Women's Development Studies.

Mazumdar, V. & Sharma K.

    1990 "Sexual Division of Labor and the Subordination of Women: A Reappraisal from India. In *Persistent Inequalities*, edited by Tinker. I.New York: Oxford University Press.

Mbiti, J.S.

    1969 *African Religions and Philosophy.* London:
Heineman.

Meli, F

    1988 A History of the ANC: South Afruica Belongs to us. Harare: Zimbabwe Publishing House

Mendosa, E.

    1977 Elders Office Holders and Ancestors Among the Sisala of Northern Ghana. *Africa*, 46, 57-65.

Mernissi, F.

    1976 "The Moslem World, Women Excluded from Development." In *Women and World Development.*New York: Praeger Publishers.

Mies, M.

    1986 *Patriarchy and Accumulation on a World Scale: Women in the International Division of Labor.*
London: Zed Press.

    ____. 1988 "Women's Work and Capitalism. " In *Women: The Last Colony* M. Mies, M.,

Bennholdt-Thomsen V, and von Werlhof, C. eds. London: The Zed Book Limited.

_____1988 "Social Origins and the Sexual Division of Nature" In *Women: The Last Colony*. London: The Zed Book Limited.

_____. 1988 "Class Struggle and Women's Struggle in Rural India" *In Women: The Last Colony*. London: The Zed Book Limited.

_____.1980 *Indian Women and Patriarchy*. New Delhi: Concept Publishing Company.

Mies, M., Bennholdt-Thomsen, V., von WerlhoF C. 1988 *Women: The Last Colony*. London: The Zed Book Limited

Mills, W.
1959 *The Sociological Imagination*. New York: Oxford University Press

Mitchell, C.
The Meaning of Misfortune for Urban Africa. In *African Systems of Thought*
Fortes, M. and Dieterlin, G. eds. London: International African Institute.

_____. 1969 *Social Network in Urban Situations*. England: Menchester University Press.

_____. 1970 Towards a Sociology of African Independency. *Journal of Religion in Africa*, III: 99. 2-21.

Mofokeng, T.
1990 Black Theology in South Africa: Achievements Problems and Prospects. In *Christianity in South Africa*. edited by Prozenky, M. Berglei: Southern.

Mokoka, H.
1967 *Dipuku tsa Bapedi*. Pretoria: Bosele Printers.

Molland, E.
1955 *Christendom*. London: Oxford University Press.

Moller, H.J.
1992 *God en die Voorouergeeste in die Lewe van die Stedelike Bantoe*. Pretoria: Human Science Research Council.

Mönnig, H.O.
1967 *The Pedi* Pretroria: Van Schaik Limited.

Morgan, S.
1989 *Gender and Anthropology*. Washington D.C: AA Association.

Morris, C.
>1962 *The End of the Missionary? A Short Account of the Political Consequences of Missions in Northern Rhodesia*. London: Cargate.

Muntemba, M.
>1960 "Women and Agricultural Change in the Railway Region of Zambia: Dispossession and Counterstrategies, 1930-70." In *Women and Work in Africa*,.edited by Bay, E. Colo.: Westview Press.

Murdock, G.P. 1949 *Social Structure*. New York: Macmillan.

Murphee, M.
>1969 *Christianity and the Shona*. London: Anthlone Press.

>____. 1971 Religious Independency Among the Budja Vapostori. In African Initiative in Religion, edited by Barret, D.B. Nairobi: East African Publishing House

Mzimba, L.
>1940 The African Church. In *Christianity and theNatives of South Africa* edited by Taylor, J.D. Pretoria: Van Schaiks.

Nash, J. & Kelly, P.
>1983 *Women and the International Division of Labor*. Albany: SUNNY Press.

Nash, J. & safa, H. eds.
>1985 *Women and Change in Latin America*. Mass.: Bergin and Garvey.

Ndiokwere, N.I.
>1981 *Prophecy and Revolution-in the Role of Prophets in the African Independent Churches and in Biblical Tradition*. London: Oxfrod University Press.

Neame, L.E.
>1905 Ethiopianism: *The Danger of a Black Church. Empire Review*. New Nation News Paper. Johannesburg 1998,

Ngubane, H.
>1977 *Body and Mind in Zulu Medicine*. Cambridge: Cambridge University Press.

Nida, E.A.
>1971 New Religion for Old. In *Church and Culture Change in Africa*. edited by Bosch, D.J. Pretoria: Lux Mundi.

Norbeck, E.
　　　1961 *Religion in Primitive Society*. New York:
　　　Harper and Row.
Norton, G.R.
　　　1940 The Emergence of New Religious
　　　Organizations in South Africa. *Journal of the Royal
　　　African Society*.
Nthabu, B.Y. (now Mosupyoe)
　　　1989 *Meaning and Symbolism in the ZCC of South
　　　Africa..* University of California,
　　　Berkeley.
Obbo, C.
　　　1980 *African Women*. London: Zed Press
　　　_____. 1990 "East African Women, Work, and the
　　　Articulation of Dominance." In *Persistent
　　　Inequalities*, edited by Tinker. I. New York: Oxford
　　　University Press.
O'Dean, T.F.
　　　1966 *The Society of Religion*. Englewood Cliffs:
　　　Prentice Hall.
Ogbu, J.U.
　　　1974 *The Next Generation: An Ethnography of
　　　Education in an Urban Neighborhood*. New York:
　　　Academic Press.
Ogbu, J. U
　　　1977 "African Marriage Family, Fertility and
　　　Economics" In *Current Anthropology*. 18 (2). 259-
　　　287
Ogbu, J.U. and Simons, H.D.
　　　1994 *Cultural Models of School Achievement: A
　　　Quantitative Test of Ogbu'sTheory*. University of
　　　California at Berkeley.
Okeyo, A.P. (Formerly Pala).
　　　1961 *Towards Strategies for Strengthening the Position of
　　　Women in Food Production*. Nairobi: Institute
　　　of Development Studies.
Ollman, B.
　　　1971 *Allienation*. Cambridge: Cambridge
　　　University Press.
Omoyajowo, J.A.
　　　1984 *Cheribum and Seraphim: A History of An
　　　Independent Church*. New York: Lagos.

Omoyi, B.A.
    1905 *A Defense of the Ethiopian Movements.*
    Edinburgh.

Ong, A.
    1987 *Spirits of Resistance and Capitalist Discipline:*
    Factory Women in Malaysia. New York: State
    University of New York Press.

Oppong, C. ed.
    1983 *Female and Male in West Africa.* London:
    George Allen and Unwin

Ortner, S.
    1974 "Is Female to Nature as Nature Is to Culture."
    In *Women Culture and Society* Rosaldo, L. &
    Lamphere, eds M. Stanford: Stanford University
    Press.

    ____. 1984 "The Founding of the First Sherpa
    Nunnery, and the Problem of "Women" as an
    Analytical Category." In *Feminist Revisions*, edited
    by Arbor, A. Women's Studies Program, University
    of Michigan.

Ortner, S. and Whitehead,
    1981 *Sexual Meanings.* Cambridge: Cambridge
    University Press.

Oosthuizen, B
    1968 *Post Christianity in Africa: A Theological and*
    Anthropological Study. Stellenbosch: Peabo
    Publishing Company.

Otto, R.
    1967 *Naturalism and Religion.* London: Williams
    and Norgate.

Pala, A.O. (now Okeyo)
    1977 "Definitions of Women and Development: An
    African Perspective" *Signs:* 3(1): 9-13.

Papanek, H.
    1973 "Men, Women and Work: Reflection of the
    Two person Career."*American Journal of Sociology*
    78 (4):852-872.

    ____. 1977 "Development Planning for Women" In
    Women and National Development: The
    Complexities of Change. Chicago: The University of
    Chicago Press.

    ____. 1979 "The 'Work' and 'Non-Work' of
    Women," *Signs*: 4(4):775-781.

    ____. 1990 "To Each Less Than She Needs, From
    Each More Than She Can Do: Allocation,

Entitlements, and Value." In *Persistent Inequalities*,
edited by Tinker, I. New York: Oxford University
Press.

____. 1974 "The Search for Origins." In *Critique of
Anthropology Women's Issue* 9 and 10: 3.

____. 1975 *Towards an Anthropology of Women*.
New York: Monthly Press Review.

Parson, T.
1967 *The Social System*. London: Cohen and West.

Parson T and R Bales
1955 *Family, Socialization and Interaction Process*.
Glencoe, Illinois: Free Press

Patel, R.M. (Adaptation by Shamsi A.)
1990 *The Making of the Mahatma Based on
Gandhiji Ni Sadhna*. Ahmedabad: Prashant R. Patel

Pauw, B.A.
1960 *Religion in Tswana Chiefdom*. London:
Oxford University Press.

____. 1963 (a) African Christians and their
Ancestors. In *African Independent Church
Movements* edited by Hayward, V.E.W. London:
Edinburgh House Press.

____. 1974 Ancestor Beliefs and Rituals Among
Urban Africans. *African Studies*, 33.

____. 1975 *Christianity and Xhosa Tradition*. Cape
Town: Oxford University Press.

Peaden, W.R.
1970 *Missionary Attitudes to Shona Culture 1890-
1923*. Salisbury: Central African Historical
Phamphlets.

Peel, J.D.Y.
1968 *Aladura: A Religious Movement Among the
Yoruba*. London: Oxford University Press.

Perrin-Jassy, M.F.
1971 *Communication with an African*. Zaire:
Bandudu.

Powdermaker, H.
1966 *Strangers and Friend: the Way of
Anthropologist*.

Price R and Roseberg C eds
1979 *The Apartheid Regime: Political Power and
Radical Domination*. University of California
Berkeley:
Institute of International Studies

Ramose, M.B.
　　　　1987 *Kgotso Ga e Ate*. Unpublished Manuscript:
　　　　University of Zimbabwe.
　　　　____. 1988 *The Ontology of Invisible Beings*.
　　　　Unpublished Pro Manuscript, Zimbabwe University.
Ranger, T.
　　　　1963 The Early History of Independency in Southern
　　　　　　　Rhodesia. In *Religion in Africa* edited by Watt,
　　　　　　　W.M. University of Edinburgh: Center of
　　　　　　　African Studies.
　　　　____. 1970 The African Voice in Southern
　　　　Rhodesia. Evaston: Northwest University Press.
　　　　____. 1975 *Dance and Society in Eastern Africa*
　　　　1890-1970. London: Heineman.
Resknin B, and Padavic,
　　　　1994 *Women and Men at Work*. Thousand Oaks:
　　　　Pine Forge Press
Rigby, P.
　　　　1968Some Gogo Rituals of Purification. In *Dialectic*
　　　　in Practical Religion edited by Leach E.R. England:
　　　　Cambridge University.
Robertson, C. Berger, I.
　　　　1986 *Women and Class in Africa*. New York:
　　　　Africana Publishing Company.
Rosaldo, M. & Lamphere, L.
　　　　1974 *Women, Culture and Society*. Stanford:
　　　　Stanford University Press
Rubin G.
　　　　1975 "The Traffic in Women: Notes on the Political
　　　　Economy of Sex. In *Towards an Anthropology of*
　　　　Women. New York: Monthly Review Press
Sacks, K.
　　　　, 1979 *Sisters and Wives*. Connecticut: Greenwood
　　　　Press Inc.
Safa, H.I.
　　　1977 "Introduction" In *Women and National*
　　　　Development: The Complexities of Change.
　　　　Chicago: The University of Chicago Press.
　　　　____. 1987 "Women and Change in Latin
　　　　America" in Latin America:
　　　　Perspectives on a Region ed. J. Hopskin. New York:
　　　　Holmes and Meier.
　　　　Sahlins, M.
　　　　1976 *Culture and Practical Reason*. University of
　　　　Chicago Press.

_____1981 Historical Metaphors and Mythical Realities: *Structure in the Early History of the Sandwitch Island Kingdom.* Ann Arbor: University of Michigan Press

Schapera I
1953 *The Tswana* London: International Institute:

Schlosser, K.
1958 *Eingeborenenkirchen in Sud-und Sudwest Afrika.* Inhre Geschichte und Sozialstruktur, Kiel.

Scott, H.
1984 *Working Your Way to the Bottom: The Feminization of Poverty.* Boston: Pandora Press.

Scott, J. and Tilly A
1975 "Women's Work and and the Family in the Nineteenth Century Europe." In *Comparative Studies in Societies and History* 17:36-64 Sechaba: *An Official Organ of the African National Congress South Africa.* United Kingdom: Sechaba Publication 1987 June Vol 22 No 6 and Decemeber Vol 22 No 12,1989 Feb Vol 23 No 22, September Vol 23 No 9 and October Vol 23 No 10 1990 August Vol 24 No 8

Sibisi, H.
1977 "How African Women Cope with Migrant Labour in South Africa" In *Women and National Development: The Complexities of Change.* Chicago: The University of Chicago Press.
South African *Bantu Authorities Act,* 1951 no 68

Sundkler, B.
1948 *Bantu Prophets in South Africa.* London: Oxford University Press
_____. 1961 *Bantu Prophets in South Africa* 2nd edition. London: Oxford University Press for the International African Institute.
_____. 1976 *Zulu Zion and Some Swazi Zionists* London: Oxford University

Star News Paper
1985 April 15 Johannesburg

Stein, C.
1992 *Spiritual Healing: A Comparison Between New Age Groupd and African Initiated Churches in South Africa.* Pretoria: University of South Africa

Thorbek, S.
1987 *Voices From the City* London: Zed Book Ltd.

Tinker, I. & Bramsen, B.

    1976 (a) *Women and World Development.* New York: Praeger

Tinker, I.

    1976 (b) "Women in Developing Societies: Economic Independence is Not Enough." *In The Foundation For Equal Rights* edited by Chapman, R

    ____. 1983 *Women in Washington: Advocates for Public Policy* Calif.: Sage Publications.

    ____ . 1990 *Persistent Inequalities.* New York: Oxford University Press.

Urdang S.

    1989 *And Still they Dance* New York: Monthly Review Press.

Van Warmelo, N.J.

    1953 *The Bantu Speaking Peoples of South Africa,* edited by. Hammond-Tooke, W.D. London : Routledge and Kegan

Van Wyk, J.H.

    1965 *Die Separatisme en Inheemse Kerklike Bewegings Onder die Bantoe van die Sothogroep,* 11: 855-856.

Wadley, S

    1980 *The Power of Tamil Women* Syracuse: Maxwell School of Citezenship and Public Affairs

Wallace A.

    1956 *Religion: An Anthropological View.* New York: Random House

Warren, K.B.

    1986 "Capitalist Expansion and The Moral Order: Anthropological Perspectives.' In *Christianity and Capitalism : Perspectives on Religion, Liberalism and Economy.* Chicago: Center for Scientific Study of Religion.

Weber, M.

    1993 *The Theory of Economic and Social Organization,* edited by. Parson T. New

    1994 York: Oxford University Press

Wellesley EditoriaL Committee

    1977 Women and National Development: The Complexities of Change. Chicago: The University of Chicago Press

West, M.
> 1975 *Bishops and Prophets in a Black City*.
> Claremont, Cape Town: David Phillip Publishers

West C and Zimmerman H
> 1979 "Doing Gender' In *Gender and Society* 1; 125-51

Westmore, J. and Townsed, P.
> 1995 "The African Women Workers in the Textile
> Industry in Durban." *South African Labor
> Bulletin*. 2
> (4): 18-32.

Wilson, M. and Thompson, L.
> 1971 *The Oxford History of South Africa*. Oxford:
> Oxford University Press

Workers' Union 1997 and 1998 July. Cape Town: SAMWU

Wright, C.
> 1989 Precursors to adjustment, Revitalization, and
> Expansion: an under the carpet view of the
> education crisis in Sub-Saharan Africa. In *Zimbabwe
> Journal of Educational Research*. Volume 1.
> Number 1 Reconstruction and Development
> Programme" 1994 Johannesburg: African National
> Congress

Zion Christain Church:
> 1985-1996 *ZCC Messenger*. ZCC Publications

APPENDICES

Appendix A: Map of Apartheid South Africa

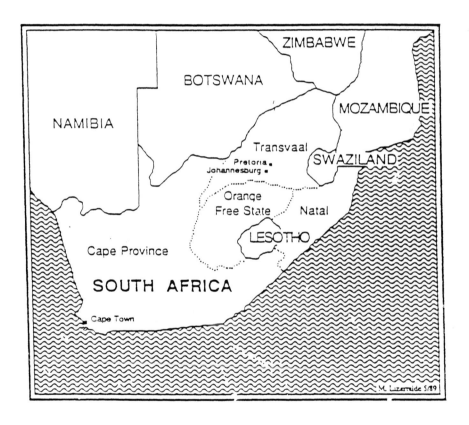

Appendix B: Map of Current South Africa

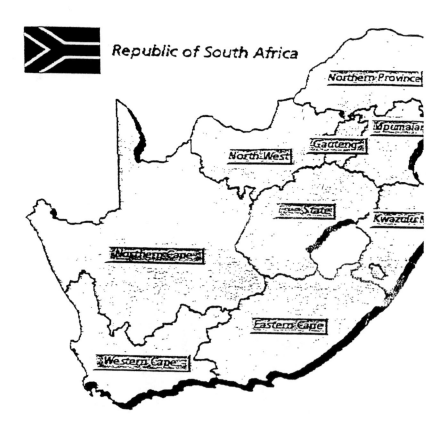

Republic of South Africa

Appendix C: Map of South Africa from the Bapedi History

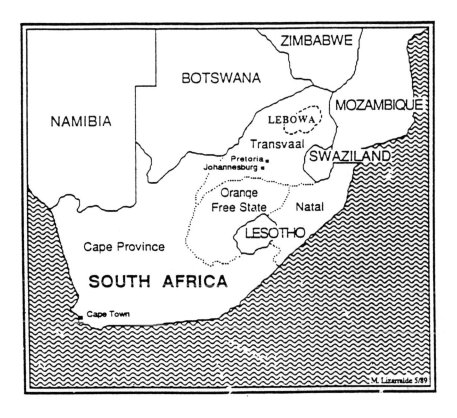

Appendix D: Map of Zion City Moria

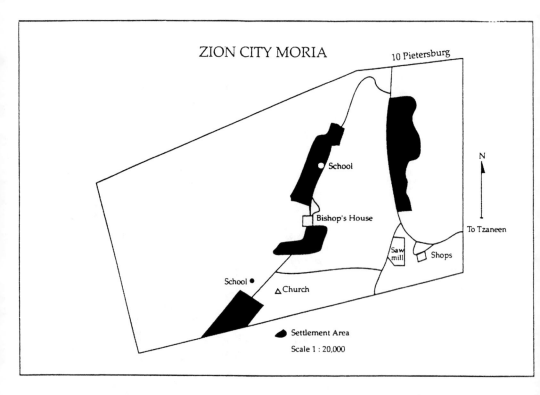

Chart 1.1

The Origin of the African Independent Churches and Features

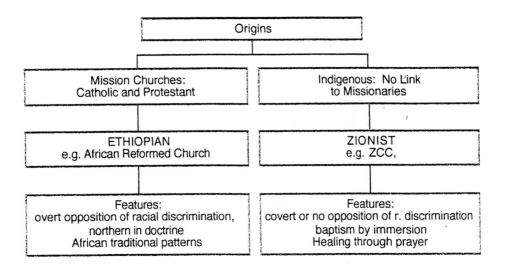

Chart 1:2
The Historical Origin and Development of the ZCC

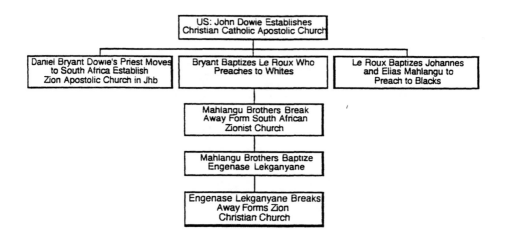

Chart 1:3
Membership of Different Denominations and ZCC
(also published in the ZCC messenger 1992)

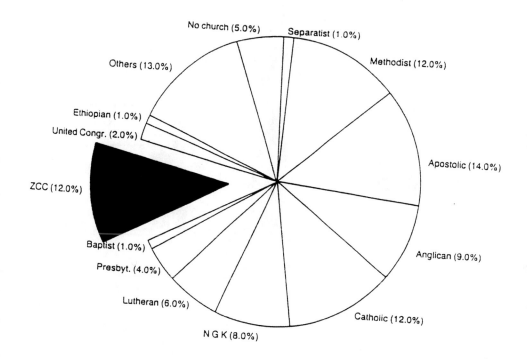

Chart 1:4
ZCC Retention Rates in Education
((also published in the ZCC messenger)

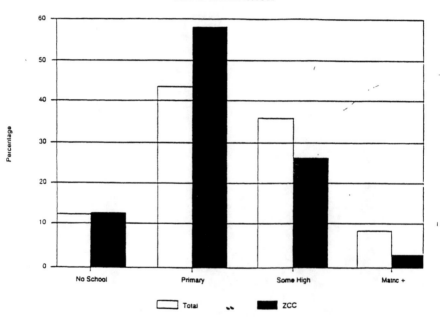

ZCC Education

LIST OF TABLES

Table 1:1
Social Identity of Informants: A-F

Social Identity of Informants							
Name Assignec	Age	Gender	PR	Level of Educ.	Occupation	Urb. or Rural	Union Aff.
Amr	45	Female	Ratjiepane	8th grade	Office Cleaner	Rural	Yes
Ar	58	Female	Hammans.	5th grade	Office Cleaner	Rural	Yes
Ayu	22	Female	Garankuwa	DO 9th grade	FW	Urban	Yes
Br	62	Female	Hammans.	2nd grade	Sells Food	Rural	No
Bu	50	Female	Garankuwa	5th grade	Laborer	Urban	No
Byu2	28	Female	Att/ville	DO 11th grade	Laborer	Urban	Yes
Byu	33	Female	Mabopane	10th grade	Hosp. Laborer	Urban	Yes
Bu3	51	Female	Garankuwa	4th grade	Laborer	Urban	No
Cmr	47	Female	Hammans.	DO 1oth grade	Hosp. Laborer	Rural	No
Cmr2	40	Female	Hammans.	7th grade	FW	Rural	No
Cmru	45	Female	Mapobane	Compl. HS	Teacher	Urban	Yes
Cmru3	45	Female	Garankuwa	Compl. HS	Teacher	Urban	Yes
Cmu	40	Female	Garankuwa	DO 12 grade	Clerk	Urban	Yes
Cmu2	39	Female	Mabopane	DO 10th grade	Clerk	Urban	Yes
Cyu	20	Female	Garankuwa	DO 10th grade	FW	Urban	Yes
Cyu2	21	Female	Garankuwa	11th grade	Adult. Liter.	Urban	No
Cr	60	Female	Ratjiepane	5th grade	FW	Rural	Yes
Cyr	18	Female	Ratjiepane	9 grade	Prophet	Urban	No
Dmr	45	Female	Ratjiepane	8th grade	Laborer	Rural	Yes
Dr	59	Female	Ratjiepane	3rd grade	Prophet	Rural	No
Dr2	50	Female	Hammans.	4th grade	Prophet.	Rural	No
Dmu	46	Female	Garankuwa	DO 12th grade	Hosp Laborer	Urban	Yes
Du	50	Female	Att/ville	6th grade	Laborer	Urban	Yes
Du2	53	Female	Att/ville	6th grade	Proph.	Urban	No
Dyr	18	Female	Ratjiepane	12th grade	Student	Urban	No
Dyu	17	Female	Mabopane	11th grade	Student	Urban	No
Eyu	26	Female	Garankuwa	DO 9th grade	FW	Urban	Yes
Eyu2	21	Female	Mabopane	DO 7th grade	Adult. Liter.	Urban	No
Fu	52	Female	Garankuwa	No School	Adult. Liter.	Urban	No
Fu2	50	Female	Garankuwa	No School	Adult Liter	Urban	No
Fyu	26	Female	Soshanguve	DO 10th gade	Adult. Liter	Urban	Yes
Fmu2	35	Female	Mabopane	10th grade	Laborer	Urban	Yes
Fyr	15	Female	Ratjiepane	10the grade	Student	Rural	No
Fyu	26	Female	Soshanguve	DO 10th gade	Adult. Liter	Urban	Yes
Fyu2	18	Female	Mabopane	12th Grade	Student	Urban	No
Fyu3	24	Female	Mabopane	9th grade	Adult. Liter.	Urban	No
Fyu4	20	Female	Mabopane	10th grade	Adult. Liter.	Urban	No
Fyu5	30	Female	Mabopane	DO 11th grade	Adult. Liter.	Urban	No

Table 1:2
Social Identity of Informants: G-Ly4u

Name Assigned	Age	Gender	RR	Level of Educ.	Occupation	Urb. or Rural	Union Aff.
Gmr	48	Female	Ratjiepane	11th grade	Laborer	Rural	Yes
Gmu	49	Female	Garankuwa	Compel. Hs	Teacher	Urban	Yes
Gmnr	47	Female	Ratjiepane	6th grade	PW	Rural	Yes
Gr	50	Female	Hammans.	5th grade	PW	Rural	No
Gyu	29	Female	Garankuwa	9th grade	Maid	Urban	No
Gyu2	31	Female	Garankuwa	8th grade	Maid	Urban	Yes
Hu	58	Female	Att/ville	10th grade	Maid	Urban	No
Hyu	35	Female	Garankuwa	9th grade	Taxi Owner	Urban	No
Hyu2	39	Female	Garankuwa	11th grade	Hosp. Laborer	Urban	Yes
Jr	58	Female	Ratjiepane	3rd grade	Hosp. Laborer	Rural	Yes
Jr2	56	Female	Hammans.	5th grade	PW	Rural	No
Jmr	49	Female	Pietersburg	2nd grade	Laborer	Rural	No
Ju	57	Male	Att/ville	6th grade	High Priest	Urban	No
Jyu	25	Female	Garankuwa	11th grade	Hosp. Laborer	Urban	Yes
Kmu	42	Female	Mabopane	9th grade	Laborer	Urban	No
Kr	50	Female	Ratjiepane	5th grade	Maid	Rural	No
Ku	53	Female	Garankuwa	7th grade	Maid	Urban	No
Kyu	16	Female	Att/ville	10th grade	Student	Urban	No
Kyr	13	Female	Hammans..	8th grade	Student	Rural	No
Kyr2	14	Female	Ratjiepane	8th grade	Student	Rural	No
Kyu2	35	Female	Soshanguve	11th grade	Laborer	Urban	Yes
Kyu3	33	Female	Soshanguve	11th grade	Clerk	Urban	Yes
Kyu4	25	Female	Mapopane	11th grade	Maid	Urban	No
Lmu	46	Female	Att/ville	Compel.. HS	Teacher	Urban	Yes
Lr	67	Female	Ratjiepane	2nd grade	Prophet.	Rural	No
Lr2	51	Male	Hammans..	3rd grade	Priest	Rural	No
Lu	57	Male	Soshanguve	Doctorate	High Priest	Urban	No
Lu	62	Female	Garankuwa	2nd grade	Sells Food	Urban	No
Lu2	50	Female	Soshanguve	Compel.. HS	Teacher	Urban	Yes
Lu3	56	Male	Mabopane	3rd Grade	High Priest	Urban	No
Lyu	34	Female	Att/ville	10th grade	Taxi Owner	Urban	Yes
Ly2u	33	Female	Garankuwa	11th grade	Clerk	Urban	Yes
Lyu3	28	Female	Garankuwa	8th grade	Maid	Urban	Yes
Lyu4	32	Female	Att/ville	DO 8th grade	PW	Urban	Yes

Table: 1:3
Social Identity of Informants: Lr-Pmu

Name Assigned	Age	Gender	RR	Level of Educ.	Occupation	Urb. or Rural	Union Aff.
Lr	62	Female	Ratjiepane	2nd grade	Sells Food	Rural	No
Lu3	58	Female	Mabopane	4th grade	Laborer	Urban	Yes
Mr	50	Female	Hammans.	5th grade	Laborer	Rural	No
Mr2	57	Male	Hammans.	7th grade	Priest	Rural	No
Mr2	57	Female	Pietersburg	4th grade	Laborer	Rural	No
MMu	48	Female	Mabopane	10th Grade	Clerk	Urban	Yes
MMu2	39	Female	Att/ville	Compl. HS	Teacher	Urban	Yes
Mmr	46	Female	Ratjiepane	9th grade	Laborer	Rural	No
Mu	55	Female	Garankuwa	DO 12th grade	Maid	Urban	Yes
Mu	59	Male	Mabopane	4th grade	Priest	Urban	No
Mu2	53	Female	Mabopane	2th grade	Sells Food	Urban	No
Mu3	54	Female	Garankuwa	6th grade	Laborer	Urban	Yes
Myu	25	Female	Att/ville	7th grade	PW	Urban	Yes
Myu2	12	Female	Att/ville	7th grade	Student	Urban	No
Myu3	15	Female	Soshanguve	9th grade	Student	Urban	No
Myu4	33	Female	Att/ville	DO 12th grade	Clerk	Urban	Yes
Myu5	23	Female	Att/ville	6th grade	PW	Urban	Yes
Myu6	33	Female	Garankuwa	8th grade	PW	Urban	Yes
Myu7	36	Female	Mabopane	7th grade	Taxi Owner	Urban	No
Myr3	12	Female	Ratjiepane	7th grade	Student	Rural	No
Nmr	46	Female	Hammans.	Do 12th grade	Laborer	Rural	Yes
Nr	47	Female	Hamanns.	8th grade	Sells Food	Rural	No
Nyr	23	Female	Hammans.	DO 12th grade	Clerk	Rural	Yes
Nyu	20	Female	Garankuwa	DO 12th grade	Clerk	Urban	Yes
Nyu2	21	Female	Mabopane	DO 12th grade	Hosp. Labore	Urban	Yes
Nyu3	18	Female	Mabopane	12th grade	Student	Urban	No
Nyu4	23	Female	Mabopane	College	Student	Urban	No
Nyu5	17	Female	Mabopane	11th grade	Student	Urban	No
Nyu6	30	Female	Garankuwa	DO 6th grade	Maid	Urban	No
Omr	45	Female	Ratjiepane	3rd grade	PW	Rural	Yes
Omr2	40	Female	Ratjiepane	2nd grade	PW	Rural	Yes
Pu	50	Male	Garankuwa	8th grade	Priest	Urban	No
Pmr	45	Female	Ratjiepane	7th grade	Laborer	Rural	Yes
Pmu	46	Female	Att/ville	Compl HS	Nurs. Ass	Urban	Yes
Pmu2	47	Female	Garankuwa	Compl. HS	Teacher	Urban	Yes
Pmu3	47	Female	Att/ville	Compl. HS	Teacher	Urban	Yes

Table: 1:4
Social Identity of Informants: Pyu-Ymr

Name Assigned	Age	Gender	RR	Level of Educ.	Occupation	Urb. or Rural	Union Aff.
Pyu	24	Female	Mabopane	DO 12th grade	Adult. Lit.	Urban	No
Qr	45	Female	Ratjiepane	3rd grade	Laborer	Rural	Yes
Qu	50	Female	Soshanguve	8th grade	PW	Urban	Yes
Qu2	50	Female	Garankuwa	10th grade	PW	Urban	Yes
Rr	50	Female	Ratjiepane	6th grade	Laborer	Rural	No
Rr2	51	Female	Petersburg	7th grade	Laborer	Rural	No
Smu	43	Female	Garankuwa	10th grade	Laborer	Urban	Yes
Smu2	43	Female	Garankuwa	6th grade	Sells Food	Urban	No
Syr	10	Female	Hammans.	6th grade	student	Rural	No
Syu	24	Female	Garankuwa	DO 12th grade	Adult. Lit	Urban	No
Syr2	11	Female	Garankuwa	7th grade	Student	Urban	No
Sr	57	Female	Ratjiepane	9th grade	PW	Rural	Yes
Tyu	26	Feamle	Garankuwa	DO 4th grade	Maid	Urban	Yes
Tyu2	24	Female	Garankuwa	DO 6th grade	Adult lite	Urban	No
Tr	58	Female	Pietersburg	6th grade	PW	Rural	No
Um2	45	Female	Att/ville	5th grade	Laborer	Urban	Yes
Umu	34	Female	Garankuwa	5th grade	Laborer	Urban	Yes
Vmr	42	Female	Ratjiepane	4th grade	Laborer	Rural	No
Vmr2	41	Female	Ratjiepane	3rd grade	Laborer	Rural	Yes
Vmr3	40	Female	Ratjiepane	3rd grade	Laborer	Rural	Yes
Wr	55	Female	Pietersburg	5th grade	Laborer	Rural	Yes
Wu	58	Female	Garankuwa	11th grade	Laborer	Urban	Yes
Wr	50	Female	Ratjiepane	6th grade	PW	Rural	Yes
Wr2	50	Female	Ratjieapne	10th grade	PW	Rural	Yes
Xr	54	Female	Ratjiepane	6th grade	PW	Rural	No
Xu	50	Female	Att/ville	11th grade	Mnstr. Wife	Urabn	No
Ymr	35	Female	Ratjiepane	11 grade	PW	Rural	Yes

1:5
ZCC Adult Literacy and Education: Rakopi Center
(also published in the ZCC messenger)

ZCC LITERACY CAMPAIGN AND ADULT EDUCATION: RAKOPI CENTER						
				1990		
AGE	LITERACY	PREPARATORY	COURSE I	COURSE II	NEEDLEWORK	TOTAL
21-30	5	3	4	3	12	27
ALL WOMEN						
				1991		
AGE	LITERACY	PREPARATORY	COURSE I	COURSE II	NEEDLEWORK	TOTAL
21-30	5	4		5	15	29
ALL WOMEN						
		RAKOPI ADULT EDUCATION CENTER SUMMARY OF RESULTS				
				1990		
	NO WROTE	NO PASSED	% PASSED	NO FAILED	% FAILED	DROPOUTS
LITERACY	3	3	60	1	40	1
PREPARATORY	2	2	67	1	33	1
COURSE 1	4	2	50	2	50	
COURSE II	2	2	100			
COURSE 111	11					
NEEDLEWORK						
				1991		
	NO WROTE	NO PASSED	% PASSED	NO FAILED	% FAILED	DROPOUTS
LITERACY	5	4				1
PREPARATORY	4	3		0		
COURSE 1						2
COURSE II						2
COURSE 111	6	Subjects				1
Supervising Teacher: Mr. D. Seabi						

ZCC Adult Literacy and Education: Vaalbank Center
(also published in the ZCC messenger)

ZCC LITERACY CAMPAIGN AND ADULT EDUCATION: VAALBANK CENTER						
	ADULT ZCC VAALBANK--KWANDEBELE					
LITERACY	PREPARATOR STD 1- 2 CONTINUATION					
		STD3	STD4	STD 5	STD 8	STD10
35	22	14	8	11	13	7
					/	
		TOTAL 110				
	Supervising Teachers Mahlangu and Mackay					
Explanations: Standard(std) 1 is an equivalent of third grade						
	Standard 2 is an equivalent of fourth grade					
	Standard ten will then be twelve grade-final year of high					
Compiled with the help of Mr. Mamabolo						

1:7
ZCC Adult Literacy and Education: Siyabuswa Center
(also published in the ZCC messenger)

ZCC LITERACY CAMPAIGN AND ADULT EDUCATION : SIYABUSWA				
	SIYABUSWA ZCC ADULT LITERACY CENTER			
	LITERACY	CONTINUATION CLASSES		
	9	STD I	6	
		STD 2	9	
		STD 3	4 &5=14	
		STD 6	4	
		STD 10	7	
		TOTAL	56	
Supervising Teacher: Mr J. Mahlangu				
EXPLANATIONS: Standard 1-10 are equivalents of the United States				
	third grade to twelfth grades			
Compiled with the help of Mr. Mamabolo.				

1:8
ZCC Adult Literacy and Education: Soshanguve
(also published in ZCC Messenger)

	SOSHANGUVE ZCC ADULT CENTER			
	1994–1997			
GRADE I	GRADE II	STD 5	STDS 8 & 10	
14	13	7	38	
	TOTAL		72	
Supervising Teacher: Mr. M. D. Zulu				
Explanations:				
STD 5 = US 5th grade				
STD 8 = US 8th grade				
STD 10 = US 10th grade				
Compiled with the help of Mr. Mamabolo				

1:9
ZCC Adult Literacy and Education: Denilton
(also published in ZCC Messenger)

ZCC ADULT LITERACY CENTER: DENILTON			
	KHOBOKWANE: DENILTON		
	LITERACY	CONTINUATION	
	121	0	
SUPERVISING TEACHER: B. A. MOHLAMONYANE			
Compiled with help of Mr. Mamabolo			

1:10
ZCC Adult Literacy and Education: Existing and Earmarked
Venda
(Also published in ZCC Messenger)

ZCC LITERACY CAMPAIGN AND ADULT EDUCATION : VENDA CENTER				
EXISTING AND EAR MARKED VENDA CENTERS				
DISTRICT	CENTER NAME			
Thohoyando	Sibasa	Illiterate	Continuation	
Thohoyando	Sibasa	97	62	
Ndzihelele	Raliphaswa	80	20	
	Mauluma	30	15	
	Phadzima	50	0	
	Maelula	15	0	
	Fondwe	40	0	
	Khalavha	0	0	
	Maelula	0	0	
	Mphephu	60	0	
Vuwani	Tshakuna	0	15	
	Tsianda	0	17	
	Ndzwerani	0	25	
Tshitandan	Ramahatsha	30	28	
TOTAL		402	183	
District Co-ordinator Mr. A.J. Mukhondo				
68% of Coninuations are women				
Compiled with the help of Mr. Mamabolo